THE
JESUIT
ETHOS

THE JESUIT ETHOS

A SOCIAL AND SPIRITUAL HISTORY

JEAN LUC ENYEGUE, SJ

Paulist Press

New York / Mahwah, NJ

Cover image by j.chizhe/Shutterstock.com
Cover design by Joe Gallagher
Book design by Lynn Else

Library of Congress Cataloging-in-Publication Data available upon request.

ISBN 978-0-8091-5621-4 (paperback)
ISBN 978-0-8091-8782-9 (e-book)

Published by Paulist Press
997 Macarthur Boulevard
Mahwah, New Jersey 07430
www.paulistpress.com

Printed and bound in the
United States of America

*To John Padberg, SJ, and John O'Malley, SJ,
for their significant contributions to Jesuit history
and for their friendship*

CONTENTS

FOREWORD

A popular African proverb counsels that until the lion learns to write, the tale of the hunt will always glorify the hunter. There is an unspoken assumption that the Society of Jesus—the order of Jesuits—is intrinsically a European phenomenon. The tale of its Spanish founder, Saint Ignatius of Loyola (1491–1556), and its history, mission, traditions, and spirituality have always appeared as the preserve of European historians, chroniclers, and interpreters. This perspective is reductionist. The story of the Jesuits is a universal patrimony albeit spawned in a particular historical context and geographical space.

Over the last one hundred years, as Christianity's center of gravity has shifted dramatically from the Global North to the Global South, the voices of the latter's scholars have become prominent as authentic and credible interpreters of Christianity's origins, teachings, and progress. The Society of Jesus has experienced a similar trajectory of displacement of its center of gravity. Younger members of the order are to be found more in the Global South than in the North. In the next thirty years, more than half the total number of Jesuits will live and work—or come from—South Asia and Africa.

This stunning historical and demographic development has multiple implications. The responsibility for narrating and interpreting the tale of the Society's origins, progress, and achievements in history now falls largely on Jesuits from the Global South. Expectedly, such narratives will no longer conform to a Western paradigm. They will unfold in a wider and more inclusive framework that takes account of the astonishing revirescence of the Society in the South rather than its inevitable obsolescence in the North.

To the astute observer, nothing in this trajectory should be surprising. From its inception, the order and its members have always crossed boundaries to expand the vision and realize the mission of the Jesuits. In some sense, what the Society of Jesus is becoming today was sown in its origins and nourished in its history. At no time in this history was the order the exclusive enclave or monopoly of a particular nationality, continent, or ideology. One of its originators and Ignatius's earliest companions, Jerónimo Nadal (1507–1580), famously declared that for Jesuits "the world is our house." Not only did this global vision enlarge the space of Jesuit mission, but more importantly, it transcended closed and narrow interpretations and narratives, leaving room for historians to craft fresh, living histories of the lives and times of Jesuits across the globe.

Thus twenty-first-century Jesuits and their partners in mission are no longer just inheritors of a venerable tradition; they are fervent architects of vibrant religious and social tales of peoples, events, and places that matter to the understanding of the Jesuit ethos or ways of proceeding. Strikingly, history told through the lenses of an expanded and inclusive paradigm offers a more honest and sobering account. From the perspective of the Global South, the spiritual and social history of the Society of Jesus—and indeed of Christianity as a whole—cannot escape the burden of accounting for the cruel reality of colonialism and violent imposition of a foreign religion, which, in many instances, was the first fateful taste of baptism by converts. Yet, as many modern historians of African extraction, like Jean Luc Enyegue, show, we are no longer bound to the dynamics of this historical violence. We are capable of reading history as our-story and interpreting it in our language and on our terms.

Enyegue's social and spiritual history of the Jesuits epitomizes this approach that honors the virtue, sanctity, holiness, and flaws of our ancestors and the import of their cultural and religious backgrounds. The outcome of Enyegue's tale is both refreshing and surprising, consoling and shocking, personal and authentic. History has always taught that Jesuits came from Loyola, Manresa, Montserrat, La Storta, Rome; Enyegue's enthralling tale demonstrates that we also come from Ethiopia, Cameroon, Congo, Zambezi, Peru, Brazil, Japan, India, and China. Anything short of this comprehensive vision is a truncated and false narrative.

In the final analysis, this social and spiritual history shows that the Society of Jesus was born from a place of vulnerability or lameness but grew doggedly through multiple encounters in time and space to attain a solid and successful global missionary footprint. That is the genius of the Jesuit ethos—never one thing but a fascinating spiritual and social specimen of creative fidelity to the past and audacious pilgrimage toward the future.

Agbonkhianmeghe E. Orobator, SJ
President of the Jesuit Conference of Africa and Madagascar

INTRODUCTION

Recent historians have framed a Jesuit ethos in terms of "Jesuit ways of proceeding." Some see in these "ways of proceeding" some "Jesuit thought," which, according to George E. Ganss in his foreword to Joseph de Guibert's *The Jesuits: The Spiritual Doctrine and Practice*, was the primary goal at the creation of the Institute of Jesuit Sources.[1] Interestingly, Joseph de Guibert gives reasons why "ways" is plural. It is, he says, the result of a "spirituality developed continually through history; and from the different characters and persons or the different graces they received there sprang naturally many varieties in the manner of living it out or of teaching it."[2] Pedro Arrupe, the charismatic Superior General of the order from 1965 to 1981, acknowledged this diversity in the concrete exercise of his office: "It is evident," he wrote, "that to write a letter to the entire Society is never very easy. I must present the universal values—those which, precisely, nourish the union of minds and hearts—and accept the different concrete attitudes which will result from them."[3]

The plurality of origins and opinions was already highlighted in the *Formula of the Institute*, as if the unicity in the Jesuit way of proceeding, its ethos, is to be found in the constant quest for the unity of minds and hearts of all the members. Ignatius of Loyola made the "way" the expression par excellence to define the Jesuit organization. The Society of Jesus was, to Ignatius and the first Companions, primarily a *"via quaedam ad Deum"* (a way toward God). This "way" makes the organization itself a pilgrim, discerning body, thus in tension between a centralized government, collegial ways of deliberation, and the multiplicity of apostolic commitments among different peoples, races, languages, and cultures.

Nowhere has the Jesuit ethos, however, been more renowned than in their education. There is a Jesuit *Ratio Studiorum* for leaders of Jesuit educational institutions. It exposes the method, content, and aims of Jesuit education. Claude Pavur's translation of the *Ratio* calls it "the official plan for Jesuit education," which, in 1599, "formally constituted and established as a unity an international network of schools that had already begun to be put under the auspices of the Jesuit order."[4] Imagining how Ignatius would have perceived the *Ratio*, Pavur believes that the founder of the Jesuits "would have found in this text unmistakable marks of his own lived experience and his own spirituality."[5] In a recent publication, Pavur made the link more explicit. The *Ratio* is intimately linked to the *Spiritual Exercises of Saint Ignatius*, as both documents pursue the Jesuit goal of "learned devotion" (*docta pietas*), which is to rouse in the human soul "the knowledge and love of our Maker and Redeemer."[6]

The pilgrim and discerning nature of the institution is what helps update it as historical contexts evolve. It was the case when, already in the early days of the order, education erupted to become the main apostolate of the Jesuits. Under the impetus of Saint Ignatius of Loyola (1491–1556), the Jesuits' involvement in the education of youth from 1548 onward was unprecedented for a religious order, especially for their contribution to the development of science, art, and culture.[7] Some historians consider this unexpected irruption of education into the Society's ministries as a true revolution.[8] This apostolate remains at the heart of the Jesuits' identity. Today, its various components constitute a worldwide network that includes hundreds of primary, secondary, and tertiary institutions.

Because the social impact of Jesuit education, as well as of its other ministries to the poor and commitment to social justice,[9] is undeniable, historians have developed, even without explicitly acknowledging it, a social approach to Jesuit history. This paradigm is developed alongside others such as institutional, cultural, and global history. Jesuit history, as this book shows, is also a spiritual history. It thus signals the irruption of a paradigm sidelined by historians since the beginning of the modern era.

The social and spiritual reinterpretation of the history of the Society implies a reevaluation of the traditional social paradigm. It also implies the expansion of this paradigm to social phenomena highlighted by current historiography, including infirmity and spirituality. The social and spiritual history of the Society of Jesus is indispensable in order to better account for the belonging and appropriation, by the Global South, of an institutional and religious tradition born in a world context that is dominated by the expansion of the European West and rationalism but that today must reckon with a demographic shift toward a marginalized and poor Global South,[10] which approach to history is naturally linked to spirituality.[11]

The social paradigm is not entirely absent from classical Jesuit historiography. In his *First Jesuits*, for example, John O'Malley presents the Society first and foremost as "a body" within the church, one whose reforms, especially in education, can be compared to a revolution.[12] The American historian also notes the vagueness surrounding the life of Saint Ignatius. For him, as for Robert Maryks,[13] following David Myers,[14] it is difficult, almost impossible, to find the historical Ignatius. The *Autobiography* of the future saint is not really one. Even the author of the *Many Lives of Ignatius* remains anonymous. The *Autobiography* seemed so problematic to Jesuit superiors in the 1560s that it was withdrawn from circulation in the 1570s, each copy confiscated and locked up by Superior General Francisco de Borja. In its place, and providing the authoritative account of Ignatius's life until the twentieth century, was the more thorough but far more polemical biography published by Pedro de Ribadeneyra in 1572.[15] Faced with the limitations of the historical-critical approach to give an accurate account of the historical figure of Ignatius, these historians came to see the *Autobiography* and *Many Lives* not as history books but as spiritual writings—hagiographies that could be used by catechists to edify children.[16]

O'Malley does, however, maintain explicit contact with the social history of the Society. Like social historians, the first Companions remain for him, above all, a "group" that, on April 19, 1539, decided to elect "an equal among" its members, Ignatius, as its superior. And it is this decision, collective rather than dependent on the individual Ignatius, that will make history. In another detail of social history, O'Malley mentions the age of the new general, fifty, as if to emphasize that Ignatius, at the time of his election, had enough strength to govern "a growing religious order." In fact, the first general's skill in government was primarily manifested in the choice of his team of collaborators. He surrounded himself with men of great quality such as Juan de Polanco and Jerónimo Nadal, whose solidity quickly eclipsed the first ten Companions of Paris.[17] Some of them were descendants of *conversos*, a social group being targeted by laws of purification in place across Europe.

Thanks to these early Companions and the rapid worldwide expansion of the Jesuits, the order embarked resolutely on the first globalization. The first Jesuits had the support of the Catholic kings of Spain and Portugal to gain access to the ends of the world, their peoples, cultures, and their wealth. They brought with them not only a vision of Catholicism, knowledge of art, music, architecture, and science, but also a humanism that placed them in a favorable position regarding new cultures.[18]

With giant steps, the Jesuits explored and discovered, for the West, the New World, its peoples and its cultures. Their "discoveries" helped in the elaboration of maps, revolutionized the social and human sciences in Europe, and inspired new enterprises. By adapting to new cultures, even accommodating them,[19] the Jesuits reformed world Catholicism with one foot inside, through exemplary loyalty to the papacy and the church, and another foot outside, the one that opened the way to the unknown proper to the New World. They undertook this mission boldly, sometimes at the risk of perishing.[20] In this tension, the Jesuits also developed a mode of governance of a global organization through a meticulous codification of communications. José Casanova and Thomas Banchoff have studied this first globalization.[21] Luke Clossey has analyzed it in the modern missions of the Society.[22] And John McGreevy has demonstrated its rebirth after the Jesuits were reestablished in the nineteenth century.[23] In this paradigmatic revolution, even the enmity toward the Society, global in its manifestations,[24] is analyzed meticulously.

The global paradigm of Jesuit historiography raises other questions: who is seen and who is not seen? Who speaks and who is silent? Who is heard and who is not? Globalization, according to Melinda McGarrah Sharp, is indeed allowing more people to be seen, especially among those who are traditionally excluded.[25]

Introduction

Through the development of Jesuit missions both within and outside of Europe, these voices and realities, which the new globalization has now confirmed, have helped shape the history of the Society. The Society has debated them at the highest level of its governance. So it was with Jews, schismatics, heretics, Muslims, Moors, and so on, in the sixteenth century. The same groups remain at the heart of the current debate on globalization, its hopes, and its many discontents. These realities have also often resisted it. In this confrontation, the order has been able to adapt locally.

Since its conception, the Society has had to negotiate with the different marginalities that make up the modern world. This experience has made it more resilient in the face of the first criticisms of a monolithic world order. It also enables the Society to respond effectively to the current challenges of globalization. The Society's handling of early globalization, its management of distance and difference, and its effective governance can only heighten the interest of globalization historians in its institute and its spirituality.[26] The Jesuit organization can inspire regional and global governance. Today's globalization and its malaise may also contribute to a reform of the institute in the direction of a greater consideration of its social and religious impact, as well as its demographic reality, because everything seems to indicate that Christianity is moving toward a church of the poor and one of greater spiritual sensitivity.[27]

The Society is certainly made of men who, with their collaborators, have a considerable social and historical impact. But the history of these men, by their own admission, starts from a common spiritual experience. Their historical value therefore goes beyond the merely social. It is also religious. The history of the Jesuits is therefore also spiritual, anathema to the schools of modern and contemporary history, leading even Walter Ciszek, a saintly Jesuit, to apologize for sharing about his time of persecution in Russia.

This history, like that of most religious institutions, touches on an aspect of human experience that modern and contemporary historiography have often avoided. The French historian Pierre-Antoine Fabre has recently noted this uneasiness. Asking whether it was possible to separate the *Spiritual Exercises*, understood as the "fundamental center of the spiritual life of the Society," from Ignatius, the founder of the Society, Fabre answered in the affirmative.[28] For, he says, the Society, as an institution, is an open work that has eluded Ignatius. This admission is part of the dance and ballet of globalization, whose lived history is sometimes unspeakable.[29]

For an institution like the Society of Jesus, social history and spiritual history are therefore inseparable. Peter N. Stearns believes that the former focuses on marginalized groups far removed from the centers of power. It focuses on the processes of change rather than the description of events. From then on, "individuals, events and precise dates mattered less, and ideas no longer functioned independently of social interaction."[30] Understood in this way, social history, on the one hand, is concerned with issues of class, race, ethnicity, and, more recently, age. However, it gives less space to individual biographies.[31] This social history must be completed by institutional history. For institutional history allows the historian to analyze at the highest level the procedures that lead to decisions whose social impact is undeniable. Institutional history also makes it possible to value the representativeness in decision-making better.[32]

The recent spiritual history, on the other hand, was born in the medical world. It emerges in the face of the unspeakable suffering of a patient. It is based primarily on the realization by one physician that "most patients want to be asked about their spiritual beliefs or non-beliefs, and that many consider it rude for health professionals to ignore this important element of their well-being."[33] It is no coincidence, then, that spiritual history is found in the study of cannabis, a symbol of a certain ecstasy and a "real" beyond the explicable. This reality is part of "peak" experiences, of "feelings of wonder, awe, reverence, humility, deep gratitude and surrender."[34]

Words, philosophers believe, cannot fully grasp this reality, that of the peak experience. They can only re-present it, awkwardly or, one could say, under the effect of cannabis. As he concluded his book *He Leadeth Me*, Walter J. Ciszek wrote, "I have written in this book about the will of God and his providence. I am afraid some readers may feel that I have made too much of it, and to them I can only apologize….But I have written only what I know and what I have experienced…how I managed to survive the years in Soviet prisons and the labor camps of Siberia."[35]

Ciszek shows that the peak experience can be isolated by methods and strategies. It exists, nevertheless, dominant, in the human, the nature, and the social. Moreover, the truth of these experiences "cannot be expressed by words because the divine is uncreated, undifferentiated, indivisible, un-manifest, unnamable, without form, the foundation of the being."[36] Even the archive, in this context of spiritual history, has a spiritual character. People are sometimes interested in it "to counterbalance a feeling of uncertainty about the future."[37]

According to Piret Paal et al., "Spiritual history is the process of interviewing patients, asking them questions about their lives in order to better understand their needs and resources."[38] It begins with a series of questions to help the clinician create a caring environment that encourages the patients to share their beliefs, hopes, fears, and concerns. The essential purpose of this spiritual history is "to go beyond words within the unfolding situation and offer a relationship."[39] In the more distant past, however, it is possible to find traces of spiritual history among the Jesuits, especially in the first hagiographies on Ignatius of Loyola, or even their approach to the history of Black people and non-Europeans, such as those published by José de Acosta and Alonso de Sandoval.

In Sandoval's account, Ethiopia refers to the entire African continent and the eastern regions of the world. The Black peoples live there. His history of Ethiopia thus excludes the northwestern part of the continent, which he associates with the Berber and Arab peoples (with lighter skin). On a spiritual note, the Ethiopians possess the virtues of generosity, divine knowledge, and spiritual humility.[40] The history of these virtues that has long served as the basis for ethnological research cannot be separated from the spiritual history, shall we say, of institutions that claim to be fundamentally religious. In his analysis of gender, spirituality, and economics in Gambia, Assan Sarr makes this direct link between the spiritual and social history.[41]

Such research remains rare, however, and does not sufficiently capture the human, therapeutic, and spiritual value of history. The reason for this void is that professional historians believe that such spiritual conjectures psychologize history. This, at least, is the perception attributed to Jesuit Jeffrey von Arx by Simon Skinner in a review by von Arx of Newman's biography.[42] Skinner does not hide his condescension for these ecclesiastical historians, "sympathetic to the confession," and without a true critical spirit.

In a recent publication, a case was made for an intrinsic, and necessary, relationship between history and value.[43]

Making spiritual history, therefore, runs the risk of the same
criticism from professional historians. And yet, Fernand Braudel,
a leading historian of the Annales, recognizes that all history is the
daughter of its time:

> Its concern is therefore the very concern that weighs
> on our hearts and minds. And if its methods, its pro-
> grams, its tightest and most reliable answers yesterday,
> if its concepts all crack at once, it is under the weight of
> our reflections, of our work and, even more, of our lived
> experiences.[44]

The experience of which the French historian speaks is the
one shared by a humanity used to a certain amount of cruelty. It is
the lived reality of the frontiers, among the subaltern layers of any
civilization. It is located both inside and outside the most industri-
alized regions of globalization. It constitutes the substance of the
very being of other regions that globalization leaves behind. Even
the elite of this region is subaltern when it is transported into the
globalization of the affluent.

Braudel observes that in reading Gaston Roupnel's *History
and Destiny* from the margins of the global conflagration of the
1940s, of which he himself was a prisoner, history is "a shifting,
moving spectacle." He refuses to believe that history is driven
above all by dominant social forces or by the spiritualism of German idealism, or even by the techno-scientific world. History finds
its meaning in the relationship and dialogue of human beings "with
the earth that bears them and nourishes them," in short, with their
destiny.[45]

Frontier historiography thus seems to overcome the dominant historical-critical complex and its inability/refusal to grasp
the historically spiritual. On the contrary, in her study of "the [rit-
ual] practices of the African American church," Barbara A. Holmes
argues that the Black church has both an actual and a meta-actual
form:

It inhabits the imagination of its members in ways that are far beyond its scope. Although it is no longer a truly invisible institution, it will always be so to some extent because it embodies a spiritual idea. This idea is based not only on history, but also on the stories and myths of an oppressed people.[46]

Moreover, the Cameroonian-born Jesuit historian Engelbert Mveng, son of the Annales school of history, had to make a detour into historical poetry to express the same historical facts that could escape the language of the historical-critical method.[47] For the African "real" is inseparable from the spiritual. Africans claim to be fundamentally spiritual. And their daily life is always tragically shifting. "Things" in Africa speak as loudly as "beings."[48]

It is with this socio-spiritual approach that this work reads the life of Saint Ignatius of Loyola, founder of the Jesuits and, from there, the history of the Jesuits. Better than any of the early Jesuits, he was able to navigate the first globalization in its various facets, its elitism, illness, infirmity, pilgrimage, diaspora, suspicion, imprisonment, and finally to arrive at a model of leadership capable of holding together the progress of globalization and its discontents.

1

THE STORY OF
A LIMPING SAINT

A castle, the only fortress in the city, was Pamplona's most important line of defense, with tall and strong towers to watch out for enemies. On top, the soldiers aligned along the battlements. Some were armed with arrows, others with powder guns. A little cannon at the center pointed to the direction from which the French soldiers were approaching. All the soldiers were afraid. They knew the battle against André de Foix was lost. Should they dare to fight, they might well die.

In a corner of the tower, Iñigo, also afraid, was collecting his thoughts. This time of his life was not the future he had dreamed for himself. His was meant to be a future with glory and renown, a future in the court. But nothing seemed to work for him as planned. He had lost too many people in his life: a father, a mother, three brothers in bloody wars at the service of the king. His last hope, which was dashed, was to be a courtier. Juan Velasquez de Cuellar, his mentor and treasurer in the court, had just lost his position and favors in the court. Iñigo's new master, Duque of Nájera, was now losing the battle of his life.

As Ignatius would later ask in his *Autobiography*: *Quid agendum?*, "What to do?" Using the imagination he recommends in the *Spiritual Exercises*, one can hear a voice rising within him, a voice he cannot resist. He is a Loyola, for God's sake. And the Loyola family does not back down from a battle, especially if this battle is in defense of the king. The voice persists and seems to overtake his body, heart, and mind, as if it were a calling. He stands up, determined as he moves to the center to talk to a terrified commander. We are told that "he offered him many reasons" to defend the castle. But before the battle, he turns to his comrades of arms to confess his sins.

Ignatius dictated his *Autobiography* between 1553 and 1555. In it he recounts that on May 20, 1521, during a battle between the loyalist forces of Castile, for whom Ignatius was fighting, and the rebellious forces of Navarre, supported by Francis I of France, a cannon fired a ball that ricocheted off a wall. A piece of shrapnel landed on Ignatius's leg and shattered it, severely injuring his other leg. These French forces, with heavy artillery, wanted to "liberate" Navarre, which had been annexed by the kingdom of Castile nine years earlier.

A handful of resistance fighters loyal to the king of Castile had taken refuge in the citadel. After seeing the enormous superiority of the enemy, the soldiers fighting under the Castilian flag wanted to surrender. One man, however, persuaded them to defend themselves to the end, for the sake of honor. This man, Iñigo López de Oñas y Loyola (1491–1556), was the thirteenth and last child of a family of small Basque nobility, long in the service of the king of Castile. He was thirty years old at the time of the battle. He would later take the name Ignatius out of devotion to the martyr Ignatius of Antioch. When he fell, he, the besieged, who had been the soul of the resistance, immediately surrendered.

From these first lines of the *Autobiography*, the first Companions are identified as Ignatius's comrades in arms. In a sign of what would be his leadership style in the Society, he inspired them to follow him in the battle. He also confessed to them, once they had agreed to follow him and become his subordinates.

Ignatius, the *Autobiography* narrates, offered many reasons to defend Pamplona's fortress. The good leader needs a speech to inspire his troops so that they can fight for him. In this case, the frightened soldiers were ready to fight for Iñigo, their new captain. Words of this speech might be those contained in the address of the supreme commander in the "Meditation of the Two Standards"

[EE 135–48]. As Ignatius invites the retreatant to consider his/ her state of life in the *Spiritual Exercises* [EE 135], he has him/ her go through this moment in Pamplona. This time, Christ is the captain and supreme commander and Lord, calling the retreatants for battle against Lucifer, the captain and commander of this world and its vanities. The address that Christ makes to his "servants and friends whom he is sending on this expedition" has replaced the castle and its stones with human beings: "He recommends that they endeavor to aid all persons, by attracting them, first, to the highest degree of spiritual poverty and also, if his Divine Majesty would be served and pleased to choose them for it, to no less a degree of actual poverty."

Further, in the same address, Ignatius's vain desires are replaced with a "desire of reproaches and contempt, since from these results humility" (EE 148). This first paragraph, therefore, also set the goal of the *Autobiography*, which is connected to the end of the *Spiritual Exercises*. The main question addressed to the retreatant is to move from a person driven by worldly vanities, having a vain and overpowering desire to gain renown (*Aut.* no. 1), to "overcoming oneself, and order one's life, without reaching a decision through some disordered affection" (EE 21). He frames it in terms of surrender of one's own will and interest to the will of God.

After the speech, Iñigo confessed his sins to his comrades. In the *Spiritual Exercises*, this might correspond to the three degrees of humility. Praised as a captain with a group of devoted followers, Iñigo humbled himself. Concerning the first degree of humility, he later wrote, "Even though others would make me Lord of all creatures in the world, I would not enter into deliberation about violating a commandment either human or divine" (EE 165). In the second, "he would not desire or feel himself strongly attached to have wealth rather than poverty, or honor rather than dishonor, or a long life rather than a short one" (EE 166). Instead, "I desire to be regarded as a useless fool for Christ, rather than a wise or prudent person in this world" (EE 167). The commander gains respect by confessing to his subordinates and winning them over through the means of humble service.

However, the bullet remained, piercing tissues of human body and shattering bones. It hit Ignatius in a leg, "shattering it completely, and since the ball passed through both legs, the other was likewise severely wounded" (*Aut.* no. 1). The consequences of a bullet are nothing to celebrate. We are told that Ignatius "fell wounded" and led the other soldiers to surrender to the French. He is called "a wounded man," "transported on a litter." His condition got so serious that the physicians and surgeons "summoned from many places, agreed that the leg should be broken again and the bone reset." Ignatius calls what follows "a butchery." And it was "repeated." We are told again later, that the situation got worse to the point that Ignatius was unable to eat and showed signs that he was approaching death, with the physicians not expecting him to pull through and advising him to make his confession, which he did.

The cannonball moment is therefore speaking to today's world, its wars, wounded and shattered legs and lives, the generosity of its physicians, as well as their powerlessness, to the despair of people suffering the consequences of these wars, and the parents and siblings in hospital waiting rooms being informed by doctors that there is nothing left to be done to save their beloved one.

At this point, the retreatant could ponder two points in the *Spiritual Exercises.* First, a meditation about the first, second, and third sins, "seeing in imagination the physical place where that which I want to contemplate is taking place…and consider my soul as imprisoned in this corruptible body, and my whole compound self as in exile in this valley of tears among brute animals" (EE 47). They would further consider how the angels, "created in grace, not wanting to better themselves by using their freedom to reverence and obey their Creator and Lord, fell into pride, were changed from grace to malice, and were hurled from heaven to hell" (EE 50). Ponder how these many people, in some cases through no fault of their own, are now clothed, like Adam and Eve, "in garments of skins and expelled from paradise (their homes), living out their whole lives in great hardship, deprived of any kind of justice" (EE 51). These images represent "our Lord suspended on the cross" before our very eyes (EE 53). And from there, "ask God what I want and desire" (EE 48), and secondly, "What have I done for Christ? What am I doing for Christ? What ought I to do for Christ?" (EE 53). For Ignatius, these are the images contemplated by the Holy Trinity at the hour of the incarnation.

The victors, however, treated the valiant fighter who had stood up to them with panache with great respect. After a fortnight in Pamplona, where the doctors put the bones back in place as well as they could, the French had Iñigo carried on a stretcher to his family castle, Loyola, next to the town of Azpeitia, some one hundred kilometers from Pamplona. Frenchmen, the enemy, took care of a wounded Ignatius and treated him with courtesy and kindness. This is typical of the Spanish *caballería*, nobility. We can think about it in terms of the laws of war, where they apply. However, the fact that Ignatius's narrative, written by a Portuguese, is mentioning the nationality of the soldiers who cared for him is not accidental. It identifies the actual enemies facing the kingdom. It also speaks to an issue dear to Ignatius and to all his followers: the constant quest for the unity of minds and hearts among the members of the Society.

Rarely has a cannonball been so talked about in the history of Christianity. It was not the only one that was shot that day, and Ignatius was certainly not the only one wounded. There might even have been worse outcomes, with dead soldiers on both sides. Yet, historians highlight this moment as significant because Ignatius's wound in Pamplona is a turning point for his conversion. It turned his life around, and the church later considered this life exemplary and worthy of history. As his bones healed, we read in the *Autobiography*, an inner work slowly started taking place within him. Ignatius reordered his scattered life. He pondered the seeds of the *Spiritual Exercises*: the secret of the Jesuits.

IGNATIUS IN THIS FIRST GLOBALIZATION

Ignatius was plunged, like many young people in today's world, into the heart of the upheavals of the world of his time. This time was above all a time of adventure and migration. The spiritual dimension of these migrations included pilgrimages and missions among the infidels. The time of Ignatius, especially that of his birth in 1491, was a time of great popular piety coupled with great national expectations. The *Reconquista* began centuries earlier, probably with the nostalgia for the reestablishment of the

Hispanic-Visigothic kingdom in the eighth century. By 1265, the great *Reconquista* was over, and except for Granada, the remaining part of the Peninsula, including Portugal, the Crown of Castile and Leon, from Galicia to Murcia, from Vizcaya to Seville, already exhibited the regional areas that are still alive today. Navarre, Aragon, Catalonia, Valencia, and Mallorca had territories that have not changed, or hardly changed at all, and formed historical realities whose evolution has continued uninterrupted until present-day Spain.[1]

This restorative dream eventually gave rise to a national and religious identity of which the Spaniards could be proud. The crowns of Castile and Aragon united in 1482, giving Spain "Catholic Kings" eager to make it a powerful, Catholic nation. It was in Granada that the last battle took place, at the very moment of Ignatius's birth in 1491. Some sources suggest that his father, Don Beltrán, took part in the last battle of Granada, justifying his absence at his wife's bedside during his birth.[2]

James Brodrick describes very well the advent of this new Spain, its optimism, adventurism, and vitality. It carried a sense of mission to extend its influence over the whole world and, with it, the Catholic faith: "Poets, historians and visionaries saw in their dreams a new Jerusalem, purged of the infidels and flying on the dome of the Holy Sepulcher the flag of Spain."[3] This was the advent of what has been called Spain's imperial and Christian Golden Age.[4] In its white splendor, it sometimes showed little tolerance for what was less firmly Catholic and Western.

A few years later, after the founding of the Society in 1539, joining the Jesuits meant joining this new world and its unlimited horizons.[5] The Iberian influence extended to the distant lands of Africa, Asia, and America, under a new regime of patronage skillfully elaborated by the popes and the new Catholic kings. With the papal bull *Inter Coetera* of 1493, Alexander VI consecrated Spain and Portugal, then rivals, as the preferred daughter and son of the papacy. His successor, Julius II, gave them control over education with another papal bull in 1508.

These papal acts caused some discontent among both the old and the new powers. The eldest daughter of the church, France, did not seem to understand this infanticide. She did not participate in the victory of Granada, nor did she finance the expedition of

Christopher Columbus. This was interpreted as a sign of its disinterest in the American adventure. However, the papal decision remained unacceptable to France. Its king, François I, it is said, expressed his opposition sarcastically when he asked the Spanish ambassador to show him the testament of Adam that excluded France from the cutting of the world's cake.[6]

France soon mounted a resistance for control of the Mediterranean. During the battles it undertook in Italy against Spain, two of Iñigo de Loyola's brothers fought and died: the eldest and heir of the family, Juan Pérez, and another, probably Beltrán, the fifth in the line of succession. As a sign of the loyalty of the Loyola family to royalty, and as a prelude to the response that Ignatius would later propose to the call of the temporal king, Juan Pérez "will have given up everything, marriage, inheritance, his life, for the king."[7] Another brother died in Hungary, confronted by the Turks, and one, finally, died, far from Europe, in the Spanish war against the Indians in America.[8]

Further south, in North Africa and beyond to the kingdoms of the Congo, Monomotapa, and especially Ethiopia, as far as Asia, a missionary enterprise was launched from the Iberian Peninsula by the Portuguese Capuchins and explorers. Ignatius, who became the founder of the Jesuits and their first Superior General, undertook to continue it.

The Portuguese had been in Elmina (Gold Coast) since 1482, before moving to São Tomé the following year, where they had fortresses for the slave trade. São Tomé became a diocese in 1534. It covered the entire southern half of West Africa. Around the same time, Diego Cão arrived in the Kingdom of Kongo in 1483. And, in 1491—the year of Ignatius's birth—the princes Mani Soyo and Mani Kongo (Nzinga Nkuvu) were baptized. Nzinga was given the name João I, in honor of the reigning king of Portugal, João II. On June 4, that same year, his son, Mvemba Nzinga (Afonso I), was also baptized with his mother. Then in July, the first church was opened in Mbanza Kongo.

Afonso reigned from 1506 to 1543 and remained committed to Christianity until his death. During his reign, Kongolese Catholicism was marked by a strong adherence to the monarchy and a notable commitment to the Kongo ruling class. Kongo had an elected governing council, a kind of constitutional monarchy.[9] The churches in the kingdom's capital, its rituals and priests, its new symbolic identity, and the major Christian festivals were all part of the national and royal life cycle. At the same time, Mbanza Kongo became São Salvador, a sacred city of churches, the heart and symbol of modern Kongolese and African Catholicism. There was also a large Portuguese community, most of them Christians, who lived off the slave trade and had Black concubines.[10]

In 1546, three years after Afonso's death, the bishop of São Tomé ordained a young mestizo, "Diogo Gomes, who was born in São Salvador and became an excellent priest and, later, a Jesuit. He composed the first Kikongo catechism, printed in Lisbon, which, however, does not seem to have survived long for use in Kongo."[11] But until 1591, the year in which Filippo Pigatetta published his *Relatione del reame di Congo*, Kongo was essentially unknown in Europe, even in Rome. It was confused, as was Benin, with the Christian kingdom of Prester John, in western Ethiopia. Africa, for the West, was a homogeneous block, a country.

In the east of the continent, Yohannes Bermudez, a Roman Catholic layman residing in Ethiopia, was chosen to replace Abuna Marcos, weakened by age, as Abuna of Ethiopia (that is, ambassador). Because of the Arab blockade, Marcos could not obtain a new appointment from Alexandria. Just after his enthronement in 1535, Bermudez was sent to Rome to inform the pope, and João III of Portugal, of the Ethiopian king's willingness to recognize his supreme authority and submit to him. However, in exchange, he wanted urgent military aid.[12] Jean-Baptiste Coulbeaux thinks that Claude (Glaodios as he calls him) had a genuine interest in the Roman faith. To prove it, Glaodios approved the appointment of Andres Oviedo as the new patriarch.[13]

Ignatius himself wanted to go to Ethiopia. But Pope Julius III refused.[14] Having become Superior General, Ignatius sent the first Jesuit missionaries to Ethiopia. It was after his death, however, that they finally managed to settle there and became pioneers in the European discovery of Ethiopia. The early Jesuits in the country are described as "highly educated men" who "wrote systematic accounts of the country, its history, its administration, its ethnography and its wildlife."[15]

A TIME OF DISILLUSIONMENT

The last born of the Loyolas, therefore, had models of warriors and adventurers to imitate. His father, however, seemed to have other ambitions for his youngest son, and had his head tonsured. Some say that it was the custom that the youngest son be consecrated to God. Others see in it the concern of the father to ensure the clerical benefits to the youngest of the sons, failing to make him a scribe.[16] Both hypotheses are not to be excluded. One might also see in it the protective desire of a father who dreamed of new opportunities for his son in the service of the court, but far from the service of the weapons and the adventures without return to the Americas. It is difficult to know if the young man consented to this rather familial project. What is certain is that the wound of Pamplona allowed Ignatius to rediscover this clerical vocation, this time despite the opposition of his older brother.

Around 1507, after the death of his father, who had fought in Granada in 1492, Ignatius was adopted by a family friend, Juan Velásquez de Cuellar, treasurer at the court of King Ferdinand of Castile. The education he received there was that of a courtier. In a world dominated by an adventurous spirit and where family relationships were a key to success, Ignatius grew up as an orphan. He passed through the hands of three tutors, each of whom had a considerable influence on his character.

However, the interest in Ignatius's infirmity goes beyond his simple story of conversion. Ignatius, the limping saint, is a new school of history that completes a strand of social history. The history of the infirmity is concerned with a socially marginalized and historically ignored category. This category is, however, inseparable from the history of the church, notably that of the saints and their miracles. Moreover, Ignatius the lame speaks differently to the recipients of the Jesuit apostolate today.

While doing my doctoral studies at Boston University, I served as a teaching assistant for a course on "Spiritual Guidance in Christian Traditions" by Professor Claire Wolfteich. We invited William (Bill) Barry to speak to us about the Ignatian tradition. Bill was a leading authority on the subject. And the students were given some excerpts from the booklet of the *Spiritual Exercises*, with specific questions about its structure.

At question-and-answer time, a student asked Bill if the *Exercises* discriminated against the disabled and vulnerable. Bill gently dodged the "bullet," making some points by sharing his own vulnerability as a recovered alcoholic. But the bullet hit me in the heart, because more than one student had a disability. Turning to me, Bill, who was also my spiritual advisor, asked if I had anything to say. I told him that in the Central African culture where I came from, children do not speak after their elders. At his insistence, however, I replied that I could not resist thinking that Ignatius himself was lame, that this whole enterprise began because a bullet had broken his leg and seriously wounded the other. We had complemented each other perfectly. The students seemed more than satisfied, and the class fell into a profound silence.

Following the cannonball moment in Pamplona, Ignatius's foot remained "short," very ugly for the one who dreamed of being a knight, and unbearable therefore for this medieval. It is not the only place in which Ignatius links ugliness and disability. Indebted to a certain medieval conception, the handicap was perceived as a consequence of sin, sometimes associated with cases of demonic possession.

If the cannonball shattered the knight's military dreams, this physical ugliness shattered the charming heart of the seducer who dreamed of a princess. Voluntarily, "he decided to martyr himself: he asked the doctors to cut the bones that protrude." Then followed a long convalescence of nearly a year.

While he waited to recover, Ignatius wanted to kill some time. To do so, he wanted to read some novels of chivalry. Instead, he was given *a Life of Christ* and *Lives of Saints*. Physically, he was subjected to a new butchery because he did not wish to belong to that category, that of the invalids. Through the readings and because of his immobility, he saw himself forced to make the inner journey, to confront a past that he would have liked to leave behind forever. He read in Spanish, not in Latin as a well-educated nobleman would. This reveals another handicap, that of letters, at an age as advanced as his and for a man of his blood and rank.

But Ignatius did not give up his dream. He had desired to be at the service of a princess whose mother was a prisoner because she had a disability, Joanna the Mad. The princess in question was the Infanta Catalina. She was not the one of Aragon (1485–1535) and daughter of the Catholic kings Isabel of Castile (1451–1504) and Ferdinand of Aragon (1452–1516), and who later became queen of England.[17] Rather, it was the Catalina who, on September 17, 1525, became queen of Portugal by marrying João III.[18] Ignatius would have seen her, and would have fallen in love with her for the first time in Tordesillas, while he was accompanying one of his tutors, Duke of Nájera.

Although it remained fictitious, Jean Lacouture goes so far as to imagine the great benefits that such a romance between Ignatius and the queen brought to the Society in Portugal and to the world. In his imaginary story, the heroine and wife of John III is "the same Catherine who, as a little Infanta of Castile walled up in Tordesillas at the side of the mad queen, her mother, met the cripple of Pamplona, Iñigo, the youngest of the Loyolas."[19] The queen might have known of the feelings that the founder had brought to her. She could well have read the *Hechos del Padre Ignacio* (Acts of Father Ignatius) shortly after his death, and Luis Gonçalves da Camara, a Portuguese, worked in her Lisbon court before the late death of Catherine (1578).[20]

The memory of this past and her beautiful ladies now left Ignatius dry and sad, with the sadness of sin. This sorting out of the forces that build us up and those that destroy us is discernment. It leads to a decision of conversion: for Ignatius on his convalescent bed, as for the retreatant of the *Exercises*. Just as the medieval crusaders who, at the instigation of the pope, went to Jerusalem to give themselves a chance of redemption, Ignatius also resolved to go there, to do penance and help the souls. Ignatius had not yet finished recovering from his wounds in the castle when his brothers observed the change. Ignatius would thus have converted. He himself admitted to having a great "repugnance" for his sins. This same repugnance he would later ask of the penitent in the First Week of the *Spiritual Exercises*. It was to be obtained as a grace. For sin, as one of the greatest physical and social handicaps of the time, was as ugly, purulent, and contagious as leprosy. And the Jesuit who created division in the Society must be rid of it like the plague. It produced in the soul the same feelings that the new physiognomy of his foot produced in him: ugliness and repugnance.

The Duke of Nájera, his last tutor, knew that Ignatius felt better. The latter told his brother that he wanted to join him in Navarre (*Aut.* no. 12). His brother, however, knew Ignatius's true intentions. He tried to dissuade him. In vain! So, Ignatius left the family castle, where he would never set foot again. Even when, thirteen years later, after his studies, he returned to his village of Azpeitia, he stayed in a hospice and witnessed his new life by teaching catechism to the children. He headed to the east coast, to Catalonia, to take a boat to Jerusalem. He first stopped for a while at the great Marian shrine of Montserrat, where he made a general confession of his life and did some spiritual exercises under the guidance of a French Benedictine.

On the eve of the Feast of the Annunciation of the Lord, March 25, Ignatius spent a night of prayer in the chapel, like the knights going on crusade, sometimes standing, sometimes kneeling. He gave the abbey his mule and his sword and left for Barcelona after exchanging his fine nobleman's clothes with those of a poor man he had met. Passing through Manresa, a small town near Barcelona, he felt the desire to pause there, and to write. In fact, he would stay there for almost a year, where the work of God continued in him and reached a peak in the form of an illumination.

SEE ALL THINGS NEW IN CHRIST

At Loyola, during his convalescence, Ignatius had decided to change his life, especially by following the example of the saints, to do as they did, or even better than they did! To do great things for God was his project. What he was going to learn at Manresa was to let go of his own project and let God accomplish his. He stayed in the hospice and spent his time in a life of prayer and rigorous austerity. The people of Manresa were impressed by this man whom they called "the man in the sack" because of his pilgrim's habit made of coarse cloth, his hair and nails that he never cut, his austere diet, his nobility that showed through in spite of himself in his way of living and speaking.

God was going to make Ignatius go through a hard test of purification. Sometimes he experienced great joys, favors from

God, inner illumination, sometimes he went through darkness, morbid recollection of the sins of his youth, doubt, disgust, even the temptation of suicide (*Anfechtung*). Thus, Ignatius gradually learned to let go of his plan for God and let God realize his plan for him. Ignatius slowly discovered this plan in the form of a growing desire to help souls, as he put it. From then on, this would be the driving force behind his entire existence and all his choices.

In 2021, the Jesuits and their collaborators decided to celebrate a jubilee to mark the 500th anniversary of Ignatius's conversion and canonization. The jubilee activities were organized around the theme of conversion: "Seeing All Things New in Christ" (2 Cor 5:17). This expression is Pauline. It is also a crucial experience in the life of Ignatius. It corresponds to the Cardoner's illumination:

> He sat down for a little while with his face to the river—Cardoner—which was running deep. While he was seated there, the eyes of his understanding began to be opened; though he did not see any vision, he understood and knew many things, both spiritual things and matters of faith and learning, and this was with so great an enlightenment that everything seemed new to him. It was as if he were a new man with a new intellect. (*Aut.* no. 31)

Recent historiography, especially the work of Sabina Pavone, shows that the formulation of this experience in the *Autobiography* could have been borrowed from the Middle Ages. The Dominican sister Maria de Santo Domingo (1485–1524), a Spanish mystic of the fifteenth century, *Alumbrada, avant la lettre*, claimed to communicate directly with Christ and the Blessed Virgin. In front of the Inquisition tribunal in Salamanca, the same one that judged Ignatius a few years later, she defended herself energetically and without fear, under the guidance of the Holy Spirit, believing that one did not need to be educated to speak about the things of God. With the unconditional support of Ferdinand of Aragon and Cardinal Francisco Jimenez de Cisneros of Alcala (1436–1517), she was cleared in 1510.[21]

In the same way, the Cardoner was, for Ignatius, an experience of pure grace. It came after a year of doubt and anguish that had brought him to the brink of suicide. According to the historian Alain Woodrow, "The content of the experience escapes us and the 'objective' historian will remain hungry. The fact remains that its effects are definitive. At the end of his life, Ignatius would confess that he did not seem to have received as much in the course of his entire existence as he had received on this single occasion."[22]

It is not a question, it should be specified, of a vision as at La Storta in 1537, but of an illumination of the intelligence.[23] This illumination carried with it the risk of the illuminism. At stake against Ignatius before the inquisitors was the pneumatology of Ignatius. Although Ignatius referred directly to the Holy Spirit throughout all the *Exercises* only six times (plus five times quoting Scripture), he was the object of at least eight trials until 1545, suspected of illuminism.

The experience of Ignatius, and the novelty that he represented, had something of "Protestant" or, better, of pre-Pentecostalism. At the time, it carried the danger of John Hus and John Wycliffe, medieval theologians, whose sermons greatly influenced the sixteenth-century reformer Martin Luther. These two theologians, when confronted by their inquisitors, relied on Christ as their only judge. Believing that the Spirit could communicate directly to the faithful soul, they rejected all ecclesiastical and hierarchical mediation.

Ignatius avoided this trap, first, by going to Rome to obtain permission from the pope to travel to the Holy Land. He further developed this *sensus ecclesiae* in the meditation to have the true sense with the church militant. At the time Ignatius proposed this meditation, he was aware of the Protestant risk; he also knew the church that Protestantism vomited. The *sensus ecclesiae* was therefore inseparable from the *sensus fidei*.

Moreover, where the *Anfechtung* had led Luther to deny the importance of works for the good of souls by relying on grace alone, Ignatius turned to the sacramental life and to the apostolate. Certainly, like Luther, he received grace in all its brilliance and purity, understanding the things of faith as well as of the world, of this world and all that inhabits it. His illumination, however, was different from all others of his time because it was apostolic and because it remained ecclesial. Ignatius maintained the importance of penance, confession, almsgiving, and charity as helpful means or ways to save one's soul by continually reforming one's state of life. His fidelity to the church of his time was equally an admirable evangelical action. It places the mercy and motherhood of the church at the heart of the founding of the Society and its spirituality. In face of Mother Church, confronted by corruption and moral decay, Ignatius had the choice of being the child who goes out of his way to expose the sins of his mother on Instagram or Twitter. He decided, instead, evangelically one might admit, to stay home and care for the sinful and ailing mother. Fidelity to the church thus depersonalized the invitation to "see all things new in Christ." For, as Peter Faber, quoted by Pope Francis, said, "Those who wanted to reform the Church were right, but God did not want to correct it with their methods." The Spirit who makes us see all things new "makes us men of the Church—not clerics, but ecclesial."[24]

Finally, Ignatius's illumination was also associated with the mystery of the cross. The Cardoner found its full meaning in the vision of La Storta where, in 1537, God the Father placed Ignatius with his Son carrying his cross. Once again, Ignatius was on his way to Rome, the path of the church. Put with the Son carrying his cross, the Jesuits would interpret this new experience as a call to serve under the banner of Christ. This service was carried out in a society that worked on this earth and was understood in contrast to the "angelic" Society, that of Ignatius's contemporaries Oviedo and Onfroy.

EXPELLED FROM JERUSALEM AND THE RETURN TO SCHOOL

Going on pilgrimage was part of the popular devotions of medieval Spain, inspired by centuries of *Reconquista*. To take the road to Jerusalem had been, since the time of Pope Urban II, a spiritual crusade, linked to penance and even the practice of indulgences. The *Reconquista* also meant widening one's horizon, a road to discovery of new spaces and cultures, as well as conquering oneself so as to keep oneself from the corruption of this world by deciding without disordered attachments. This would be the aim of the *Spiritual Exercises* (EE 21) and that of a missionary Society that Ignatius helped create: one that is dedicated to the good of the souls.

Jerusalem was, above all, the Holy Land, a devotion in itself. It represented the power of the relics, the dispensers of Christ's protection to the crusaders and of his redemptive power over sinners. This place par excellence of popular devotion remained under the vigilance of the Franciscans and Dominicans. They forbade Ignatius to settle there again. Like his leg, his dream, his life project, was broken.

Ignatius had to return to school. Already, at the beginning of his conversion, he read in Spanish and took notes (*Aut.* no. 11). This was the best education that, with a rather checkered childhood, he could have afforded. He received it, first, from Maria Garín, his adoptive mother until the age of sixteen, when his father joined his mother in the afterlife, fourteen years after her premature death. Garín was poor, but she had a respectable education, as did many Spanish girls who benefited from the educational reforms of Queen Isabella. This education, in the Basque country at that time, was received through literacy campaigns but also through the new communal schools, the parochial schools being reserved only for future clerics like Ignatius, and the monastic schools for candidates to the monastic life or the sons of the nobles who founded these monasteries. Moreover, Garín had a good memory. It was from her, acting as a witness to the canonization of Ignatius, that we have the date of birth of the Saint, around October 23, 1491.

To eradicate ignorance, that spiritual poverty capable of undermining the beauty of a soul like the plague, one had to work for the redemption of humanity. An essential part of this work, education was therefore key for the consolation of souls and for their salvation. If we read the *Formula of the Institute*, approved later in 1540, this relationship between education and salvation is contained in the works of charity. These make explicit the earlier apostolate of the instruction of children and the ignorant. The candidate to the Society will be convinced, we read, that he

> belongs to a Company instituted above all to devote itself principally to the good of souls in Christian life and doctrine and to the propagation of the faith, by public

preaching and the ministry of the word of God, the Spiritual Exercises and works of charity, and namely by the Christian formation of children and the ignorant [unlettered persons/rudos], and the spiritual consolation of the faithful by means of confessions.

This paragraph offers a literary conclusion. It begins with the good of souls and concludes with the good of souls. The love that is expressed more by deeds than by words in the contemplation *ad amorem*, and that is therefore sacramental, is accompanied by an agenda of social transformation at the heart of which are the education of children and the ignorant and the sacrament of reconciliation. It was not by chance that the first Companions placed so much importance on the ministry of preaching and confessions.

In the Middle Ages, the goal of any confession was the satisfaction of the penitent. But for the penitent to be satisfied, his confession had to be complete, and the penance given to him by the priest had to be proportional to the fault committed. Now, human memory is fallible. The probability of an incomplete confession was therefore very high, increasing scruples among the poor penitents. This resulted in literary productions (confession manuals), but also a need on the part of both the clergy (then often illiterate) and the faithful for a basic knowledge of arithmetic and proportions. This was how scientific education developed in the Middle Ages, how the first rationalist currents developed, which we already find in Thomas Aquinas.

A good education eliminated scruples, gave satisfaction to the penitent, ensured the validity of absolution, and was essential to the salvation of souls. For Ignatius, therefore, education went beyond mere scholarly erudition. It was part of the works of charity and essential to the good of souls.

The new man went to Jerusalem in total trust in God (without money). The ecclesiastical masters of the holy places, the Franciscans, prevented him from staying there. As a result, he returned to Barcelona. There, a decisive question arises for him: *Quid agendum?* "What is to be done?" What did God expect of him? Ignatius understood that, in order to help souls, he absolutely had to go through the detour of studies leading to the priesthood. Hence, in 1526, he began his studies in Spain, Alcalá, at the age of 35.

THE SCHOOL OF HUMANISM

Aware of the value of education, Ignatius put himself at the school of modern humanism. After a brief stay in Barcelona, where he applied himself to learning grammar, he went to Alcalá. Out of curiosity, pious women gathered around Ignatius, looking for new experiences. Some of them had spiritual ecstasies and seizures, even fainting. According to Stefania Pastore, these behaviors were foreign to the communitarian and elitist spirituality of the *alumbrados* such as María de Cazalla.[25]

But his main mission was to study. For three years, Ignatius took everything from the ground up, with children. This period in Alcalá represents "the first test for Loyola's religious program in an extremely sophisticated and vital environment that originally looked upon his religiosity with a somewhat reserved eye."[26] There, Ignatius met Juan de Ávila and Manuel de Miona, who would later become a Jesuit, in Paris in 1541. The latter introduced Ignatius to the works of Erasmus and the doctrines of the *alumbrados*.[27]

Pastore highlights another aspect that later marked the history of the Society with marginalized populations in Europe. Alcalá was the city of the Complutensian Bible, and the street where the small hospital where Ignatius resided and served was the Jewish center of the city, where most inhabitants and their descendants had converted to Catholicism. To these Black and Jewish minorities were added the *beatas*, "female and lay tertiaries to whom the path of perfection formerly reserved for religious was now open."[28]

The spiritual experiences of the *beatas* and *alumbrados* had global implications. It represented then, and now, the existence of a Christianity of trances at the threshold of modernity. The *beatas*, in fact, "fall into ecstasies and crises, and fainting spells, which put the women of Alcalá, whom Loyola initiates in his exercises, to a great test."[29] Alcalá established in Ignatius "the conviction of a universal call to perfection…which is mixed with the certainty that any person can reach a meditative state."[30]

Such connections were likely to arouse the interest of the guardians of orthodoxy. Ignatius was questioned by the Inquisitor Juan Rodriguez de Figueroa (1490–1565), who forbade him to preach. Having ignored this first warning, he was arrested and imprisoned for forty-nine days in 1527.[31] The surviving evidence from the trial describes Loyola and his early followers as appearing barefoot, dressed in "beige robes" down to their feet "in the manner of the apostles." Their preaching referred to a primitive apostolic age marked by simplicity, purity, and divine illumination.[32] Among these early Iniguistas were Calixto de Sa, Lope de Cáceres, Juan de Arteaga, and Juan de Reynalde.[33]

TRIALS IN SALAMANCA

Persecuted in Alcalá, Ignatius continued his intellectual journey at the University of Salamanca, the most prestigious in the Iberian Peninsula during the fifteenth and sixteenth centuries.[34] The University of Salamanca was a global institution. It was networked with branches in Spanish America and the Philippines. The Dominicans reigned supreme, imposing Thomism, although humanism took its first steps there around 1538.[35]

The university also represented the spirit of the *Reconquista* under whose shadow it was created in 1254 with the support of the king and the approval of the pope. By the middle of the fifteenth century, its organizational chart already projected the structure of a modern university, with a rector, a chancellor, an academic council, and a student council. Their roles were well distributed. The most illustrious among the students received the title of doctor, a title by which the student scholar also acquired a certain nobility of soul.[36]

Ignatius arrived at the university campus without fanfare. Four Iniguistas preceded him there. While praying in a church, a woman, who had probably followed them from Alcalá, recognized him and directed him to the rest of the group. He made his regular confession at the Dominican convent (monastery) of San Estéban, and it was his confessor who informed Ignatius, barely ten days after his arrival in the city, that the fathers of his community had invited him to dinner. Once at the table, Ignatius realized that it was a trap and that he was really facing an inquisition on the content of his spiritual conversations. The ones with his confessor? Or with other people? In only ten days, who could have informed the Dominicans of these "things they would like to learn about him" (*Aut.* 64)? Ignatius gave them an account of everything, "how little he had studied and on what little basis" (*Aut.* 64).

The prior of the convent, Diego de San Pedro, was attending a conference in Valladolid, probably about the *Relectiones Theologicae* (1528–1539) by Francisco de Vitoria (1483–1546). It discussed the legitimacy of the colonial conquest as a papal donation, which granted the Spaniards and Portuguese the right to occupy the indigenous lands and evangelize their inhabitants, who were considered "subhuman (homunculi), illiterate and impious (Sepùlveda)."[37] Parallel to these worldwide intellectual and academic debates, the sub-prior was questioning a beggar who, by his own admission, "did not know what the doctors said about these things" (*Aut.* 68), and about the dress of his Companion Calixte.

Two forms of Catholicism met with these early controversies. There was an authentic, orthodox, and Dominican Catholicism, and a mass-spirit-filled Catholicism bordering on heresy. In the eyes of his inquisitors, Ignatius concentrated in his person a cheap, "illiterate," and "impious" Christianity (because he was suspected of heresy) that was to be fought in the same way as the impiety of the Indians or the Saracens. The criterion of authenticity was not, however, the purity of the gospel or baptism with the Holy Spirit, which the Inquisition feared, but Thomism and Scholasticism.

Ignatius's encounter with the Inquisition in Salamanca thus staged a glocalization in which the battles being waged by the Spanish crown in the Indies were being fought in a convent in Salamanca against a Spanish nobleman who had become poor and was being held prisoner by the fathers for twenty-two days. The evangelization itself became an extension of the construction of the Spanish nation begun with the *Reconquista* and in which both hispanicizing and catholicizing merged. Having found Ignatius innocent, the Dominican fathers reduced his actions to those of a catechist, at best to popular pastoral ministry. He could teach "the catechism" and "speak of the things of God," but he should not "define," proper to the masters and doctors, until he had done at least four years of theology.

"C'EST PARIS!"

Seeing the difficulties that were presented with trials questioning his orthodoxy, Ignatius decided to continue his studies at the University of Paris. After earning a Master of Arts, Ignatius left for Paris, "alone and on foot" (*Aut.* 73). Arriving there on February 3, 1528, he was welcomed by a group of Spanish students.

Paris was the seat of the best university in the world. Europeans of various nationalities abounded. The Deliberation of the First Jesuits of 1539 offers a portrait of this multicultural Paris. Among the first Jesuits were Savoyards, Flemish, Spaniards, Portuguese, and so on. Since the thirteenth century, those with a Master of Theology had watched over academic orthodoxy under the direction of the Chancellor.[38] Soon, Ignatius and his followers faced their inquisitive wrath.[39]

University studies in Paris were expensive. By moving to an urban environment, the students found themselves in an economic system in which money was king. They could no longer rely on the resources of their rural environment that allowed for a self-sufficient domestic economy. According to Serge Lusignan, by refusing the economic support of land ownership and by choosing to live in the cities, the mendicant orders "were necessarily part of an economic system based on money, which, for their part, they obtained by begging."[40] Fake clerics also swarmed the city, eager to profit from this professional begging.[41] Colleges and hospices for poor students multiplied. But such structures tended to discriminate against people with physical disabilities.[42]

In Paris, Ignatius had to live on alms, as did half of the Parisian population, which was then living below the poverty line, with worrying levels of unemployment.[43] He experienced homelessness because he was unable to pay his rent. Confronted with these conditions, he experienced "great inconvenience for studies" (*Aut.* 74). He gave the Exercises, took care of the sick, wrote to friends of the Portuguese court to obtain scholarships for students at the University of Paris. In search of a patron to support him, he already imagined what obedience would be like in the Society once it was founded: "When the master gives me an order, I will think that it is Christ who gives me an order; and when another gives me an order, I will think that Saint Peter gives me an order" (*Aut.* 75).

It was there, in Paris, that God gathered the first Companions to whom Ignatius gave the Spiritual Exercises. Favre was the first to experience the power of the Exercises, which he began to give to many others even before he left Paris. Master Francis Xavier was won over almost at the same time. After him came Master Diego Lainez, who, like Xavier, came from Spain. Lainez was already educated in the arts and lived in the same inn as Iñigo. Iñigo befriended him and gave him the Exercises. It was Lainez who brought Master Salmerón, his friend from Spain.

According to Juan de Polanco's account, it was around this time that Nicolas Bobadilla arrived from Spain. He asked for Iñigo, who had a reputation for helping many students. Iñigo provided him with a certain comfort that allowed him to stay and study at the University of Paris. After them came Master Claude le Jay, then Master Simon Rodrigues, who "before meeting Iñigo *erat vir desideriorum* ('was a man of desires'), though perhaps not so much *secundum scientiam* ('according to knowledge')."[44] Talking and conversing with him, Ignatius made him join the group. Two others, Master Pascase Broët and Master Jean Codure, were won over through Favre, after Iñigo's departure for Spain.

These are the ten Companions who were there when the Society was instituted and confirmed. Favre and Xavier, with whom Ignatius shared the room, have all been canonized, a clear sign of the effectiveness of the Exercises as a path of conversion. John Calvin stayed at this same college, and his ideas continued to make their way to the University of Paris. It was not surprising, then, that Ignatius wrote his "Rules for arriving at the true meaning of the Church militant" when in Paris.

On August 15, 1535, the first Companions made their vows at Montmartre. On their way to Rome, the Companions stopped in Venice. It was a pivotal city, where the cultures of Renaissance Italy abounded, but also business, diverse cultures and religions, and great poverty. While in Venice, Ignatius wrote the Principle and Foundation of the *Exercises* (EE 23). This was his theological synthesis. The Companions also practiced works of charity there. They decided to leave Venice, dividing into different groups according to their affinities: Iñigo, Favre, and Lainez in Vincentia; Xavier and Salmerón in Moncelese; Jean Codure and Diego de Hoces in Treviso; Claude le Jay and Simon Rodrigues in Bassan; Pascase Broët and Nicolas Bobadilla in Verona.

After Lent, in the year 1538, they all met in Rome, staying first in a house called Trinity. They preached in various churches and taught Christian doctrine to children and heard confessions. Once Ignatius's plan for the new institute was accepted in 1540 ("the finger of God is there," the pope is said to have said), Ignatius finally reluctantly accepted the office of Superior General. For sixteen years, he would remain in Rome, where he would be in contact with his Companions sent to different regions of the world, while at the same time writing the *Constitutions* in accordance with what the new order was experiencing, notably the important development of colleges, which was not foreseen at the beginning.

In addition to his office as Superior General, Ignatius also began the work of Saint Martha's, where the women of "bad life" were gathered. After having withdrawn from sin, according to their devotion, they became nuns or got married. The house reintegrated more than a hundred women into society. The Companions worked hard to help the poor. There was a great famine in Rome, leaving the poor starving, cold, and abused in the streets. They even took some of the poor into their homes and gave alms to many others. This work of charity increased so much that in a house they had in the tower of Narangola, they had up to two hundred, three hundred, and even four hundred poor people, to whom they first provided a house, heating, and as many beds as they could find, for the healthiest among them with straw.[45]

THE ENCOUNTER WITH THE MOOR

Judged as a second-rate Catholic by the inquisitors in Alcalá, Salamanca, and Paris, Ignatius was not the last on the scale of religions, races, or social classes. The episode of his encounter with the Moor seems insignificant in the *Autobiography* (*Aut.* 15–16). It is, however, a distinctive phenomenon of this first globalization. On his way to Manresa, the Narrative tells us, Ignatius meets a Moor, a "Mudejar." These were the free Muslims of Castile who, after they had enjoyed great freedom of law and worship, were gradually marginalized at the turn of the fifteenth century. The Mudejars were imposed "a strict apartheid with regard to the residence of the Muslims, [who then] lived in morerías or mourarias separated from the rest of the city."[46] The creation of a spotless Catholicism was already underway.

It is possible that the Moor here is a Morisco, a Muslim converted to Christianity, but whose faith was still marked by Muslim dogma on Catholicism. This generated debates and even conflicts about the virginity of Mary.[47] Nothing is said about the education of the Moor, who nevertheless seems to have had arguments. Ignatius, however, was without theology; and his enlightenment at the Cardoner had not yet taken place. He had had only a few previous visions, at the beginning of his conversion, and above all, the catechism lessons of his childhood.

If the Muslim believes that the Virgin could have conceived without knowing a man, he refuses, however, to believe that Mary remained a virgin after giving birth (*Aut.* 15). This was a theological position common to some Morisco circles in Castile. They even used it sometimes to provoke pious Catholics, in this climate of *Reconquista* in which the Virgin Mary had become the patron saint.[48] Dozens of mosques were dedicated to her in reconquered regions. For these crusaders, the virginity of Mary was more than a matter of piety. She represented a fortress that only Christ could breach.[49] She was the symbol of the new Spain, Catholic, and immaculate in its aspiration to get rid of everything that was not Catholic and orthodox.

In his *disputatio* with the Moor, Ignatius was unable to convince him. Furthermore, having won the argument with Ignatius, the Mudejar went ahead of him faster, thanks to his donkey. This situation highlighted a double infirmity for Ignatius: his lack of argument, and the physical weakness of a man once a knight and who now limped after being wounded in Pamplona. Ignatius might have been deeply disturbed for this double "failure." He had to satisfy his anger against the Moor by defending the honor of Our Lady. He would kill the Moor if he could find him. At the crossroads, not knowing which road to take to find his new enemy, Ignatius relied on his mule. It was up to him to choose whether to follow the village road or the one that went toward the urban center. Like the later Jesuit apostolate, the mule chose the urban center and abandoned the village (*Aut.* 16). In the city, where, as in most of the large European cities, thrift shop vendors abound,[50] Ignatius purchased new clothes. He dressed in sacks, with a stick and a gourd, and took on the habit of a pilgrim.

Ignatius's devotion to the Virgin was well rooted in the family, its militarism and spirit of conquest. Ignatius's brother dedicated himself to the Virgin before dying in battle in northern Italy. Ignatius's father fought in Granada, the seat of Marian devotions for fighting soldiers and captives. Ignatius himself wanted to kill the Moor who had dishonored Mary; he consecrated himself to her and gave her a singular place in the resurrection narratives of the *Spiritual Exercises* and the consecration of the Jesuits through their religious vows.

Through this encounter with the Moor, we also see a powerful phenomenon in early modern world Christianity, namely, a Christianity of captives. Europeans are held in North and East Africa by Asian Muslims, who are themselves segregated in Europe. At the same time, Muslims and Europeans held Africans captive in East Africa and sold them into slavery in the Americas, where the prevention of Indian enslavement and the baptism of Black slaves became the first Jesuit version of liberation theology. This Christianity of captivity would mark the history of the Society, not only its beginnings in Africa in the sixteenth century but also in nineteenth- and twentieth-century America.

IN THE VORTEX OF THE "FIRST GLOBALIZATION"

Ignatius was born at a time when a new world was evolving with unlimited horizons for the Spanish. Spain seemed ready to become the superpower. If the unity of the crown and the church had been achieved, many young people (including the nobles) were still disoriented, their lives butchered. This disruption was first social, because Ignatius was an orphan of his parents and brothers, carried away by endless wars, and a sanitary system to be perfected. His childhood was the symbol of a system of patronage that protected noble children and guaranteed them a future in the court or in the priesthood. It was also, unfortunately, the symbol of an itinerant poverty: that of the orphans of war, of the mad or imprisoned princesses, of the adventurers across deserts and oceans, without hope of return. Ignatius was the symbol of the opportunities of globalization and its discontents.

Ignatius's conversion marked his true passage into adulthood. Above all, it involved an immobilization. If the initiatory suffering was not foreign to him, the cannonball succeeded in immobilizing him, making him physically dependent, at the mercy of the choices of others for his distractions, but also and above all, of his interior world, which could not be contained. It was also a conversion of dreams, for Ignatius had to move from a love of the world and its glories to a love for the world, from his self to God, and finally from God to himself. Faced with a boiling and bursting world, Ignatius rediscovered interiority and sought the soul of an ever-expanding Spain. It was necessary to discern well so as to make wise choices. He found a principle and foundation on which to build the edifice of his life. Ignatius was converted to himself, to God, to the human, to creation. He saw all things new, with the general optimism of a powerful Spain but also the realism of a life tested by the fire and losses of globalization. He was aware of the infinite mercy of God, who could speak to the heart of the global subject.

Ignatius then went through an intellectual conversion: from Azpeitia to Barcelona, then Alcala, Salamanca, and Paris. His dream, a divine inspiration that bordered on illuminism, was put to the test by the Inquisition. He intellectualized his charisma. The instruction of the God who spoke directly to the heart of the modern person was theologized in a process of corrections-ratifications-confirmations. This intellectual conversion was an openness of mind, an attention to the signs of the times, an ability to adapt, to redefine the choice, to rely on others, for the greater service of God, in the church and to the most vulnerable.

Ignatius had to convert his life project constantly. He moved from itinerancy to the sedentary life of a religious order with constitutions and a great bureaucracy. Ignatius's governance was halfway between curialism and conciliarism. It was a solidary and centralized governance in a globalized world. Education became one pillar; missions was another. Both represented the reign of accommodation.

This inner journey, these constant changes of the project cultivated in him a sense of discernment. We gradually see a portrait of Ignatius as a saint, beginning with his first Companions. The life of Saint Ignatius that Diego Lainez, Juan de Polanco, Gonçalves da Camâra, or Pedro de Ribadeneira wrote was a life written for the good of souls and with a view to canonization. These early biographies were characterized by a progressive setting aside of Ignatius and by his exaltation. Focusing on his impact on the church and society, Ignatius emerged as a reformer *ad intra*. His miracles formed the background of a popular and devotional spirituality. He became a saint for the new globalization, in its rationalism and in its Pentecostalism.

POPULAR LESSONS OF A LIFE

There are traces of this historiography of Saint Ignatius from the margins, although none of them has really been systematic. Jean Lacouture recalls a visitor to Padua who presented Ignatius as "a Spaniard who was small in stature, a bit lame, and had joyful eyes."[51] Later in his text, referring to Ignatius's convalescence, Lacouture speaks of the "cripple of Azpeitia."[52]

James Brodrick also recounts that one of the many people who came to him for spiritual and temporal help in Paris became very melancholic and asked Iñigo to sing a little for her and dance as they did in the Basque country. She believed such a gesture would cheer her up and console her. Iñigo sang and danced at once, "even though he was slightly lame." This had such an effect that his melancholic friend "began to get rid of the depression that was eating away at her heart, until she was completely cured in a few days."[53]

Ignatius of Loyola, the founder of the Jesuit order, was lame, and it is not for lack of literature that this seems like glowing news. In fact, the story of Saint Ignatius's conversion is well known to us, and it keeps repeating the founder's infirmity. The work of the Jesuits, as the different general congregations remind us, consists in the defense of the faith and the propagation of justice that it implies. It requires that, in the ennoblement and elitism for which

Paul Grendler reproaches Jesuit education,[54] they never forget that Ignatius was *rudo* and never forgot the *rudos*. It was he who put together the instruction of children and of the *rudos* as the constitutive ministry of the Society. By recovering the *rudo*, Ignatius therefore made the Jesuits friends of the poor. For as Father Arrupe said, "Where there is suffering, there is the Society." Pope Francis took up this intuition of Arrupe's in his address to the fathers during the opening of the 36th General Council of the Jesuits. Being friends of the poor, serving them, can lead to the supreme sacrifice if that is the desire of the Divine Majesty.

Although we know that he was noble by birth—and the language of nobility would itself be difficult to understand for a child of Douala, Bangui, Soweto, Bombay, Manila, and Bogotá in the twenty-first century—Ignatius was also a roughneck, and the physiognomy of his family could resemble in many ways our African families. It was a large family, as he was the last born of eleven children. Doña Marina Sáenz de Licona gave birth to him on the second floor of the family castle in Loyola, in 1491. Others, whom we call cousins of the village—neighbors, and other friends—also lived there.

It was this fellow that had a cannonball break one leg and wound another in 1521. Ignatius's wound was not simply physical. It was a world of dreams and ambitions that collapsed. Ignatius, in fact, touched the bottom of the abyss, being the object, in the sculpture designed in memory of this incident by the City Council of Pamplona, of the pity of a dog, like the poor Lazarus in the Gospel of Luke.

It was in the abyss that God came to seek Ignatius. He sought him out first by enlisting the help of Ignatius's enemies in his work of grace. They were the ones who transported him to the family castle. This incident represents the catalytic moment of Saint Ignatius's conversion. Because of this incident, the bull of canonization of Saint Ignatius, in 1622, described him as a man called "from the honors of the world and the earthly militia"[55] to a holy life that led to the founding of the Jesuit order.

Saint Ignatius's entry into history had an epic character, that of a battlefield, Pamplona, where the hero was defeated but managed to attract the sympathy of his enemies.[56] His exit from the stage was not his death as such, if not his canonization, since this was the moment when, as a historical event, the parenthesis opened in Pamplona was closed. As in any tragic spectacle, the day of Ignatius's canonization also offered a spectacle, defined by contemporaries as one of the most spectacular liturgies that Rome had ever known.

In addition to the immense procession and the splendor of the liturgical vestments and royal finery, there was above all the irruption of the baroque in the liturgical chant performed, a great novelty, by the students coming from the colleges of the religious order that the hero of the day helped to found. The solemnity of this canonization of Ignatius also brought together great nations that were once enemies. Each of them had pushed for the canonization of Ignatius and wanted to recover this jubilee moment, in Rome, to generate a dynamic of reconciliation in their own nation.

This epic character of the conversion and canonization of Saint Ignatius also became a mark of Ignatian spirituality. Joseph de Guibert, in a retreat given to the priests in 1940 amid a world war, called this spirituality "military-christological." Through it, Ignatius also impressed upon the Society the obedience of its members, their simplicity of life, the discipline of its pedagogy, the search for excellence, and so on. This spirituality exposes the retreatant to the epic battle in the heart of the world between good and evil. The Two Standards meditation, for example, offers a confrontation between two epic characters, each placed on a stage and galvanizing his troops with an equally tragic speech, in the sense that the central character aims at what Aristotle, and other tragic authors such as Jean Racine and Corneille had defined as the triple purpose of all tragedy: to instruct the listeners, to touch (move) their heart, and to convince them.

THE PILGRIM LIVED ON ALMS

Following the rules for the discretion of the spirits in the *Spiritual Exercises*, Ignatius dedicates several paragraphs to the rules to distribute alms (EE 338–44). Looking at the structures of these rules and the language they use, Ignatius seems to offer a practical summary of the *Exercises*. He establishes a parallel between the rules to distribute alms, the principle and foundation, and both the election and the reform of one's state of life (EE 184, 189). By giving alms following the proper rules, the retreatant confirms the election already made and renews it in a concrete and practical way. Giving alms also sets the tone for the apostolate of the Society toward the poor and in their defense. Jesuit Superior General Peter-Hans Kolvenbach understood this link when he wrote,

> In the old economic order [time of Ignatius] it was by means of alms that the good will of the rich helped to correct excessive social inequality, though of course in a very imperfect way. Saint Francis, the poor man of Assisi, had people pray every day so that thanks to the rich we could continue to be poor…. (Kolvenbach, *The Road from La Storta*, 254)

Ignatius was himself an almsgiver, starting to be so for the first Companions during their studies in Paris. He did not want poor people to beg; they were to be helped, begged on behalf of. Men who had responded to the call of becoming "professional beggars" should therefore take the place of the poor and beg on their behalf, for the love of God. On his return to Venice (1537), with other Companions, they lodged in a hospice for the poor. They no longer sought alms for themselves but in order to help others. He went on securing alms for the colleges to help train future almsgivers, so that they could take care of the poor. During the winter of 1538–1539, the Jesuit house in Rome hosted about four hundred poor, and Ignatius cared for them himself.

Because of his injury and infirmity, Ignatius belonged to a social category that is often dependent on others. He is a beggar who turns his back on the nobility and its privileges to identify with the "little people." When we talk about the medieval "little people," Kouky Fianu argues that we are talking about "individuals in a modest economic situation (*pauperes*), involved in manual labor (*laboratores*), bathed in an oral culture (*illitterati*) and without any particular legal status."[57] Ignatius, a poor man, sets out on his journey, conversing about the things of God with those he meets, gradually depending on begging, whose professionalism is strengthened by a network of benefactors. Moreover, at the end of the Middle Ages, infirmity plays a key role in investigations concerning the penitential practices of a putative saint.[58] Thus, there is no shortage of people who see this sacked, lame, seductive, austere, and God-hungry man as a living saint.

According to the manuals of the confessors and the synods of the church in the thirteenth century, for example, "disabilities often resulted from sexual intercourse during forbidden periods."[59] Therefore, since Peter Lombard, physical defects were eliminated from the glorious bodies of the resurrected,[60] and the maintenance of the body in its perfection was a proof for canonization. The infirmity that Ignatius bore in his flesh was accidental. Nevertheless, the popular perception of a certain abnormality surrounded him. By freely assuming this infirmity as a beggar, Ignatius transformed his infirmity from a symbol of sin and demonic possession into a criterion of holiness. He no longer had to fight against it in the search for an aesthetic perfection that could make him useful in the service of his princess.

Nor could his advanced age be an obstacle to Ignatius's intellectual formation.[61] At a time when life expectancy in England, for example, averaged about thirty-five years, Ignatius began a new life of studies at exactly that age. He did not join just any school. He had to face the demands of the modern humanities, and in the most prestigious of universities, the one in Paris where people considered to be infirm were expected to "work" for their survival by begging in the streets.[62]

Rather than worrying about his own body, Ignatius found consolation in another, that of Christ. The suffering body of Christ for whom Ignatius could now endure humiliation and persecution, and whose love constituted the grace of the third week of the *Exercises*. Ignatius not only experienced physical persecution behind bars in Alcalá and Salamanca, but also the accusations of the inquisitors that were sometimes aimed at his fundamental spiritual experience. This was not an isolated case since these same inquisitors also attacked the frequent practices of confession and communion encouraged by Ignatius. They suspected that the spiritual practices promoted by Ignatius were in line with the ideas advocated by Juan de Ávila (1499–1569).[63]

Not surprisingly, the regular Eucharist became the center of Ignatius's life. For the medievalists, it was considered "the center of the conscience of Christians and of social unity."[64] This devotion to the Eucharist was associated with the radical option he contemplated in following Christ. Indeed, it was while meditating on poverty that Ignatius shed the most tears in what remained of his spiritual journal. He meditated on the question before, during, and after the eucharistic celebration. Faith and charity, therefore, went hand in hand. Both the reformers and the counter-reformers debated the relationship between faith and work. The humanists reserved charity for those who were truly in need and did not tolerate professional beggars.[65]

Yet, with his devotion to the Eucharist, the sacrament of reconciliation, the saints, the Virgin Mary, and so on, Ignatius shared the most popular devotions of emerging Christianity. The said devotions were fed by an environment of sin. The "unrest and lawlessness of the time had led to a general loosening of morals that required time and the efforts of many great reformers to counteract and cure it."[66] This universal awareness of sin may also have inspired Ignatius's conviction of a universal call to perfection.[67]

During the eleven months he spent at Manresa, Ignatius experienced his own limitation and obscurity, the radical inadequacy of granting himself forgiveness, and the enormous resistance that exists in every human to be docile and available to the divine will and to be placed fully in the hands of God. It was in these first two periods that Ignatius experienced the Exercises of the First Week.[68] He hit rock bottom at Manresa. His disgust for sin was sometimes confused with his disgust for himself. He had suicidal thoughts, fed by his powerlessness to overcome sin and, no doubt, the experience of a never-satisfying confession. Sin, he would later write in the *Exercises*, is ugly and contagious like the plague. It covers the whole history of the individual, all the spaces occupied and at all times. Like the plague, it makes the body purulent (EE 57–58).

As in medieval times, Ignatius therefore asks the exercitant to count his sins, in detail and in an exhaustive, complete manner. This detail is autobiographical. At Manresa, he made a general confession. He also experienced incompleteness and scruples: Had he counted correctly? Did he count everything? Was the penance proportional to the sins committed?[69] Ignatius took on the figure of the daily penitent found in most of the world's churches, whose last confession was in the last hour and who frustrated the rationalizing priest. He had no confession manuals. Scruples were gnawing at him; first as a penitence in the face of the magnitude of his sins, then as a great temptation that wore him down from within and led him to the bottom of the abyss and to destitution.

Martin Luther suffered from the same *Anfechtung*. It was this experience of radical powerlessness that led him to believe in the power of grace alone. No amount of effort, no matter how spiritual, could pull him out of this fundamental lukewarmness of the soul. It was the abyss before him. Like him, Ignatius also threw himself into it, and believed that only God could save him. Only, this God acted in the concrete person of his confessor. If he did what his confessor asked, Ignatius was convinced, he would be doing God's will. From this experience, Ignatius was "awakened" to the gratuitousness of God's grace, to the unconditionality of God's love, and to the uselessness of his own justice, assurance, and personal security.[70] It was only after this purifying experience of absolute powerlessness that Ignatius had his illumination in the Cardoner. It was here that his path separated from Lutheranism. It was also the first concrete expression of his *sentire cum ecclesia*, exactly in a context in which this scandalous church needed to be reformed from the head to all its members.

Gone were the days when, on his convalescent bed, his ego made Ignatius think that he could do what a Francis of Assisi or a Dominic de Guzmán had done before him, or even do better than them. This time, Ignatius had to face his powerlessness to overcome himself and order his life without deciding under the influence of disordered attachments of which he was a victim: the attachment to himself, to his desire and will. Even when he decided to go to Jerusalem, or to follow Christ "alone and on foot," to give up his name, his title of nobility, his clothes and coat of arms, he was still the center. Throughout his time at Montserrat and until he experienced his powerlessness at Manresa, it was Ignatius who decided and wanted to do great things for God, to build him a temple like David in his time. Such a project of the self toward God, without return, was doomed to failure. It left victims on the road, like the poor man to whom he gave alms of his luxurious clothes and who was taken for a bandit (*Aut.* 18). In the hole of his own misery, among the monasteries and caves of Manresa, his soul, he admitted, was still "blind," one of the worst medieval handicaps. But it was filled with the burning desire to follow Christ. For this reason, he decided to do all these penances and other works of charity (*Aut.* 14).

CONCLUSION

In opting to "see therefore all things new in Christ" during the Ignatian Year (2021–2022), the Jesuits have decided to place themselves once again under the banner of the cross, in the church and with an attitude of faith, so that their gaze may be converted to live a life of grace. It is a matter of not separating Pamplona from Rome. For the cannon and the ball and chain are not enough. They cause human misery and do not deserve to be celebrated in themselves. Pamplona only finds its full meaning in the journey that goes from Loyola to Rome, passing through Manresa. To Paul VI, who asked the Jesuits gathered in the General Congregation (GC) on December 3, 1974, "Where do you come from?," Arrupe, in the name of the Society, answered, "We come from Loyola, Manresa, Montserrat, La Storta, Rome." Rome, where they placed themselves at the service of the pope and which was the place of Ignatius's ministry as General of the Society.

To understand the theme of conversion through these stages that we have skimmed over is to live it on an individual level, letting the Spirit illuminate the intelligence of the Christian of today as at the Cardoner. It is also to live this conversion collectively, in the light of the vision at La Storta, where the community of the first Companions was already complete, just before their deliberation that gave birth to the Society. It is therefore together, collectively, that the Jesuits, in this social and spiritual history, embrace conversion as an individual, collective, and institutional process. In this way, they accept to be placed with the Son carrying his cross and to keep their gaze fixed on him who gave his name to the Society. The vision at La Storta reminds them that the Society was created by divine means and can only be preserved by divine means. It is with this grace that they look at our world with hope, despite its many enticements. It is a world, GC 34 would say, "where it is sometimes difficult to believe that God is good, that a good God exists." Those who have made this journey with Ignatius, in all their social, spiritual, emotional, and even institutional infirmities, discover their mission as messengers of peace and reconciliation, bearers of hope through their ministry of consolation.

2

THE FORMATION OF A GLOBAL ORDER

THE SOLEMN VOWS

Once everyone had gone to the sacrament of reconciliation with a brother, Ignatius, the newly elected Superior General, opened the celebration of the constitutive Eucharist of the Society. Although the order had received papal approval a few months earlier, on September 27, 1540, it was from this Eucharist that the professed Society was born. The bull of establishment and confirmation of the Society was issued on the date indicated therein, September 27, 1540, with a limited number of sixty professed members. Later, in a new confirmation of the bull, on March 14, 1544, this number was opened completely. Following the briefs of June 3 and 5, 1546, spiritual and temporal coadjutors were admitted.[1] However, it was on April 22, 1541, that the constituted body of the Society was officially formed.

The rite of profession is universally repeated today. At the Eucharist, before receiving communion, holding the paten in his right hand and the text of his profession in his left, Ignatius was the first to read the formula of vows and, turning to his five Companions present, took communion. Jean Codure, Pascual Broët, Claude le Jay, Alfonso Salmerón, and Diego Laínez each read the same formula, and each took communion from the hands of the general they had just elected.

According to Pedro de Ribadeneira's account, Ignatius embraced each of his Companions with great devotion and tears. His tears were mixed with the more dramatic tears of Codure, who "pushed such cries to God that we thought at any moment to see him failing and as if bursting, collapse, by the excess of his emotion."[2] Four months later, on August 29, 1541, Jean Codure died. Later, Favre, Bobadilla, Xavier, and Rodrigues took the same vows. Xavier, symbolically, pronounced them on Indian soil in 1544.[3] It was a prophetic sign of the global expansion to come.

This expansion was done with zeal, despite the dangers of an unknown world that began to emerge in the writings that the first Companions sent to Europe. To venture into the islands, Xavier recognized from the Moluccas, was very dangerous. The native peoples were constantly at war with one another. It was the characteristic of what Europeans considered a barbaric race, illiterate and lacking a written language. The inhabitants of these islands did not hesitate to poison those they hated. They lacked food, water, and grapes to make good wine and oxen to provide meat. There was a mountain that spitted fire and huge amounts of ashes. On the banks of the sea, quantities of fish, dead from pollution, were the joy of the starving populations.[4]

Xavier's description of the Indigenous peoples was paradigmatic of the commonly told stories about the Indigenous peoples of Asia and Africa. It spoke of their habits and customs, at least as the explorer perceived them and believed he understood them. It also talked about the cuisine, the climate, the geography.

For anyone who has, for example, read the history of Cameroon by Engelbert Mveng, the first Cameroonian Jesuit, what Xavier reported could well apply to the Atlantic coasts of Africa discovered by the Carthaginians five centuries before Christ and rediscovered by the Portuguese at the end of the fifteenth century. At the foot of the "Mountain of God, unique on the west coast of Africa,"[5] are the bays of Ambas and Biafra, not far from the Atlantic Ocean where the Wouri River flows. Later, toward the end of the fifteenth century, the Portuguese named the place after the shrimp that the Wouri River poured onto its banks: Rio dos Camaroes, "River of Shrimp," "Camerones," "Cameroons," "Kamerun,"

"Cameroon." Pacheco Pereira believed that it was Fernando Poo who, around 1472,[6] gave the name of Rio dos Camaroes to the mouth of the Wouri that he had just discovered.[7]

In contrast to Mveng's reconstructed account of the great civilizations around Mount Cameroon, which has been part of Ethiopia since Pliny the Younger,[8] Xavier's account of the Moluccan Islands in 1548 represented the Moors as barbarians. Mveng was downstream of a project of historical reconstruction aimed at asserting Africa's place in history independently of the ahistorical barbarism of modern accounts of Africa. With no ill intent on his part, Xavier reported what the shock of a first encounter produces in every explorer, missionary, or member of a humanitarian organization who steps out of his or her comfort zone. He used these images to appeal to the heroism and missionary awakening of those he left behind in Europe. Francis Xavier believed that he had to share this ocean of misery with them so that missionary candidates could grasp the urgency of the mission and, above all, understand the deep source of his own spiritual consolations. Somebody, Xavier sighed, may lose his sight because of the abundance of tears of consolation.[9]

As the Carthaginians, Greeks, Portuguese, and other Western peoples followed one another to the coasts of Africa, Xavier was not the only one interested in the Moluccan Islands. Thanks to the new route around the African Cape of Good Hope, Europeans such as Xavier flocked to Asia in search of spices, new markets, adventure, and the evangelization of peoples. A caravan of Portuguese and Spanish immigrants—seven ships in all—landed on the islands of Amboina, where Xavier had just baptized some children. In front of the Christian villages that he had founded, Francis overflowed with admiration. The Moors who lived on the islands had learned the creed, the commandments, the Our Father, the Hail Mary, the Confiteor, and to sing sacred hymns. Although he may have written a catechism (*doctrina*), it was this sung method that was most successful.[10]

The king of the Moluccas, a Moor, considered himself a vassal of the king of Portugal and was proud of it. He spoke Portuguese. If he was open to the conversion of at least one of his sons, he himself resisted becoming a Christian. For, like many Africans today, although this chief was circumcised as a child, he had many wives, a hundred in total. This number far exceeded the four acceptable by the Qur'an, the teachings of which were followed by some of his people. The king was, however, a religious man. He asserted that Moors and Christians all believed in the same God, and that, one day, Christians and those of his religion would become one.[11]

Xavier was able to evangelize the Indian region of Goa. And from the Moluccan Islands, he set his course for Japan. The inhabitants of this country, unlike the Indians and the Moors, were "curious," "eager to know the truth," and "reasonable." This open-mindedness, he thought, would favorably dispose the Japanese people to the message of the gospel. In fact, Xavier seemed to have concluded that the Society could grow and maintain itself with the natives of India.[12]

In this letter from Cochin in 1548, Xavier, who had left Europe six years earlier, spoke of the Society above all as a spiritual body. It was made up of the Companions—his friends and brothers—to whom he owed everything. He loved them so much that, in his solitude, he cut out the handwritten names of each of them and attached them to his neck to keep him company. He used these names as a source of energy and inspiration. He tenderly evoked the late Favre and the Company in Heaven, and he declared his unfailing love for the Company on Earth. Woe to him, he said, if he should ever forget it!

In those days when a letter took eight months to travel between Europe and India, it was this mysticism of brotherly love that reduced the distances. The virtual dimension that cemented this brotherhood was combined with the tireless deployment of Xavier's physical body for the mission. This was supported by an effort to maintain the handwritten correspondence that Ignatius immediately undertook to codify. He would make it the foundation of the overall governance of the Society.

Through correspondence, Ignatius "maintains good will, regulates domestic life, directs zeal….He exercises government with that great and strong soul which he wishes for the General in the *Constitutions*."[13] In the beginning of December 1542, he wrote, in a few days, two hundred and fifty letters. The Society's archives in Rome have preserved more than seven thousand of his letters. Like a spider's web of airlines in the skies above the world, so was the network of correspondence of the Society, which very soon became universal.[14] Rather than a traffic policeman, it needed a general with world dimensions.

A GENERAL FOR THE WORLD

In 1548, Ignatius was in the seventh year of his generalate, and the Society in the eighth since its approval by Pope Paul III in 1540. He prayed and worked on the *Constitutions*. The educational project of the Society was consolidated. After the first experiences in Goa and Valencia, the opening of the college in Messina represented a radical change in the identity and mission of the order. The Parisian method was introduced, as well as the system of boarding schools combined with day students.

Among the pioneers of this important project, Ignatius chose an international group of well-trained Jesuits and scholastics. As John O'Malley acknowledges, never has so much talent been assembled in one project.[15] There are some great names from the first generation of Companions: André des Freux the Frenchman, Peter Canisius the German, Benedetto Palmio the Italian, Jerónimo Nadal the Spaniard and director of the project,[16] and Annibale Coudret the Savoyard. They arrived in Messina during the Octave of Easter 1548. They were warmly welcomed by the city and all its inhabitants, led by the Viceroy and Queen Eleanor.[17]

In Messina, Ignatius also saw a great opportunity to recruit and, above all, train young Jesuits in the face of the growing demands from all over Europe. Not surprisingly, the first principles of the *Ratio Studiorum*, the primer of Ignatian pedagogy, were developed there.[18] The scholastics of the Society achieved great success in Valencia, Coimbra, Louvain, Padua, and Bologna, and other requests arrived for Sicily and Northern Europe.[19]

Among the many candidates who entered the Society in 1548, the majority were recruited directly by Ignatius himself or at least accompanied by him. Everard Mercurian became the fourth Superior General of the Society. Francisco Borgia, his predecessor as General, also took the secret vows in 1548. The recruitment tool par excellence was the Spiritual Exercises and the Formula of the Institute inserted in the bull of Paul III. Using these two sources,

Ignatius "put in the heart of all his people deep and overbearing sentiments, an ardent love of Jesus Christ and of souls, which impelled them to face all the work, all the contradictions, all the sufferings, with the most generous joy."[20]

Once the candidates were admitted into the Society, Ignatius treated them with mercy and tenderness. However, he did not hesitate to send away those who seemed less willing to follow the Society's way of life. Poverty is to be loved like a mother. But Ignatius also believed that "those who left everything to follow the Lord seemed to him to deserve every expense."[21] Obedience was nonnegotiable for the preservation of the order, but regulations were not enough. It was necessary to explain and persuade. He sometimes publicly corrected the most deserving to serve as an example to others. Moreover, in a world where the church was facing Nicolaism and other nepotisms, Ignatius wanted to see the Jesuits live in the purity of angels. He asked for the dismissal of a brother nurse admired by all for his goodness and humility, but who, while massaging the foot of a sick man, had raised his hand a little higher than he should have.[22]

The efforts of the General to keep the Society away from scandals did not, however, save it from fierce enemies. In Salamanca, the Dominican Melchior Cano accused them of being anti-Christ. In Alcalá, the rector of the college, Francisco Villanova, was dispatched to put out another fire at the university. In Paris, the king approved the project with letters of patent in 1551 and 1553, but the parliament, the archbishop, and the university disapproved. For them, the Society represented a threat to ecclesiastical peace, to the monastic profession, and to the faith itself.[23]

In the face of these threats, Ignatius sought allies to defend the Society, pontifical confirmations of his Institute, the Exercises, and so on. He sometimes kept a low profile when the enemy, through his influence, could harm the Society, leaving time to diffuse the tension. Above all, he believed in God and his providence. The Society, he wrote in the *Constitutions*, was created by divine means. It can only be kept in good condition by the same means (*Const.* 840).

Acts of confirmation of the new order also existed. Paul III approved the *Spiritual Exercises* in 1547 and their first edition was printed in Rome the same year. Julius III confirmed the Society with the bull *Exposcit debitum* of July 21, 1550. The Roman College opened in 1551, and Ignatius even began to dictate his *Autobiography* in 1553. However, Juan de Ávila, who had been following the progress of the Society for a long time, gave up the idea of creating his own congregation. He recommended his followers to the Society, ratifying that it had established itself among the great religious orders.[24]

In fact, as early as 1548, Ignatius had Antonio Araóz, Provincial of Spain, write that it was formally forbidden to receive people who had belonged to other religious orders. This prohibition came at a time when groups of Barnabites, Theatines, and other congregations wanted to merge with the Jesuits for greater apostolic effectiveness. Ignatius politely dodged the offer, inviting his own to show the utmost respect for other congregations. He justified his refusal on three points.

First, out of fidelity to the *Constitutions*, which did not admit persons who had been previously admitted to another congregation. He refused the amalgam of diverse origins and the inconstancy of persons who had not persevered in another congregation. Second, Ignatius believed that all other congregations were created by God, with their own identity and mission. It was therefore not up to him or any other human being to undo what God had so well established. Finally, the merger would deprive the Society of its freedom of action.[25] It could become mired in internal identity crises, to the detriment of the mission. Ignatius valued the integrity of the Society's project, and even defended it against those on whom he relied for its expansion: clerics, kings, and other benefactors.

The constitution of the group as a religious order was born of the desire to remain united in a context of dispersion. One year after this solemn profession, the Society was established in the great capitals of Catholic Europe: Rome, Paris, Lisbon, but also in Goa. Only seven years later, in 1549, it had three provinces: Portugal, Spain, and Goa. The order had 25 houses in 1550, 27 in 1551, 40 in 1552, 45 in 1553, 50 in 1554, and 61 in 1555. When Ignatius died in 1556, he left 76 houses grouped into twelve provinces, a thousand religious spread throughout Italy, Germany, the Netherlands, France, Spain, Portugal, Brazil, Japan, India, and even on the roads to Ethiopia.[26]

THE DRAFTING OF THE *CONSTITUTIONS*

The object of history, said Marc Bloch, "is, by nature, man. Let us say rather the men." And "behind the institutions, which seem almost entirely detached from their founders, there are men, and it is men that history seeks to grasp."[27] Take Luther, Calvin, Loyola, Bloch adds, "the first duty of the historian who would like to understand and explain them would be to place them in their environment, where they are immersed in the mental climate of their time and confronted with problems of conscience that are quite different from ours."[28] Bloch even went as far as to believe that if the Society of Jesus were to reveal its "secrets," some of which are contained in its *Constitutions*, it would contribute to solving many of the enigmas of the modern world.[29]

When he wrote the *Constitutions*, Ignatius did not act as a historian. Although he drew on the rules of older religious orders, Benedictine, Franciscan, and Dominican, his focus was not on the "man" in Bloch's sense, but on the institution and its ability to meet the challenges of a world in turmoil. In fact, he inserted in these *Constitutions* the secret that would allow the Institute to maintain its unity in the context of the first globalization and its malaise. His job was to constitute "a body for the spirit," to insert a "spirit" into a text to make it a living text, a way of proceeding. It was a question, Dominique Bertrand states, of "institutionalizing a charism."[30]

It was therefore a question of forming a "body" for the mission in a fragmented world. The word is used fifteen times in the *Exercises*, forty-nine times in the *Constitutions*. In fact, the project of the *Constitutions* was one of incorporation, from admission to the novitiate (first and second parts), their preservation and progress to definitive incorporation (third to sixth), their mission *ad extra* as well as the way in which the institute could maintain itself and keep itself in good condition (seventh to tenth). They conceived the Society as a project that constantly sought to "be one for the mission."

According to André de Jaer, one listens to the Spirit when reading the *Constitutions*, for they are "approved by the Church as a way of living the Gospel, 'a path to God.'"[31] Writing them was a prayerful task, for Ignatius said Mass every day to present his text to God and the point on which he was writing, and expected confirmation from God.[32] This text, especially on the question of poverty, is soaked with the tears of the founder of the Jesuits. The *Spiritual Journal*, we read in a commentary, "is crossed by tears that seem to complete the course of it, in the second notebook preserved, by erasing the traces of writing, like bodily erasures."[33] It is not only the text that was crossed out, but it was also Ignatius's sight itself that was suppressed little by little, as if by a blindness. And so, the eyes of Ignatius, as well as those of the later reader, could be opened to the Spirit that alone allows one to grasp the great secret: God, whom Ignatius wanted to see at work in the institution as the source and guarantor of the same. In paragraph 134 of the *Prologue*, we read,

> Although the Wisdom and Goodness of God our Creator and Lord must maintain, lead and advance this tiny Society of Jesus as He deigned to bring it into being, and on our part the interior law of charity and the love that the Holy Spirit imprints in hearts must help for this…we judge to have Constitutions. (*Const.* 134)

The "secret" of the Jesuits, so sought after by friends and enemies alike, was therefore God. Ignatius sometimes seemed to see in the "smallness" of the Society the metaphor of the divine seed. The "little" Society may well become great and have under its branches thousands of Jesuits working in hundreds of works; but it was to remain "little," because it should never be an end in itself.

It was this secret that served as the condition of possibility for the interculturality of the Society and thus for its universal claim. Marc Bloch believed in this, he who, in his apology for interculturality, called on his fellow historians in Oslo in 1982 "to stop locking themselves into national conceptual universes, but to agree on common terms."[34] For the task of history is to forge a way of living together.[35] The first globalization, like the current one, claimed to rely on a deterritorialization that allowed to go beyond national borders and nationalistic ideologies.[36] It also created conditions in which transnational processes connected diverse histories and made them interdependent.[37]

Ignatius was aware of the strength of nationalist pressures in the Europe of his time. And he knew that within the young Society itself, these nationalistic dynamics were already unleashed and dangerously threatening the edifice of the Institute. The encounter with other nations and cultures—among them the Turks, the Moors, and the Indians—only increased this unease. More than the text, then, it was the spirit of the text of the *Constitutions* that counted. Xavier, on his way to India, had not yet seen the approved text. But he knew the spirit. He acted accordingly in the recesses of sixteenth-century Asia.

Nationalisms and the Union of Minds and Hearts in the Society, 1539–1639

Among them there were French, Spaniards, Savoyards, Cantabrians: we were divided in opinions and views which differed from our status, and we all had one and the same thought and will, which was to seek 'the good pleasure and the perfect will of God,' according to the aim of our vocation...[38]

This 1539 text from the "Deliberations of Our First Fathers" insists on the diversity of origins and opinions among the first fathers, and on the fact that the decision to found the Society "was the very fact of having deliberated in common."[39] An analysis of the nationalist question in the first century of the Society thus helps better to understand the means that the first Companions used to overcome nationalisms and thus grow in the direction of a greater union of minds and hearts.

From this analysis, it emerges, first, that the initial miracle of Saint Ignatius was to have put into his context "a team of rivals,"[40] united by their rootedness in Christ and their zeal for mission. Second, by showing the perennial danger of nationalism and ethnic tribalism in the history of the Society, we discover that the manifestation of these same phenomena in religious life in Africa today are not inevitable. On the contrary, the origins of the Society represented an example of overcoming differences and exploiting the rich diversity that these differences implied for the greater service of God and the good of souls in our societies.

Two questions arise from this analysis: How did Ignatius build a team of rivals around himself? And how did the "synagogue of the Jews" formed by the first circle of Ignatius's followers implode at the turn of the first century of the Society? The analysis of the nationalist question thus allows us to take seriously the nationalist and tribal threat to African Christianity, which is perceptible in the divisions between the left- and right-wing Christianities in the West.

FORMING A TEAM OF RIVALS

The context for the creation of the Society, it has often been noted, was the fact that the pope had begun to disperse the Companions, and there was the problem of how to maintain or not maintain the bond that already existed between them. This tension between a body *ad dispersionem* and a body deeply united for mission is at the heart of Jesuit identity. It is also true that the idea of a Society that is primarily *ad dispersionem* has sometimes taken over the practices of the order to the point where recent General Congregations have insisted on "community as mission."

And yet, from a political and ethnic perspective, nothing predisposed Ignatius to treat Xavier or Faber, or even Laínez or Polanco, favorably. In fact, Ignatius's friends strongly discouraged him from going to Paris,[41] because a war was raging between France and Castile, a war that Ignatius himself had been a victim of in Pamplona. These wars in Europe were fueled by well-established ethnic stereotypes and clichés. Since the thirteenth century, the Charter of the University of Paris, where all the first Companions had studied, offered an unflattering portrait of the nations involved:

> The English [were] drunks and had tails; the sons of France were proud, effeminate, and carefully adorned like women. The Germans were furious and obscene at their parties; the Normans, vain and boastful; the Poitevins, treacherous and always adventurous. The Bretons were reputed to be fickle and changeable, and were often blamed for the death of King Arthur. The

Lombards were called avaricious, vicious and cowardly; the Romans, seditious, turbulent and slanderous; the Sicilians, tyrannical and cruel; the inhabitants of Brabant, bloodthirsty men, incendiaries, brigands and kidnappers; the Flemings, fickle, gluttonous prodigals, cooking like butter and lazy.[42]

Called from a world in which such clichés dominated and where their different peoples were torn apart by fratricidal wars, the first Companions therefore took to heart the challenge of uniting minds and hearts. To forge this union among themselves, the first Companions put forward the name of Jesus for the Society. It was not a question of belonging to the Society of Saint Ignatius, the Basque, but to the Society of Jesus. The text of the Deliberation shows how the Companions overcame their differences to offer themselves, with a unanimous heart, to God for the mission:

So, we too, it reads, had differing judgments, and we were eager and concerned to find a fully cleared path on which to go forward to offer ourselves as a burnt offering to our God, so that all that was ours might fade away before his praise, his honor, and his glory.[43]

In this effort to surrender themselves to God and for the mission, the text later uses sacramental language, that of marriage, to speak of the union between Companions as a mission in itself:

After the most merciful and forgiving Lord has deigned to gather and unite us together, we who are so weak and come from such different regions and cultures, we should not break what God has gathered and united, but rather strengthen and consolidate it more and more, grouping ourselves into a single body, caring for one another and in communion with one another for a greater fruit of souls.[44]

It appears, therefore, that even before the approval of the Society, the first Companions understood that it was God himself who put them together, and that this bond could not be dissolved by them under the pretext of ethnic or political differences. On the contrary, precisely because there were strong differences between them, because their world was also marked by social and political fractures, and finally, because they were aware of being fragile beings, living as a united body became imperative. The union, itself, thus became a testimony capable of doing the greatest good to the souls of the very diverse regions from which they came and to which they were sent.

In the second generation, Jerome Nadal[45] and later Francis of Borgia also insisted that the principle and foundation of this union among the members was the very name of Jesus that the Society bore. This name, wrote Borgia in 1569, "our Reverend Father proposed it on his own initiative to all his companions, pleading fervently that above all…our Society should be called the Society of Jesus. They all agreed."[46] It was therefore logical, following these deliberations of 1539 and in accordance with the spirit of Saint Ignatius, that the name of Jesus became the basis of unity of the first Companions, the name that carried them toward the mission:

> He who wishes to fight for God under the banner of the cross and serve the Lord alone and his vicar on earth, in our Society, which we wish to see designed with the name of Jesus, will persuade himself that…and he will take care to keep his gaze always fixed first on God and then on the nature of his institute, which is a path toward him, and to pursue with all his strength this end which God proposes to him.[47]

The obedience of the members was derived from this bond that united the Companions first to God and then to their leaders and to one another.

THE ENEMIES FROM WITHIN

That the Society was created out of such diversity was seen as Ignatius's first miracle at his canonization in 1622. The kings of France, Spain, and Bavaria together pushed the cause of Ignatius's and Francis Xavier's canonizations, each seeking the greatest benefit for the unity of his people. John Dryden dedicated his English translation of the *Life of St. Francis* to the Queen of England, being moved that the Queen should choose so glorious a saint as patron for herself and her country.[48]

In the fifth chapter of his biography of Ignatius, dedicated to the miracles obtained by Christians through his intercession, Pedro de Ribadeneira, one of his earliest biographers, affirms that one of the outstanding signs of Ignatius's sanctity was that he succeeded in uniting around himself, in an "extraordinary agreement of souls and hearts," Spaniards and French, in a very hostile context between the two nations.[49] That Ribadeneira spoke of the union of minds and hearts at this moment as a miracle was indicative of the growing uneasiness caused by the nationalist question in the Society at the turn of its first centenary.

Indeed, for Ignatius's successors, until the celebration of the first centenary of the Society, the union of minds and hearts could only be preserved if the "worldliness" that seemed to invade the Institute was properly diagnosed and treated with the utmost seriousness. The very survival of the Society was at stake.

On the centenary on November 15, 1639, Mutius Vitelleschi, Superior General of the Society (r. 1615–1645), addressed a letter to the entire Society. If, by misfortune, the General wrote, "some of the dust of the world has clung to us during these hundred years," then each of us, having become a victim or at least weakened by this worldliness, should return to square one: "Let us take back what belongs to us," he insisted, poverty, the spirit of obedience, and above all "those ancient virtues and holiness of our first ten Fathers, that first blessed family which, though few in number, was powerful as a whole, and which by its zeal did in a few years the work of a century."[50] It was God himself, Vitelleschi concluded, who founded the Society and nourished it with the milk of Our Lady, the Mother of Virgins. It was therefore to be maintained only by a careful and perfect observance of its rules and by the imitation of Christ.

Vitelleschi offered a formidable portrait of the first generation of Companions. He projected the image of a unified family, "powerful as a whole," holy. The fact that the General insisted on the image of a unified family in reference to the first Companions (despite the well-known cases of conflict with Bobadilla or Simon Rodrigues) came from the fact that the Society, which was living a glorious era, was also under attack from all sides. Presenting a unified front from the beginning was part of the effort to defenestrate an even more dangerous enemy, the one that came from its own ranks: the enemy within.

This alleged enemy from within had three faces. There were, for example, a handful of Jesuits whose morality and political commitment gave the Society a bad image and attracted the wrath of the powerful. There was also the case of the complacent and partisan governance of some superiors. Finally, there was the case of the perfidious *conversos* and *Moriscos* who undermined the Society from within.

Indeed, the bad example of a handful of Jesuits, Vitelleschi noted, had fueled the animosity of the enemies of the Society toward the entire body. Some superiors also showed preferences for some of their subjects. There were Jesuits who were increasingly driven by self-love, their own reputation, and their specific interests. Still others were totally consumed by the burden of daily needs and temporal concerns.[51] It was therefore imperative, Father General insisted, that all Jesuits return to a life of assiduous prayer, to the observance of the *Constitutions*, orders, and instructions, especially those concerning obedience, which among us had to be perfect, not only with the superiors within the Society, but also and above all with the Holy See.

Vitelleschi himself had succeeded the long generalate of Claudio Acquaviva. Elected by the fourth General Congregation in 1581, Acquaviva presided over four General Congregations in all. This was an unprecedented fact. Acquaviva was elected when he was only thirty-seven years old. He had the experience, however, having been alternately Provincial of Naples and of Rome, and the physical strength to handle the turbulent times of a growing Society at the turn of a new century.

Twelve years after his election as General, Pope Clement VIII called for the convocation of the Fifth General Congregation. Decree 2 created a commission of five members, presided over by Father General himself, with a mandate to examine and prevent any threat to the preservation and growth of the Society.[52] Decrees 21 and 28 forbade the Jesuits to use their privileges to read books forbidden by the Spanish Inquisition.[53] The General Congregation also forbade them to absolve heresies that King Philip of Spain considered a threat to the faith and unity of his kingdom. In short, our people could not interfere in any way with the Inquisition.[54]

Decisions were also made concerning the involvement of Jesuits in politics. For the members of the General Congregation, the union of hearts and minds among the Companions, and the very survival of the Society, required a certain balance regarding politics. Decree 47 states that the Society would hinder the realization of these goals and would expose itself to extreme peril if it were to become involved in what is secular and in the political affairs of state governance.[55] This decree is complemented by Decree 48, which asks the Jesuits to guard against friendships with secular princes and businessmen, since such connections would undermine their spiritual well-being and religious discipline.[56]

In this context, politics and the Society had a common enemy. This enemy threatened the stability of the kingdom, of the Institute, and of all Christendom. Both the politicians and the Church saw the *conversos*, Christians recently converted from Judaism, and the *Moriscos*, those converted from Islam, as the designated culprits of this existential crisis. According to decrees 52–54, the *conversos* and the *Moriscos* were agents of discord within the Society itself, a mortal threat to the continuation of its mission. A moratorium was placed on their admission to the Society. As for those already admitted, everything was done to keep them away from the offices of government. For, we read in Decree 52, that although the Society is destined to become all in and for all,

> It is more suitable to the greater glory of God and the more perfect pursuit of the end that it should possess workers who are very acceptable to other nations throughout the world and who could be more freely and reliably employed in the Church of God, and [acceptable] to those persons whose good or evil toward us has much influence in opening or keeping closed our access to the divine service and help of souls.[57]

For the Society to achieve the end for which it was created, it had to rely on the princes who were its benefactors and the secular arm used by the church for the evangelization of peoples. It was therefore imperative not to alienate such allies in the divine service and the good of souls. The displeasure and even a certain hatred against the new converts were more direct, and the remedy more surgical in Decree 54. The Jesuits of Jewish and Arab origin were treated as "deceivers, disturbers of the peace" and "authors of sedition." From then on, the General Congregation states,

> Sadly deploring the dismissal of its spiritual sons, and nevertheless weighing how much the evil which the unity, obedience, and religious discipline of the Society has endured at the hands of these men, and calculating how much the good name of its name, which generally makes its good odor in Christ exist everywhere, has been diminished among the externs, the congregation has decided that it should take steps to remedy this serious malady....The men of this race, instigators of such evils and corrupters of others, and their real accomplices as well...must all, like a plague, be separated as soon as possible from the body of the Society.[58]

In one of its 1953 editions, the newsletter of the Province of France made a distinction between the Jesuits of Paris and those of Lyon.[59] Speaking of the character of the Jesuit of Lyon in 1953, the newsletter noted his provincial spirit, his aversion to all façades, his contempt for the exterior, a certain "sympathetic disorder," and a disdain for superficial glitter that "hides well the cult of essential values." Perhaps, the article concludes, this aversion of the Lyonnais for the exterior decoration would explain "the housing crisis which prevails in the Province of Lyon."[60] The text was written in the eighteenth year of the presence of the Lyon Jesuits in Chad.

Although less obscene than the clichés of the Middle Ages, these two cases, first from the first century of the Society, then from the portrait of the Jesuit from Lyon in 1953, simply remind us that the creation of the Society was an act of overcoming deep-seated clichés and divisions. This did not prevent it from becoming a strong institution at the service of the church and from prospering in every respect. The Jesuits worked to overcome their divisions by refocusing their ethnic, cultural, and political differences on Christ and in the pursuit of their common mission for the good of souls.

The formation of the first group of Companions was a testimony to an extraordinary overcoming of the ethnic and political barriers of Europe at that time. Ignatius surrounded himself not only with other Spaniards of different political persuasions, but also with people of other nationalities. Jews, marginalized and even persecuted throughout Europe where purity laws were in force, found refuge with Ignatius. Laínez and Polanco were among their descendants. This led Robert A. Maryks to say that the early Society was a "Synagogue of Jews."[61]

James Brodrick writes that the Jesuits residing in Rome at the time of Ignatius's death represented a Pentecost of nationalities.[62] The Roman College was like "a tiny replica of Europe, *mundi quasi compendium,*" whose students could communicate "in two languages or make themselves sufficiently understood in four or five. They practiced preaching in Arabic regularly, with an eye to the Muslim world, which had been the first missionary dream of St. Ignatius."[63] There was even, at the college in Naples, "a little black boy named Peter," a young slave from Africa.[64]

THE UNION OF MINDS AND HEARTS AFTER THE RESTORATION OF THE SOCIETY

The stereotypes were not only ethnic at the University of Paris. The experts in logic, for example, who were often compared to the Egyptians, trafficked in "subtleties and sophistications, so that no one could understand their eloquent speeches in which, as Isaiah says, 'there is no wisdom.'"[65] As for those with a Doctor of Theology, "sitting as in the seat of Moses," they were puffed up with learning, but their charity was not edifying. Teaching and not practicing, they became like "brass instruments or like a clanging cymbal, or like a stone canal, always dry, which must carry water to the spice bed. In their flattery they attracted the students of others; each one seeking his own glory, but not caring at all about the welfare of souls."[66]

As soon as he was elected General of the Society in 1829, Jerome Roothaan turned his attention to the question of keeping the newly restored order in good condition. In 1830, he wrote a letter, "On the Love of the Society and Its Institute." As a sign of the times, he published a second letter on July 27, 1831, "On the Suffering and Persecution." It was because it was intimately united to Christ, the General maintained, that the Society found itself persecuted. "No one is unaware," he wrote, "that St. Ignatius prayed that the Society would not lack opposition and persecution. This prayer is certainly being answered in our day."[67] The fragile situation of the Society was described in his letter inaugurating the celebration of the third centenary of the Society. Already in 1773, "scorned and rejected everywhere, we were treated like trash, like the waste of society (1 Cor 4:13). However, God remained with us…as soon as it was restored, the hatred against it was revived. The old conspiracies, brought up to date, spread and flooded the world with libels, magazines, pamphlets and books that overwhelmed us."[68]

Roothaan believed that it was necessary for every Jesuit to be rooted in Christ and to grow in self-denial to face these persecutions and maintain the union of minds and hearts. On December 27, 1834, he wrote a letter to the whole Society on "the study and use of the Spiritual Exercises of Saint Ignatius" whose full title, he recalled, is "to overcome oneself and to order one's life, without deciding on any attachment that is disordered."[69] Self-denial, he believed, also meant striving for excellence in daily tasks and in a spirit of unity. For "the prosperity of the Society depends as much on each one in particular as on the whole community….It is like a concert: each one in particular and all together, unanimously, contribute to perfect harmony. If only one is distracted and gives a false note, confusion ensues."[70]

For the Society's enemies, there were few public acts of the Companions that were not a source of scandal, especially if the acts in question were of a political nature. In 1906, during the generalate of Luís Martín (1892–1906), the Spanish Fathers Luis Maria Ortiz and Venancio Minteguiaga published articles in the Jesuit magazine *Razón y Fe* on "El clero en las elecciones públicas" (The Role of the Clergy in Public Elections)[71] and "Algo sobre las elecciones municipales" (On Municipal Elections), respectively.[72] Both fathers defended the possibility for Catholics, in the absence of a

Jacobin capable of winning, to vote for a moderate liberal candidate. This theory of the lesser electoral evil was a heresy for the fundamentalist Catholics, led by a certain Ramón Nocedal. The latter, through another magazine, *El Siglo Futuro* (The Next Century), violently attacked the first two. General Martín, in support of Ortiz and Minteguiaga, asked the pope to arbitrate and forbade the reading of political newspapers in the houses of the Society in Spain to safeguard the union of minds and hearts.[73]

THE ADVANCE TO THE OPEN SEA

History remains the fruit of power, which itself defines the world according to its perception and interests. In this sense, the year 1492 may mark the surrender of Abu I-Qasim al-Muhli in Granada and the beginning of a new chapter of the *Reconquista* dominated by a resolutely Catholic Spain, but also confronted by the new Reformed Europe. Triumphant for the Spaniard and the white Catholic European,[74] Granada was less so for the subaltern *Converso* and *Morisco* within Europe and worse for the African and the Indian of Asia and America who would soon be colonized. This battle even invented a certain America, the one that celebrated Christopher Columbus.[75] It resulted in two approaches to history that allude to both the Hegelian approach to history as self-manifestation of the Spirit ultimately incarnated in "Big Men" (Napoleon) or Big Nations (Germany), and the Marxist approach, in which history is a product of social forces. Both Hegel's and Marx's approaches to history produce systems at the expense of certain groups of people.[76]

But underneath Columbus and the triumphalist history, there was a history of the subalterns. To his credit, Ignatius was quite nuanced in his approach to this complex world. He did not, for example, approach the Ethiopian mission as a Counter-Reformation, like the one the Jesuits were conducting in northern Europe. Instead, the Ethiopian project was intended to restore the unity of Christianity by conforming Ethiopian Christianity to the Roman. Each time, Ignatius showed an extraordinary respect for the Ethiopian political system. This was not a common attitude in his time, even within the Society.

Although Ignatius, in his letter to Canisius, seemed to refer to a "spiritual reconquest," the fact remains that he seemed to be more aggressive in his strategy in the north of Europe, at least compared to that in Ethiopia.[77] Indeed, after the defeat of Charles V in 1552, through an alliance between Henry II and the German Lutheran princes, and just before the Peace of Augsburg in 1555, Ignatius instructed Peter Canisius, first, on how he should advise King Ferdinand of Austria. The latter should "oppose Protestantism in Austria."[78]

Ignatius saw the Society's mission in the Protestant regions of Northern Europe as a "preservation," "reconquest," and "renewal" of Catholicism. He urged King Ferdinand to "keep these territories in the Catholic faith" and to "re-establish this religion in regions where it has collapsed and consolidate it where it is shaky."[79] Protestantism, he insisted, should be called by its true name, a "disease" and "heresy," not "evangelical." Ferdinand should get rid of it, without any tolerance. In Austria, the Catholic Church was engaged in a "war against all heretical errors."

Second, Ignatius's letter to Canisius proposed specific measures to stop "heresy" and cure "infection." Those suspected of heretical behavior were to be dispossessed and expropriated from their lives or property, and even sent into exile.[80] Schools and universities were not to hire professors suspected of heresy, and faculty members who showed signs of corrupt ideas were to be expelled. Heretical books were burned to prevent young people from being attracted to them. The king should show no tolerance for priests or religious who showed sympathies for heresy, for "it is better for the flock to have no shepherd at all than to have a wolf for a shepherd."[81]

Third, catechisms, syntheses of "true" doctrine and summaries of scholastic theology, should be made available to young people, who should also be instructed in the councils and synods.[82] Finally, special care should be taken in the selection of bishops. Although Ignatius did not advocate the establishment of the inquisition, he used a very combative tone in which one could recognize the hand of Juan de Polanco, but the spirit of the letter was that of Saint Ignatius. Moreover, there was also a sense of restoration.

Ignatius charged King Ferdinand, through whatever means available, with "restoring" the teachings of the true faith in Austria. It was not surprising that the theological debate in Northern Europe revolved around themes such as justification, grace, sin, and so on. The difference between this Northern European restoration and that of Ethiopia was, however, not only in the tone of Saint Ignatius's letter to Joao Nunes Barreto (1555), but also in the specific context of Ethiopia within world Christianity.

In his letter to the Negus of Ethiopia, Ignatius referred to King Claudius of Ethiopia as Prestor John.[83] Ignatius had learned about Ethiopia, its culture and religion, from Francisco Alvares's book *Faithful Relation of the Lands of Priest John* (1540) and from conversations he allegedly had in Rome with an Ethiopian monk the same year.[84] Ignatius did not seek to impose his will on the Ethiopian monarch. He simply offered some "suggestions, which may help to bring the kingdoms of Priest John into union with the faith and the Catholic Church."[85] This provision gave the Provincial of Goa some freedom to revise Ignatius's strategy if necessary. There was no reference to "war" or "heresy," with one exception about the church of Alexandria. Part of the project in Ethiopia consisted in breaking its connection with Alexandria, which was reluctant to unite with Rome. In his letter to the Negus, Ignatius used the metaphor of the oneness of the body of the church and highlighted the divisiveness of the church of Alexandria.[86]

First, Priest John was instead to be won over by respect, friendship, reason (*disputatio*), and example.[87] This change in tone is understandable. Whereas in Austria Ignatius addressed a Catholic prince asking him to reconquer a traditionally Catholic country that had recently converted to Protestantism, in Ethiopia Ignatius addressed the king who was also the head of an older Christianity, whom he wanted to reconcile with Rome.

Ignatius explicitly used the words *restoration* and many other references that alluded to the same thing, such as "union," "unity," "bringing back to uniformity," "communion," and so on. The first step in this approach was to recognize the substance of the Ethiopian prophecies so as to instruct and convince the king of the superiority of the Roman Catholic faith. For "there is no hope of salvation outside the Roman Catholic Church."[88] The king had a simple choice: join the Roman Catholics and be saved or remain outside and be damned. However, Ignatius did not understand this superiority in terms of confrontation. He simply believed that where "there is no opposition in religion, there will be a closer union of love between them."[89]

Second, Priest John was to be instructed in his rights as well as in the asymmetrical nature of the relationship he would have with the pope. As a Catholic prince, he would have authority in the appointment of bishops and patriarchs. But he would have to recognize the superiority of the Roman pontiff, Christ's vicar on earth, and his infallibility in matters of faith and morals.[90]

Third, Ignatius offered some advice on religious practices, spirituality, and rites. The Jesuit missionaries in Ethiopia should convince the king to remove certain "abuses" of the "old law" (the Sabbath law), and to moderate certain "austerities" of their rites. In addition, they should encourage "external ceremonies," "Corpus Christi processions," and promote a strong sacramental spirituality. They should celebrate Mass and "vespers," and if the king approves, use a choir with organ during these prayers. But since choir prayer "is foreign to our [Jesuit] rules," the missionaries should allow non-Jesuits to oversee these prayers.[91] Offering the example of the lives of the saints should be part of the spiritual growth of Ethiopians. The missionaries are also asked to reorganize the "calendars and feasts" in such a way as to Catholicize Ethiopian Christianity. Ignatius expected them to go to Ethiopia well stocked with liturgical objects and ornaments, including vestments, chalices, crosses, vessels for holy water, and so on. They could use them in "external worship."[92] To make this more effective, he asked the Jesuits to learn the local languages.

Fourth, a special place was given to the education of children in the mission strategy in Ethiopia. In addition, Jesuits should promote works of charity, build hospices, and work for the redemption of captives from the Moors. In this respect, Ignatius was in line with the Catholic Reformation, which began with other medieval orders such as the Mercedaries.

Briefly said, Ignatius understood "restoration" in terms of union, unity, reconciliation, and as an attempt to unify Ethiopian Christianity with Rome. What allows for some parallels between this restoration and the Catholic or Counter-Reformation is the context in Europe and the very nature of the Jesuit Institute. In practice, the charities, hospices, mental prayers, and other aspects of the spirituality of the Jesuits going to Ethiopia were indebted to the *devotio moderna* and other reforms that took place within the Catholic Church beginning in the twelfth century. Furthermore, while Ignatius sent missionaries to Ethiopia, the Jesuits were confronting and fighting Protestantism in Austria, Germany, the Netherlands, and so on. The Council of Trent was in session, and some of the liturgical, sacramental, and theological expressions in Ignatius's letter to Barreto already had Tridentine significance.

However, Ethiopia was not a Reformed Church, and Ignatius did not consider the Ethiopian enterprise to be a Counter-Reformation as such. The theological debates are christological and make no reference to themes such as justification, sin, or grace. Ignatius's instructions to the Jesuits who went to Ethiopia are aimed at unity with Rome and were primarily reparative. He uses a more cautious tone in dealing with the Ethiopians, encouraging dialogue, respect, "kindness and goodness,"[93] "compassion," and understanding in missionary strategy.

For a sixteenth-century correspondence, Ignatius shows unusual respect for the Ethiopians in a context in which, even within the Society, the classification of races seemed to put Africans at the bottom of the pyramid. Ignatius's instructions were followed to the letter in the early years of the Jesuits' presence in Ethiopia (1556–1622). But from 1624 onward, the process of "Latinization" began and led to clashes and uprisings, and finally to the expulsion of the Jesuits from Ethiopia in 1632.

THE IMPLEMENTATION OF SAINT IGNATIUS'S INSTRUCTIONS

The Jesuit mission in Ethiopia took place in three different periods, interspersed with intervening periods, during which the Turks or the hostility of the Ethiopian court often prevented the missionaries from entering Ethiopia. Officially, the first mission took shape from 1555 to 1597. This date corresponds to the death of the last missionary of this first expedition, and of the emperor, Sarsa Dengel of Ethiopia, who was then opposed to any Western influence.[94] Ignatius himself planned this mission. He appointed one of the founders of the Company, Saint Peter Faber, Patriarch of Ethiopia in 1546; but Faber died the same year. He then appointed João Nunes Barreto as his successor (in 1554), with Andrés de Oviedo and Melchior Carneyro as assistant bishops.[95]

In his letter to Barreto (1555), Ignatius concludes by stating that "all that is set forth [in his letter] will serve as a guideline." Yet, the patriarch should not feel obliged to act in accordance with it; rather, he should follow what a discreet charity will dictate to him, "taking into account the existing circumstances and the anointing of the Holy Spirit, who must direct him in everything."[96] In practice, Goa, whose Jesuit provincial "revised" the mission strategy,[97] had the upper hand in organizing the mission and implementing the strategy of this first Jesuit expedition to Ethiopia.

According to Hervé Pennec, Goa served as an intermediary between the center (Rome) and the periphery (Ethiopia), becoming, de facto, the new center of Christianity in the region covered by the Estado da India.[98] The Provincial of Goa also organized personnel movements from Goa, many of which ended in the death of the missionaries.[99]

Beginning in the 1580s, the Jesuit personnel began to change qualitatively, as younger Jesuits from Goa with strong theological credentials were sent to Ethiopia. With the occupation of the Turks, they were unable to engage in conversation with the Ethiopian court, and by the time the last Jesuit on this expedition died in 1597, there were between eight hundred and one thousand Catholics in Ethiopia, mostly Portuguese.[100] But this first expedition was primarily prospective, even though it ended with the actual entry of the Jesuits into Ethiopia. Indeed, an important result of this first expedition was the beginning of the creation of a Catholic space in Ethiopia, with the opening of a Jesuit residence in Tigre in 1566.[101] Despite these initial gains, however, they failed to make any contact with the imperial court, an essential aspect of their strategy.

The Catholic occupation of the space in Ethiopia expanded with the second Jesuit expedition (1597–1622), led by Pedro Paez. Before his arrival, there were contacts between Philip II and the Viceroy of India from 1588 to 1598, in favor of the Jesuit mission.[102] The Turkish threat being always permanent on the Red Sea, new negotiations started between Philip II and the authorities of Goa to find a passage for the Jesuits through the Ethiopian court. Unsuccessful attempts were made between 1589 and 1595. But in 1598, an Indian priest entered the court, bringing with him letters that established the first contact of the Jesuit mission with the circle of Prester John.[103]

Paez was born in Olmeda (Spain) in 1564. He entered the Society of Jesus in Portugal at the age of eighteen and was sent to India three years later as a young scholastic.[104] He was ordained a priest in Goa in 1589, where he met Alessandro Valignani, who later became an important figure in the Jesuit mission in Japan. Paez is known as the true "apostle" of Ethiopia. He was admitted to the court in 1603, along with his confrere, Father Antonio de Monserrate. His approach to the mission followed the instructions of Ignatius: contact with the king and the elite; learning the language; and *disputatio* to win the theological argument. His great success was the conversion of Krestos, a counselor to the emperor (1613), and of Emperor Susneyos himself in 1622, the year of the canonization of Ignatius of Loyola and Francis Xavier.

Throughout the 1620s and under the leadership of Paez, Susneyos showed signs of inclination toward Roman Catholicism, in terms consistent with Ignatius's restoration project. This change for the emperor, of course, was due to three events that were developing in the empire. First, the *disputatio* was bearing fruit among the king's male advisors in a well-executed plan that saw the number of Jesuit theologians in Ethiopia double from ten in 1555–1556 to twenty-five by 1630, while temporal coadjutors dropped from seven to two.[105] Second, from 1607 onward, Ethiopia was faced with political revolts. As a result, four monarchs succeeded each other on the throne from 1597 to 1632.[106] Susneyos, it is clear, needed the military support of Spain and Portugal and he knew that the Jesuits could facilitate negotiations. Some believe that Susneyos so needed military assistance from Madrid and Lisbon that, as a sign of good faith, he offered large portions of the territory to the Catholic missionaries who oversaw these diplomatic contacts with the Iberian courts. Others wonder why the emperor decided to give these lands in places close to the court and the traditional monasteries. Moreover, he affiliated these monasteries with "mother houses" run by the Jesuits[107] while creating ecclesiastical institutions also run by the Jesuits, who effectively took over Christianity in Ethiopia. Recent research on painting in the Ethiopian church has uncovered some vestiges of the syncretic nature of Ethiopian Christianity during this period.[108]

According to some scholars, Susneyos's conversion and actions were deliberate moves to consolidate his control over Ethiopian religion by "using" the Jesuits. The monks and women of the empire were increasingly suspicious of his sympathy for the Catholic missionaries and the power they were accumulating.[109]

The Jesuits had founded the first high school in May Gogwa in 1603, and a seminary two years later.[110] Moreover, they interpreted their success as a successful implementation of Ignatius's instructions. In 1624, Luis de Azevedo could happily write to the Jesuit General and declare the mission accomplished.[111]

After the death of Paez, a radical change occurred in the Ethiopian mission. The new patriarch, Alfonso Mendes, adopted a strategy of "Latinization" that had nothing to do with what Ignatius had envisioned and quickly became very problematic for the Ethiopians. In 1632, Emperor Fasiladas, the son and successor of Susneyos, expelled the Jesuits from Ethiopia, and some missionaries were killed.[112] The third mission had thus thrown away the gains that the Society of Jesus had consolidated, not only in the country, but also within the court itself. In fact, regarding this consolidation, the Jesuits had thirteen residences in 1628.[113] What was Alfonso Mendes's problem? According to Dale H. Moore,

> He had the utmost respect for the prestige of the church he represented, but little understanding of the pride and loyalty of the people he had to work with. Nevertheless, his arrival in 1623 seemed auspicious. He was well received at court, although the people in general were still hostile to the Jesuits....Mendez also had the misfortune to see a great plague of locusts visit Ethiopia the year of his arrival, and Ethiopian priests were quick to associate the two events.[114]

The arrival of Mendes marked the end of the era of Paez, the end of dialogue and compromise. The conversion of the emperor two years earlier also implied the limitation of his own power in certain aspects of religious matters. He professed the Catholic faith and simultaneously condemned essential aspects of Ethiopian Christianity such as the Sabbath. Ignatius's mission of restoration contained a veiled hope of submission, which became more apparent under Mendes and the emperor's opponents at court than during the time of Paez, who was well liked by the Ethiopians.

The conflict between Mendes and the court thus became inevitable. Mendes was hardly an exemplary Jesuit or Catholic leader. He used his friendships to seek power and ecclesiastical dignities. One of his friends, Philip IV, who was exercising his right of *padroado*, appointed him Patriarch of Ethiopia. The newly appointed patriarch wrote to Pope Gregory XV to inform him of his new appointment and to ask him for full faculties. It was only at the end that Mendes wrote to Father Vitelleschi, the then–Superior General of the Jesuits, to explain that he could not refuse his new appointment.[115]

Mendes arrived in Ethiopia accompanied by two other Jesuits who had previously served for the Inquisition in Portugal and other young Jesuits, Juan de Velasco and Jeronimo Lobo. Lobo would later become a great explorer of the source of the Nile, a Jesuit worthy of the highest praise. According to C. F. Beckingham, "None of the Jesuits who attempted to convert Ethiopia to Roman obedience in the sixteenth and seventeenth centuries, not even Pedro Paez himself, had a more exciting life than Lobo, whose adventures were far from over when he escaped to India after the expulsion of the Society by Emperor Fasiladas."[116]

Mendes used his first speech at court to outline his program for Ethiopia. This program is more like the execution of the Austrian strategy in Ethiopia:

> No cleric or monk was to offer mass or perform any ecclesiastical function until he had received faculties from him....All persons, whoever they may be, were to embrace the Roman faith on penalty of death....All clergy were now to be re-ordained, churches re-consecrated, the faithful rebaptized, fasts and feasts reorganized according to the Tridentine calendar. Circumcision— which St. Ignatius had listed among the practices to be permitted, at least temporarily—was forbidden, and the old liturgy was to be reformed.[117]

In short, everything that had happened in Ethiopia before him suddenly became nonsense. He cornered the Monophysites, and, "as theological disputes sharpened, mutual distrust and fanaticism increased."[118] The pride of the Ethiopians was wounded by seeing their emperor and nobles kneel before a foreigner and swear allegiance to a foreign ruler. At this point, the restoration envisaged by Ignatius for Ethiopia, and to some extent for Goa,[119] became a Tridentine revolution.[120] The theory of *tabula rasa* seemed to have replaced dialogue and persuasion.[121]

In 1632, Emperor Alam Sagad (Fasiladas) succeeded Seltan Sagad (Susneyos) after years of revolts and uprisings among the Ethiopians. The Jesuit missionaries were expelled from the empire. A French expedition tried unsuccessfully to recatholicize sixty-five years later, from 1698 to 1706, hoping to succeed where the Portuguese had failed.[122] The Jesuits officially returned to Ethiopia in 1945 and are still there today.

CONCLUSION

This chapter concludes the first century of the Society, from the generalate of Ignatius to that of Vitelleschi. Although there is a chapter devoted to the Society's missions among non-European populations, this chapter has sought to address two aspects of Jesuit early missiology, as conceived by Ignatius himself and executed later by the Jesuits.

Ignatius's project in Ethiopia followed centuries of diplomatic contacts between the Ethiopian court, Rome, and the Iberian Peninsula. In his project, Ignatius, convinced that the threat of the Ottomans had become a matter of survival for European culture and Christianity, saw reconciliation with Ethiopia as a strategic opportunity for Christianity and Christian Europe. In mission strategy and tone, restoration meant above all forging union/unity between Ethiopia and Rome, bringing the heterodox aspects of the Ethiopian church into conformity with Catholic teachings, persuading through dialogue, and understanding their emperor, Prester John. Until the death of Pedro Paez in 1624, the project proceeded as Ignatius had planned.

Mendes and the Jesuits who accompanied him to Ethiopia belonged to the third generation of the Society of Jesus, formed according to the *Ratio Studiorum*,[123] and had extreme views on the Tridentine reforms. Implicitly, the *Ratio Studiorum* followed the spirit and reforms of the Council of Trent, with an emphasis on Scholasticism. Depending on whether one considers Trent a Counter-Reformation or a Catholic Reformation, one can easily place the Jesuits in Ethiopia in one or the other category. However, we must remember the context in which the Ethiopian mission took place.

First, the Counter-Reformation was always about the relationship between Catholics and Protestants or Reformed churches. The Ethiopian church may have been "heretical," but it did not fall into that category. Second, the Jesuits' theological argument was part of the *disputatio*, and perhaps, as Pennec suggests, a vestige of the spirit of the age in Roman Catholicism. This context included the need for a new *Reconquista*, this time of former Catholic territories dominated by Protestants in Europe. The conquest of the infidels, starting with the Moors, under the leadership of the papacy, was also central to this strategy. Ethiopia was part of this broader strategy.

Third, the goal of the mission, even for a third generation that seems to have strayed from the original goal, was still unity with Rome: the instructions of Ignatius made this a priority; the introduction of the first Jesuits to the Ethiopian court emphasized this; and letters from the emperor of Ethiopia to Rome stressed unity with Rome.[124]

The result of the restoration movement in Ethiopia culminated in the conversion of Susneyos and the male members of his court, including his brother, Krestos. After his conversion in 1613, Krestos sent a letter to Pope Paul V in which he expressed his desire to translate the New Testament[125] and to take an active part in the christological debates that eventually won Susneyos's heart. On the day he swore allegiance to Rome, the emperor confessed all his sins, received holy communion, and repudiated all his concubines.[126] These concubines never forgave him for this mistake. They defended themselves with the support of Ethiopian monks disgusted with Mendes. They finally won, in 1632, with the death of Susneyos and, with him, the death of the Jesuit mission.

Ignatius had imagined a Catholicism of dialogue and openness. His first apostles in Ethiopia, who had known the great apostles of India and Japan, were endowed with a spirit of humanism that allowed them to adapt to African and Asian realities. Through this effort of adaptation, the principle of accommodation became a central part of the Jesuit missionary strategy.

3

THE NEW MISSION

In 2012, I arrived in my village in central Cameroon only a few weeks before my ordination to the priesthood. It had been exactly ten years since I had left the village of my childhood and its memories. I knew the names of the safari trees, the names of the forests and groves, the cries of the animals, and the names of each of the inhabitants born before 2002, the year I joined the Jesuits.

The village was ready for the party. It was everyone's business. The richest and poorest had contributed cash. Curious, I took from my mother's hands the list of those who had contributed so as to put faces to the names. Among the very first names, "Joseph: 20,000 FCFA," almost 40 American dollars! Before I could say a word, my mother reassured me: "He will explain to you himself what has become of his life."

We were still in a state of surprise when Joseph proudly announced himself, asking to see his "son," as he always called me. He was elegantly dressed, shirt on, shoes shined, head cleanly shaved. Had it not been for the voice, I would not have easily recognized the man before me. Joseph was known to live a life of alcohol, disordered love affairs, and physical indigence. He also had a sarcastic sense of humor. He called himself a "bum"!

After warm hugs, Joseph told me the cause of his change. It was more internal than external. A pastor, "one of those new revivalist churches," had come through the village. Since he had been invited by Joseph's daughter, Joseph was forced to "suffer" his sermons for entire nights. During one of these sermons, the pastor reminded him that there was no benefit for him to win the whole world if Joseph was to lose his soul in the process (see Mark 8:36).

Amid fear, anxiety, and certainty, Joseph convinced himself that he could be another man, that his present life was not a fatality, that he could live fully without being an alcoholic. He stopped drinking and returned resolutely to his wife and children. He used his meager resources to start a small business and take care of himself and his family. It was thanks to these savings that the man who had been an alcoholic and a professional beggar was able to contribute $40 to a priestly ordination. To my amazement, Joseph repeated three times: "This is just my way of supporting your mission!" He was a benefactor to the Society of Jesus.

Joseph had remained a Catholic. He regularly went to confession and had a great devotion to the Eucharist. But it was an evangelical pastor who had helped his conversion. And in later conversations, he insisted on seeing what "my Jesuit religion" had in common with all that the pastor had taught him and what the pastor had said was unique to the evangelical religion: a taste for a holy and virtuous life.

In this village in central Cameroon where everyone was born a Catholic, the new mission was launched: rural, poor, by people who were sometimes socially marginalized, and on formerly Catholic lands. From then on, Joseph's questioning crossed many hearts. The passage of the pastor had left deep traces. It took this experience with another way of being Christian for the Christian message finally to become personal for Joseph and many others.

This new evangelical way of being did not, however, lack content that was well known to classical Catholics. It is this similarity that favored the disposition of the people to the message of this pastor. Elsewhere in Africa, the faithful of *The Apostolic Church of Africa* prepare for the reception of the Eucharist at length, usually by a prayer vigil, to the rhythm of songs and hymns.[1] In another Pentecostal church in Ghana, *Lighthouse Chapel International*, the bishop teaches that the elements of holy communion effectively become the Body and Blood of Christ. But rather than using the Catholic concept of transubstantiation, he resorts to the Gospel accounts to defend the validity of this newfound devotion.[2] For them too, communion is a miracle food, sometimes therapeutic, with an efficacy comparable to anointing.

That Joseph's conversion took place in this village in which everyone remained Catholic, as well as his challenge regarding my "Jesuit religion," raised questions. Is there a study in the Society's history that addresses this global phenomenon? Is there a Jesuit response to global evangelism? What in Jesuit history is comparable to this religiosity full of emotions, devotions, sacraments, and miracles?

In this village, very few understand the word *Jesuit*. They proceed by association to define it. It is "the congregation of the Pope" (Francis). Fortunately, the pope is admired for his leadership style and perceived as a living saint. It is also the "congregation of Fr. Hebga [Meinrad-Pierre]," the Cameroonian Jesuit who was a distinguished scholar, but who was also powerful through his healing ministry, exorcisms, and miracles. It was Hebga who introduced the Catholic Charismatic Movement to Cameroon.[3] Like him, in Brazil, the Catholic Charismatic Renewal (CCR) came about largely through the influence of two American Jesuits, Edward Dougherty and Harold Rahm, and a Brazilian priest, Jonas Abid. After being baptized in the Holy Spirit at a charismatic retreat in early 1969, Dougherty shared his experience with Rahm and the two organized charismatic retreats for Catholics in the university city of Campinas and the rest of the country.[4]

In both Hebga's Cameroon and Dougherty and Rahm's Brazil, the Jesuit-inspired charismatic movement was organized around lay communities. In some cases, these laypeople lived together in community, if only temporarily, in pursuit of their sanctification. The members of these communities also shared, like the Jesuits, in the mission.[5] Beginning with a handful of people in 1969, the Brazilian charismatic movement that these Jesuits inspired grew to 10,000 adherents by 1970, 2 million by 1989, and up to 33 million by 2008.[6] This movement is now embraced by clergy who find in it an opportunity for a deepening of the spiritual life of believers like Joseph, as well as a greater sense of responsibility for one's own actions and a greater attachment to the church.[7] Charismatics also impact Latin American culture through music, lively religious rituals, and countercultural lifestyles.[8]

What happened to Joseph is a global reality. To answer the questions posed by his conversion to my "Jesuit religion," the history of the Jesuit missions serves to satisfy the demands of these new Christianities. To begin with, this history would have to shed a certain rationalizing heritage.

THE HUMANISTIC RATIONALISM IN JESUIT MISSION HISTORY

The history of the Jesuit missions, especially the well-known ones in Asia, has often emphasized methods of adaptation, accommodation, and inculturation. These methods do not hide their humanist foundations or their rationalist emphasis. In the first globalization, argues Antoni J. Ucerler, the Jesuits reinvented Christianity based on the method used by the Apostle Paul among the Athenians (see Acts 17:23–25). They distinguished between what was essential to Christianity to maintain and what was accidental as a point of adaptation. They believed especially in the light of reason. For some of them, the ancient Chinese and Japanese were saved simply by acting according to natural law.[9]

Francis Clooney recently discovered that the Talmudic translation offered by one of the Jesuit theorists of accommodation, Roberto de Nobili, was not, as he had hoped, primarily about accommodation. It also and above all contained a "rational" exposition of the content of faith, from the idea of God to revelation. But once again, for Clooney, de Nobili relied on the universality of reason and the possibility of a truth that transcends all culture and religion.[10] Heir to scholastic theology, de Nobili had assumed Thomas Aquinas's interpretation of idolatry. It was irrational, immoral, and a mistaken vision of the divine. Therefore, for him and for other Jesuits who shared this Thomistic theological training, idolatry was doomed to failure. True religion, for them, had to pass the test of reason.[11]

De Nobili shared this vision with his Jesuit contemporaries in India: Gonçalo Fernandes, Diego Gonçalves, and Jacobo Fenicio, and others. All of them, moreover, were worthy heirs of their Jesuit predecessors in Asia, namely, Mateo Ricci, who was himself a novice of Alessandro Valignano, the modern theorist of accommodation. According to mission historian Andrew Ross, the Jesuits' encounter with East Asia, from the time of Francis Xavier until the *Ex quo singulari* bull condemning Chinese rites (1742), was marked by their conviction that Christianity does not belong to a particular culture. Comparing Japanese and Chinese cultures to the Greco-Roman culture in which the first inculturation took place, these Jesuit pioneers relied on Italian humanism to replicate the same model in the seventeenth century.[12] The Jesuit vision, however, was "betrayed" because eighteenth-century Europeans could not understand it and turned against it in the controversy over Chinese rites.[13]

This interpretation, according to recent historiography, is based on a paradigm largely favorable to the Jesuits. According to Joan-Pau Rubiés, proponents of this paradigm see the overall failure of the Society's missions in Asia as the direct result of the interruption of the experiments in cultural flexibility represented by accommodation. Historians who interpret the Society's missions in this way, such as Ross, also assume a certain identity between the Jesuits and modern, even liberal, scientific values.[14] Others, such as Jacques Gernet, gave no chance of success to missions based on erroneous and sometimes embellished cultural translations that claimed to propose a uniformity that did not in fact exist within Christianity or even the Society.[15]

Recalling Liam Brockey's thesis, Rubiés argues that Jesuits did not go on mission primarily to develop science or learn foreign languages but to preach, baptize, and administer sacraments.[16] Without insisting on this religious character essential to the Jesuit enterprise, however, the author, like many others before him, ends up falling back on an intellectualist analysis of the missions. This intellectualist interpretation leads him to blame the Jesuits for the crisis of modern secularism.

Insisting that rational people governed by political systems such as those of the West were able to convert more quickly and sustainably than others who were regarded as less civilized, Valignano, Ricci, de Nobili, and others placed the criterion of civilization and natural law at the heart of their missionary efforts. This choice for the elite, observes Anand Amaladass, was deliberate. It also had the opposite effect of losing contact with the religiosity of the masses, which, in de Nobili as in his predecessors, deserved little credit.[17]

The neglect of popular religiosity had a negative impact on the appreciation of the overall mission. For, although the Jesuit accommodationists succeeded in creating a favorable context for the encounter of religions and cultures and put reason (and thus reasoning) at the center of such encounters, they also, in the process, reduced what might have been religious among the Chinese, Indians, or Japanese to a purely civil system. In doing so, they implicitly admitted that their model of Christianity remained intolerant of any true accommodation, that is, of any religious system that competed with or was an alternative to Roman Catholicism. Thus, the Jesuits simply became a vehicle for a "commercial civilization struggling to free itself from despotism and superstition, rather than an agent of Providence."[18]

The humanist and rationalist approach of Jesuit missionary historiography thus remains inescapable. Historians of Jesuit missions have so far put it at the center of any discussion in a kind of Manichean dualism: one either embraces or opposes it. However, there is another way to understand Jesuit missions. It starts with a simple, corrective observation. It is, indeed, a serious historical aberration to analyze, as Rubiés does, the Jesuit missions in Asia simply as failures. For they did have successes. In 1982, at the Macerata conference commemorating the 400th anniversary of Matteo Ricci's (1552–1610) arrival in China, Pope John Paul II (1920–2005) described the Italian missionary as "a true bridge between the two civilizations: European and Chinese."[19]

Moreover, before Valignano, Ricci, or de Nobili, Francis Xavier, whose rationalist approach was never the only force, baptized thousands. The key to interpreting these mass conversions would therefore be found elsewhere than in the praiseworthy effort of intellectual accommodation. The problem is that some historiography has favored and even isolated rationalizing accommodation at the expense of other means that were applied to these mass conversions. For example, in another article, Rubiés, recounting the deathbed conversion of Montesquieu, shows how

Jesuits who favored the rationalizing approach thought that converting one Montesquieu had more merit than converting twelve thousand as Xavier did among the Indians.[20]

Moreover, the successes of the Jesuits among peoples who, unlike the Japanese and Chinese, who were recognized by Europeans for their high degree of civilization, did not approach religion primarily with a spirit of reason have been less studied to date. When these missions have been studied, it is sometimes from the angle of civilizing missions, contemporary synonyms of the accommodationists and rationalists of the sixteenth century. For civilization was understood as being opposite to barbarism and idolatry. However, the religion of the so-called barbaric peoples (even a rationalized religion like Christianity), lived by and with emotion, was denigrated by the rationalists. Rubiés does not analyze this form of religiosity in the Jesuit missions enough and, by neglecting it, ends up falling into the secularist temptation that would have its roots in these missions.

The story of Joseph, his daughter, and her pastor thus allows us to question the other side of the story of the Jesuit missions. It is a question of situations in which accommodation was not only intellectual but also a story of conversion, of witnessing to life, of healing (sometimes simply interior healing), and of miracles, a story of living together in work, in prayer, and in the practice of the sacraments.

This pietism in history does not supplant the rationalism that has been the school of thought until now. In fact, when historiographic rationalism is understood well, it helps to avoid any temptation of religious fundamentalism. Moreover, in a context in which the growth of religion is asymmetrical to development and peace, this rationalist approach also makes it possible to comprehend religion in its rationality and institutional order as a tool for social transformation. This is what the pioneers of accommodation appreciated among the Chinese and Japanese. To recognize this is also to affirm that such a transformation is not unique to Christianity as Max Weber[21] or Michael Novak claim.[22]

RECENT CRITICISM OF THIS ELITE HISTORIOGRAPHY

Valignano, as we have seen, had great respect for the Chinese and Japanese cultures. He believed them to be civilized and similar (if not superior) to the ancient Greco-Romans, whom early Christianity had been able to inculturate. Because of this respect, Valignano believed that it was possible to build a Christian church in Japan that was Japanese and a Christian church in China that was also Chinese.[23] This admiration for Asian civilizations justified the method of accommodation that he applied to evangelize them. Valignano, like Francis Xavier before him, believed that the *gente blanca* (white people) and intellectuals were more likely to embrace a new religion. However, other races responded less to the Western intellectual and moral criteria. Africans, Indians, Malaysians, and Indonesians, for example, were deemed less fertile ground for the inculturation of the gospel.[24]

In his recent research, Eugenio Menegon shows the limits of this missionary elitism of the Jesuits in China and, in so doing, corrects the historiography that has exalted their strategies to excess. In 1746, in Fuan, it was simple people who allowed Christianity to become localized. These were "degree holders, young unmarried women from respectable families, and even lower-ranking employees in local government offices."[25] For Menegon, the Jesuits' introduction of some European scientific knowledge to the imperial court had limited impact on the technology and science of the late empire, and virtually none on education.[26] On the contrary, Fuan's experience shows "that one can be an accepted member of the local society and a Christian without adhering to the Confucianized Christianity of the Jesuit communities."[27]

Ambrose Mong seems to confirm this thesis in his justification of the failure of the Franciscan and Jesuit missions in China because of their elitism. Unlike Nestorian Christianity, which was able to establish itself firmly among the masses of the people, the modern Jesuit missions associated themselves with the imperial power and neglected to establish a mass Christianity and to build up an Indigenous clergy.[28] Mong thus adopts the classic position of cultural historians that did not leave the church indifferent in the development of its own missionary strategies. These historians observed that the end of each imperial dynasty in China brought about the fall of this palace Christianity. It would therefore have taken a marginalization of the political-ecclesial system to constitute an autonomous Chinese clergy.

Indeed, in 1688, the vicars apostolic of Thailand, Indochina, and Japan recommended the appointment of a native, Gregorio Lopez, as bishop. His Dominican confreres and other foreign missionaries objected because, among other reasons, "he did not have the theological knowledge necessary to become a bishop."[29] The Augustinians eventually brought Gregorio to China, where he was consecrated by Bernardina della Chiesa as bishop and vicar apostolic of Nanjing in 1685. Lopez would eventually ordain the first three Chinese priests in 1688 without the approval of Rome.[30]

Proponents of the latter, rather social, thesis of the history of Catholic missions in Asia believe that it was only when faced with the prospect of the collapse of imperialist enterprises that missionaries took seriously the criticisms of Christianity. This led to the promotion of a Christianity devoid of European "color" that could attract more followers in these foreign lands.[31] Other missionaries hoped to find a way to synthesize Christianity with the local tradition. This synthesis was not unanimous among the missionaries, some of whom "refused to give up their power over their congregations."[32]

The reality of the Jesuit missions in Asia, it is true, was never uniform. Nor was it a simple Manichean opposition between social classes. On the ground, these missions were extraordinarily fluid. A marginal social group, women, for example, could change the relational order in a colony and force the mission to change its strategy. Bárbara O. Reyes shows how the lives of three women, Bárbara Gandiaga, Eulalia Callis, and Eulalia Pérez, influenced the Jesuit, Dominican, and Franciscan mission projects in Baja and Alta California.[33] They were also women who orchestrated one of the theological debates that contributed to the failure of the Jesuit missions to Ethiopia in the seventeenth century[34] and to Fernando Poo (today called Bioko) in the nineteenth century.[35] In the latter two cases, the Jesuit discourse on hygiene denoted a desire for civilization, but in fact included an evangelizing background that linked hygiene and virtue in the life of the Christian.[36] As with my uncle Joseph, the interior transformation produced by adherence to Christianity was to be accompanied by an exterior transformation, both in hygiene and in morals.

Indeed, according to Tracy N. Leavelle, singular definitions of conversion as a passage of imperial subjects from "savages" to "Christians" do not adequately capture the complex processes that took place in the colonial world that served as the context for missions. Leavelle, therefore, adopts the notion of plural, dynamic, and flexible conversion that "requires an analysis of religious action—orientation and movement, song and discourse, ritual and relationships—more than a simple definition of faith and doctrine."[37] Similarly, in her analysis of the Jesuit missions in the Ottoman Empire in the early seventeenth century, Adina Ruiu offers a picture of a missionary field fraught with multilayered and enduring tensions between nations and religious denominations, and between Roman centralism and national religious initiatives supported by states.[38]

These multiple layers of power and the resulting tensions left considerable room for individual action and internal dissension.[39] As Inés Županov suggests, the Jesuit missions in both India and China were "contested." While Roberto de Nobili and Gonçalo Fernandes both believed in the importance of Brahmanism and exploited written texts as a key to understanding Indian religions and societies, they also each had different approaches:

> Fernandes was Portuguese. His missionary approach focused primarily on external accommodations. De Nobili, on the other hand, was Italian and had an aristocratic education. He understood culture that looked for universal patterns in culture, and saw Brahmins as descendants of a lost Jewish tribe and Hindu theological texts as flawed Catholicism.[40]

Differences in context and social background affected the appreciation of Indian or Chinese cultures and the extent to which they could be integrated into Christian rites. As we shall see, the controversy over rites already had its roots among the Jesuits themselves. Moreover, the liminal spaces created by these tensions also served to emancipate the mission from the colonial system and the emergence of an indigenous culture of resistance that was the basis of anticolonial nationalisms.

The approach of this book complements the rationalist approach. For just as Thomistic Scholasticism begins with a humble recognition that reason is not sufficient to account for the divine, so, too, any study of mission as a religious phenomenon cannot be satisfied with analyses that would not do justice to the-beyond-reason that, as Elisa Frei,[41] and Catherine Mooney recently demonstrated, motivated the missionaries.[42] As Inés G. Županov argues, in translating the catechism into Tamil, the Jesuits were not only imposing a colonialist model of evangelization, they were also appealing to the emotions of those they were evangelizing: "The very texture of the *Confessionario* overflows with Tamil concepts of devotion, guilt, fear of sins, sorrow, desire and hope that may only imperfectly coincide with the semantic fields of Latin or Portuguese."[43] The empire that the Jesuits were building in the sixteenth century was above all a spiritual empire.[44]

From then on, religion produced, in the peasant Joseph, an impulse toward a virtuous and happy life, a concrete act of individual conversion and social transformation. In the present context of global Christianity and its abuses, and in view of the growth of Christianity in poor regions previously classified as irrational and idolatrous, this story of missionary piety gains relevance. Undoubtedly, reason was not, and is not, the only force or faculty that, for the early Jesuits, transcended all culture. Virtue, the apprehension of a mysterious beyond—the beyond-of-reason and holiness— could have equally captivated Asian or African peoples who were neither modern atheists nor accustomed to European republicanism and its secularist inclination.

FROM EARLY JESUIT PIETY TO RATIONALIZATION

Curiously, the first historians of the Society gave an important role to the language of miracles and emotions. The *Autobiography* presents a pious Ignatius, versed in the spiritual beliefs and devotions of his time. He is practically a knight of Our Lady, a man attached to the practice of the sacraments, and a deep believer in a providential God. Thus, he would say of the Society in the *Constitutions* that it was created by divine means and could only be maintained by the same [*Const.* 840].

For the founders of the Society, its members were not only learned but also virtuous. Thanks to their exemplary lives, they were credited with an aura of sanctity during their lifetime. It was this reputation that attracted to them people seeking some good for their souls. After their death, the miracles that were attributed to the missionaries could have as much or more impact on believers and nonbelievers than any other missionary strategy. Their lives were printed and distributed for the evangelization of peoples. Their relics were "circulated to spread supernatural power and create bonds among believers, especially in newly Christianized areas."[45]

Thus, Francis Xavier had barely died on a beach on the Chinese island of Shugchuan (Sancian) on December 3, 1552, when the Society's secretary, Juan de Polanco, launched an investigation on November 21, 1555, into "Xavier's heroic virtues, apostolic zeal, holy death, and, above all, his performance of miracles, both pre- and post-mortem, which were to be collected, examined, and recorded for posterity."[46] This was immediately supported by the King of Portugal. Franco Mormando and Jill G. Thomas point out that "Xavier has been celebrated as one of the Church's most effective foreign missionaries, but even more important in the popular imagination is his fame as a miracle worker."[47] Similarly, the life of Saint Ignatius written by Pedro de Ribadeneira offers a whole chapter on the miracles of the saint.[48]

However, toward the end of the first century of the Society's existence, this history underwent a progressive rationalization. The result was the exclusion of the fanciful and the miraculous. In reaction to the profusion of legends that marked the first historiography, prominent Jesuits, including Fathers General Everard Mercurian and Claudio Acquaviva, and prominent missionary theorists such as Valignano,[49] warned against these cheap histories. The pressure to rationalize was so strong that, in 1605, Ribadeneira himself wrote a treatise in which he set out the "reasons" for the existence of the religious institute that is the Society of Jesus.[50]

This institutional dissociation from the first historiography was undoubtedly prudent. The surrounding world was becoming more and more critical, rationalistic, and hostile to the Society. There was also a rationalist turn within the Society itself that, in order to be respected by the scholars of the time, had to follow the generally accepted scientific paradigms. This shift would remain alive long after the restoration.

For instance, Luis Martin, Superior General and promoter of the publication of the *Monumenta*, asked Jesuit historians to write the history of the order in a style that even its worst enemies could respect.[51] His successor, Francis Xavier Wernz, speaking to a group of Jesuits in Rome in 1910, set forth the Jesuit ideal of authentic history. The soundness of historical research, he noted, presupposed that all things be returned to their sources. Scientific rigor and critical sense certainly presupposed piety, but "not piety without a critical spirit."[52] For, "sobriety and fairness of judgment, which lead to never telling falsehoods, to never hiding the truth; all this allows to write a true history, and not a panegyric, because only the truth is the solid foundation of the edification of ours, it alone can win the esteem of foreigners."[53]

Thus, the translations of Chinese, Indian, or Japanese classics by the Jesuit pioneers of accommodation were often directed not specifically to mass evangelization, but rather to a dialogue between European and Asian literati. While a visitor to China, Valignano recalled Rugieri to Rome. He replaced him in China with Ricci, who was his novice between 1571 and 1573. Valignano asked his protégé to retranslate Rugieri's *Thianzu shilu*, to purify it of all that was Buddhist, such as the cycle of incarnations. His intention was that Ricci's translation "might become a legitimate resource for reinforcing the Christian message" and be used in the Chinese catechism "to prevent any hint of idolatry or superstition from creeping into the catechism."[54] Jesuit translations of these classics were often precise and had a "pronounced tendency to interpret Confucian concepts in terms of the natural religion and monotheistic God of the Judeo-Christian tradition."[55] Confucius, therefore, became primarily a philosopher. If he was perceived as a saint by the *Sinarum philosophicum*, it was only because he relied essentially on human reason to lead a moral life.[56]

CANONIZATION AS AN EVANGELIZING MOMENT

While historical rationalism seemed to be taking hold in the Society, another phenomenon was emerging. As the missionary influence of the Jesuits grew, so did the number of canonizations. As the missions grew, so did the accounts of the miracles of Jesuit saints that were necessary to validate their sanctity. In what seems like an early projection into the twenty-first century, Ulrike Strasser shows that "artistic portraits of the saints served to extend the presence of the saints in time and space, linking together expanding networks of devotees and believers."[57] For reading as well as writing, copying, and printing were "mimetic technologies for producing new saints for society in the age of globalization."[58]

The lives of the first missionaries of the Society, beyond their intellect and their ability to dialogue rationally with the new cultures, were, firstly, written as lives of saints. And this sanctity had as powerful an impact, sometimes even greater, on the peoples of Africa, Asia, and America as the intellectual accommodation advocated by a Ricci or de Nobili. The canonizations of Saint Francis Xavier and Saint Ignatius (along with Saint Isidore of Madrid, Saint Teresa of Avila, and Saint Philip Neri, who were canonized the same year) was one of the most triumphant ceremonies in the history of the modern Church. The solemn procession was accompanied by music performed by the students of the *Germanicum*. The rector, Bernardino Castorio, had maintained the musical tradition established by his predecessor, Michael Lauritano, when the college was reestablished in 1573.[59] Nearby, at the Roman College, Jesuits had composed dramas and operas. It was a true exhibition of the artistic and pedagogical culture of the Society's colleges. The Jesuit theater made use of dance, spectacular scenes, but also miracles and heavenly interventions. These dramas included "ballets, large musical ensembles, and elaborate stage effects including supernatural scenes, miracles, apparitions, celestial interventions, and distortions of myths."[60]

For the Jesuits, theater, drama, opera, and other artistic performances had a missionary purpose. Long before Xavier's death, Ignatius of Loyola had authorized the distribution of his letters from the Far East among his fellow Jesuits and the Society's benefactors in Europe. The purpose of this campaign was to inspire greater missionary zeal and candidates for the Society.[61] The campaign for the canonization of Francis Xavier began with a major propaganda effort orchestrated by John III, King of Portugal. On March 28, 1556, the king sent a letter to his viceroy of the East Indies. He ordered him to begin interviewing witnesses to Xavier's apostolic activities, character, piety, and thaumaturgical powers.[62] In 1622, at the canonization ceremony at St. Peter's Basilica, artists depicted his miracles "so that the pious faithful could marvel at them and be inspired by them."[63] In the popular imagination, Saint Xavier's fame was due mainly to his miracles.

The miracles that God worked through the intercession of the saints of the Society were spread throughout the earth.[64] The King of France, in his letter of recommendation for the canonization of Saint Ignatius, encouraged it because he believed that he would be "the protector and founder of the plan he had to extirpate heresy from his kingdom." Duke Maximilian of Bavaria made a similar recommendation. All believed that their efforts to advance the canonization of the two saints would be beneficial to the peace and prosperity of their nations, as well as to their worldwide influence.[65]

The accommodationists can be credited for being concerned with rationally demonstrating the compatibility of Christianity with the new cultures and religions they were discovering. The value of this approach is therefore commendable. Yet, it also had its shortcomings. Andrés Palmeiro, Ricci's visitor to China, questioned, for example, the limited number of conversions that Ricci's elite strategy had produced. Without trying to "throw the baby out with the bathwater," it is important to emphasize that beyond all the missionary strategies that Valignano, Ricci, de Nobili, and Paéz adopted with remarkable success, the popularity of most of the early Jesuit missionaries was nonetheless sustained by the echo of their holiness and the power of their miracles. They themselves lived the success of the mission as a miracle.

THE VIRTUOUS LIVES OF THE FIRST JESUITS IN AFRICA

Ordered by Ignatius, Gonçalves da Câmara, at the head of a delegation of young Jesuits, left Lisbon. He crossed all of Andalusia and found himself on the North African islands of Ceuta and Tetuan, where one of the largest slave markets around the Mediterranean was located.[66] This was the very beginning of the Society's missions on African soil. The quality of the personnel was unquestionable, as was the extreme importance Ignatius attached to this mission. Da Câmara himself was like a true son to Ignatius. And it was to him that Ignatius dictated what today serves as his *Autobiography*.[67]

Juan Nuñes Barreto, whom Ignatius proposed as Ethiopia's patriarch, was a learned and illustrious Jesuit. He was born into a family of Portuguese nobility with great wealth and eight children, seven of whom were religious, including three Jesuits. His life, as described by Juan Eusebio Nieremberg, also provides for us a rich menu of spiritual practices and devotions proper to the nascent Society in Portugal that Saint Ignatius was forced to correct with a firm pen. However, these devotions also testify to an intellectual culture that tried to accommodate a great religious fervor. Turning to asceticism, external discipline and contemplation, some Portuguese had difficulty accepting what Nadal describes as "contemplative in action."

After studying at the prestigious University of Salamanca and then in Coimbra, where he obtained his doctorate, Nuñes Barreto entered the monastery of the Abbey of Freiras. In his biography of Nuñes, Nieremberg reports that he spent at least six hours per day in prayer. His brother, Melchior Nuñes, already a Jesuit, tried to attract Juan to the Society, but the latter hesitated for a long time. For him, the apostolic character of the Society did not satisfy his natural inclination for contemplation. This spirituality seemed to him to be *de mucho ruido y distracciones* (of much noise and distraction). To Melchior, who told him that the Jesuits were, rather, both contemplative and active, Juan found such a "mixed" life incapable of giving him the peace he desired in his solitude.[68]

It was finally through contact with Peter Faber, known for his discernment and piety, that Father Nuñes Barreto decided to join the Society. Already a priest when he entered the Society, Nuñes was quickly ready for the mission. He accompanied da Câmara on the North African expedition, where King John III needed Jesuits to work for the salvation of the Christians held captive by the Moors. Da Câmara could not stay there too long for health reasons. He also wanted to go to Portugal to recruit new vocations. As a result, Nuñes stayed on his own, doing the work of two, "for a thousand even." In the cities of Tetuan and Ceuta, Nuñes responded to the cruelty and barbarity of the Moors with humility, magnanimity, and works of mercy.

The Jesuits were, in essence, a Mediterranean order. Their headquarters were established in Rome. They also enjoyed the support of the monarchs of Spain and Portugal and looked toward evangelizing the Turks. The Institute's Formula of 1540 had identified the "Turks" as a destination for the Jesuits. A contemporary description of the African part of the country of the Turks reveals the extreme cruelty of its inhabitants. Here, arbitrary violence spared no one, not even priests. In the slave market of Tetuan, it was not only the poor condition of the sick that inspired compassion; the healthy themselves, who were innumerable, filled the places, emaciated by hunger. What the inhabitants of Tetuan had in abundance, on the contrary, were

> the curses, the affronts, the abusive words, the cruel
> blows, the unhappy floggings, the long hours of work:
> some, like beasts, brought around the millstones of the
> tahonas; others carried loads like mules, others still did
> the work of the fields, and were from sunrise to sunset
> (and even more so in Africa) picking.[69]

Here, hell is not theoretical. It is compared to the reign of cruelty, located "under the earth" and "among the wild beasts." The chaos of this slave market thus opens a window on the social relations governing this first globalization. Sometimes, it is an African shoemaker who is the master of a European slave. Sometimes, this slave is a priest. One finds another shoemaker collaborating with a Moor, selling, buying, and reselling European and Black slaves. The popular language in Cameroon calls such people "Bayam

Salam" (Buy and Sell). Ralph A. Austen gave them the more elegant name of *Middle Men*.[70]

JESUITS AS MERCEDARIANS

While much has been written about the Franciscan or Dominican heritage of the Jesuits, we discover a Mediterranean context that nourished holy vocations, including that of Peter Claver. The Mediterranean brought the Society closer to the pastoral care of slaves and prisoners. In this frontier of globalization, among these Turks, the primary mission of the Society was comparable to that of the Mercedarians, one of the hundreds of charitable associations that sprang up in Europe during the twelfth century. These institutions had hospitals, hospices, and charitable homes. Some were run under the aegis of communities of canons, cathedral chapters, or religious orders. Others were constituted by lay bodies or by confraternities organized by groups of townspeople. Most were entirely local in origin and purpose, but some were affiliated with larger groups, such as the Knights of St. John, or the Brothers of Aubrac and the Brothers of the Ransom.[71]

Nuñes Barreto, the first Roman Catholic patriarch of Ethiopia, and the first in the Society to receive ecclesiastical dignities of episcopal rank, thus learned to be a missionary in an urban center dominated by poverty, inhumane treatment of people, and violence. Some Christians, unable to bear such violence, became Muslims. To survive and carry out his ministry, Nuñes, although learned, relied primarily on his virtue. According to his first biographers, Father Nuñes occupied the position of a slave, digging the earth, carrying burdens and the stove. He not only performed the humblest services among humans, but also those of animals, "making himself the slave of the slaves, whom he had the honor of serving for the love of Jesus Christ."[72]

Nuñes spent endless hours confessing, preaching, doing charitable works, and working for the conversion of the Moors. He redeemed slaves. And this ministry required much money, which he struggled to find. He denounced the insensitivity of rich

Christians who were indifferent to so many souls who were lost for lack of money. In this battle under the two banners, the rich, Nuñes grumbled, had chosen the camp of Lucifer:

> Which makes me tremble before the great judgment of God, especially against the rich; and I know what great mercy he has shown me in leaving the world and its temporal goods, for it is far better not to have to give an account than to give a bad account of what we have.[73]

In this way, Nuñes interpreted the economic inequalities that existed in this first globalization from an eschatological perspective, that of the Parousia and the last judgment. In a homiletic style, he reminded the rich of the principle and foundation of all human existence, and warned them that an exaggerated accumulation of goods would put them on the side of the goats on judgment day:

> What excuse will these lords with their many incomes and possessions have on the dreadful day of judgment, when Christ will appear with his wounds open, demanding that each one give an account of what he has given, how he has spent it?...Let them consider all the money and treasures they spend on the construction of very sumptuous buildings, on great banquets and feasts, on brocades and tapestries; and then the souls that cost Christ our Lord his life, each of which is worth more than all that has been created. For lack of money, they are lost here, turning into Moors, enemies of their so Magnificent Creator.[74]

For Nuñes, not to redistribute goods accumulated for the good of souls is to become an enemy of God. It is to help, by omission, the advance of the Moors and their cruelty. He observes, for example, that "many young women, sexually abused by these infidels (abuse that they do not have for sins) become Moors, and after being full of lost children like them, they ask God for justice against the one who did not deliver them."[75]

MISSIONARIES TO THE TURKS — LIVING SAINTS

Beyond works of mercy and preaching, Nuñes and the first Companions attracted crowds and converted them by the example of their lives. People considered them living saints. The miracles recorded during the canonization processes, many of which served a purely hagiographic purpose, thus came to have an apostolic and missionary value. The images and parables used to talk about the miracles were inspired by the Bible.

When people saw Nuñes, Nieremberg relates, they went out into the streets and followed him (see Luke 14:25). Some kissed his hands; others clung to his robe (see Matt 9:20–22); others, probably children, clung to his lap or sat on it (see Mark 10:13–16). Even the Moorish governor looked at them with respect, his child having become an admirer of the apostle (see Luke 7:1–10).[76] It was this humility of the apostle that opened the apostolic field. Father Nuñes was so well known among the Moors that they all trusted him. Some lent him money to help the captives and sent him their slaves so that he could treat them in his hospital.[77]

Peter Claver, the model of the apostle who became a slave among slaves, was born in this Mediterranean area of slavery and trade. Heroism and martyrdom there did not necessarily consist in the beheading of the rogue missionary, but rather in a humble and poor service, without limits and without rest. Nuñes wanted to serve there until his last breath when he was called back to Portugal, at the suggestion of Saint Ignatius himself, for a mission that was considered "the greatest undertaking of all Christendom."[78]

Ignatius's first choice was Peter Faber, who in the eyes of the Society, the Portuguese Court, and others was a "reflection" of perfection and holiness. When Faber died in 1546, Ignatius turned to Nuñes, who was explicitly requested by the king. He also appointed Fathers André de Oviedo and Melchior Carnero, "both persons of great virtue,"[79] as coadjutors and consultors of the mission. Nuñes suffered so much from being raised to the ecclesiastical dignity that he begged Ignatius in vain to dispense him from it. Having rendered some services during his stopover in Mozambique, he unfortunately could not enter Ethiopia. He died in Goa on December 17, 1562.[80]

André de Oviedo, Nuñes's successor as Patriarch of Ethiopia, was also not lacking in nobility, letters, and virtues. He studied at the University of Alcalá, and then worked in Coimbra and Gandia, where he was elected by his nine fellow students as rector.[81] He was then appointed first rector of Naples, where he worked with Nicolas Bobadilla. Installed in Goa at the side of Nuñes Barreto, Oviedo was able to enter Ethiopia.

Philip II, in support of Father Oviedo's mission, sent a total of twelve letters between 1588 and 1598 to the Viceroy of India.[82] He also opened negotiations with the authorities in Goa to find a passage for the Jesuits through the Ethiopian court. There were unsuccessful attempts in 1589 and 1595. It was not until 1598 that an Indian priest was able to enter Ethiopia, bringing with him letters that would establish the first contact with the Jesuit mission.[83] The Ethiopian Negus Claudius was "a zealous adherent of the national faith. He refused to admit the authority of Oviedo."[84]

During the sixteen years that he spent in Fremona, Oviedo lived in a hut. It was round, shaped like a half-orange. The walls were made of adobe or badly kneaded mud, with no resistance to the cold, heat, and excessive storms of this land. The roof was made of straw, which made it difficult to defend against the rains. According to Nieremberg, "everything was evangelical poverty, or rather wealth hidden from the greed of those of the world: all holiness."[85] In order to write to the king, the patriarch was obliged to remove the first blank page of his breviary. Not being able to afford a similar luxury to write to the pope, he cut the margins of the breviary and sewed them into a book. The pope was moved by this and saw in it "the example of those ancient bishops of the Church, who, persecuted by tyrants, came to the greatest poverty."[86]

In a mixture of the ancient and the modern, Oviedo, no doubt emulating the Desert Fathers, was an early vegetarian. Even before the rise of the Seventh Day Adventists,[87] he hardly ate meat: "his ordinary food was a certain seed that abounds in this wild country, unappetizing and bitter, a coarse and vile food, reserved for the poorest of Ethiopia."[88] In this context of persecution of the Christians, such was the sanctity of the patriarch that even the Moors took every precaution for his protection. They were aware that God would punish them if some misfortune endangered the life of the patriarch.[89] Thus, Oviedo was able to carry out his mission with complete peace of mind. Patriarch Oviedo finally died as he had lived, in all edification, on September 14, 1567. He was almost sixty years old, having spent thirty-six in the Society and twenty in Ethiopia.

Death! This very human preoccupation that escapes all rationalism. The first pages of the history of the Jesuits took extraordinary pains to describe it. For it was their custom to constantly ask the Lord for the grace of a good death. Oviedo's death was a holy one. Although Nieremberg does not offer details about the death of the patriarch, he does it with his successor, Manuel Fernandez. The Virgin Mary, of whom Fernandez was a devotee, appeared to him herself, consoled him, before taking him for a cheerful and peaceful walk in the bosom of her Son Jesus.[90] With Francisco Lobo (Lopez), the Virgin filled his room with her presence, and took with her his soul to the mansions of the sky.[91]

The Ethiopians buried the body of Oviedo with many tears and veneration, kissing the feet of their most holy prelate, in whom they admired the most celebrated gifts among the great prelates of the church. Even the heretics mourned his death. The infidels themselves came to venerate his holy sepulcher. They offered a quantity of wheat and other fruits and products of the earth. They also burned incense and other spices and pastries in honor of the servant of God.[92]

Oviedo's relics, the Ethiopians thought, as in medieval times, gave access to the treasures of heaven, through his participation in the Petrine privileges by virtue of his episcopal rank. They also provided for the immediate needs of the Ethiopians. They invoked Oviedo to bring rain and thus free them from the miseries of drought and famine. They prayed to the saint that, if he were to free them from these plagues, they would all embrace the Christian faith. An apostle of ecology, Oviedo was also seen as a knight of peace. In this Ethiopia ravaged by wars, their massacres, the murders of kings, the incessant rebellions, and all their litany of suffering and misery, the people prayed once again to beg for a miracle from him.[93]

THE ETHOS OF THE JESUIT PATRIARCHS OF ETHIOPIA

Nuñes, Oviedo, and Fernandez were only precursors of a mission that would produce its most spectacular results with the arrival of Pedro Páez. All of them prepared the ground for this success. Above all, they all lived by the same ethos, that of the sons of Saint Ignatius and of the Society he helped to found. It is an ethos of knowledge and of holy virtues. It is an ethos of companionship and friendship made up of mutual emulation in the search for the greater glory of God and the good most universal. This ethos begins, as early as the *Spiritual Exercises*, with the victory over oneself.

One of Oviedo's Companions, Andrés Gualdames, was able to learn the language of the Ethiopians in six months with such mastery that he preached in it as if it were natural to him. Like other great Jesuit missionaries, Gualdames published in the same language. In addition to the apostolic succession that was taking place in Ethiopia, there was also a formation of disciples. For these first Companions, discipleship was practically eucharistic. It was like "drinking of the spirit of the master" and being transformed into him.[94] Those who communicated with the same body loved each other with a sincere love and became what they ate. Their death sometimes had the same sacrificial meaning. They bore witness to the faith through martyrdom! The youngest drank the spirit of the most holy elders, thus ensuring the continuity of the mission in a spirit of virtue and holiness.

This instance of virtue and miracles is in no way meant to dilute the achievements of the pioneers of intellectual accommodation or the elitist approach to converting rulers first and their peoples second. It was, indeed, during the lifetime of Pedro Páez that Western influence in Ethiopia took on a predominantly religious coloring.[95] Until 1607, Ethiopia was in turmoil, with four monarchs succeeding each other on the throne from 1597 to 1632. Malak-Sagad II was the monarch of Ethiopia when Páez entered the empire in 1603.[96] His approach followed the instructions of Saint Ignatius: contact with the king and the elite; learning the language; *disputatio* to win theological argument. The goal was unity with Rome. Páez converted first the chief steward of the palace, Takla Selassie, then the brother of the ruler, Sela Krestos. He also built the palace and monasteries, sometimes serving as a builder, mason, carpenter, and blacksmith.[97] As already noted, this phase of the Jesuit mission ended with the conversion of Emperor Susneyos in 1622, the year of the canonization of Ignatius of Loyola and Francis Xavier.[98] But because of the "Latinization" strategy adopted by the new patriarch, Afonso Mendez (1625), Fasiladas, son and successor of Susneyos, expelled the Jesuits from Ethiopia, and some missionaries were killed.[99]

By 1628, there were eleven missions in Ethiopia, led by fifteen Jesuits, five of whom had come from Europe that year.[100] But the mission also faced many obstacles. The imperial family, and especially the empress, were never really won over to the new policy. Rebellions arose, driven by what some elites and monks saw as a departure from the old ways.[101] The result of these conflicts was distrust and led to the breaking of ties with external agents. Thus, when Fasilidas succeeded his father, Susneyos, to the throne, he proclaimed that the empire would return to the old tradition: "The Alexandrian faith now reigned supreme, the Ghemb Mariam fell into disuse and Gorgora [the palace] was abandoned."[102] The failure of the mission of Alfonso Mendes, who arrived in Ethiopia in 1624, however, had the consoling point of counting Geronimo Lobo among its members. He remained in history as one of the European discoverers of the Blue Nile.[103] By the end of the mission in 1632, there were nineteen Jesuits in Ethiopia, with churches and convents.

Without the wide reach of their virtue, however, the conversion of the king made any success of the mission ephemeral. With Mendes, whose character had nothing of his predecessors, the Jesuits lost popular esteem because of his lack of modesty. Unlike his predecessors, the new patriarch had an appetite for ecclesiastical dignities. He sought and found them through his friendships. As previously noted, once in Ethiopia, he lacked discreet charity by publicly forcing the king to submit in front of a stunned and humiliated people. When the latter died on September 16, 1633, his son and successor, Fasilidas, shared the people's feelings and decided to end the intrusion of these foreign priests. Soon after, Mendes and all his Jesuits were handed over to the Turks, who sent them to the pasha of Suâkin. After a long imprisonment, they were finally ransomed and allowed to embark for the Portuguese colonies on the coast of India.[104]

Thus ended the mission of Ethiopia, by a ransom, as those first African missions had begun. There remains one constant in the execution of the Ethiopian mission. Its pioneers were generally educated men. They explored the country, studied its geography and history, its peoples and languages, and its flora and fauna.[105] Along with the holiness of a Nuñes Barreto or Oviedo, the later generations of Jesuits were also driven by an undisguised desire for spectacular conversions among the elite.

A DEDICATION TO QUEEN MARIA OF MODENA

Her sudden death on December 28, 1694, caused an immense wave of grief. For, according to Alex Garganigo, in her death as in her life, Mary II, Queen of England, remained the center of public attention, especially among English Protestants. Her funeral in Westminster Abbey gathered politicians and artists, including famous musicians singing in her memory. All consoled themselves with wax images of her, along with engravings, medals, and other media.[106]

Mary II was King James II's daughter. Her Catholic stepmother, Mary of Modena (Marie Béatrice), died later in exile on May 7, 1718, after she and her husband, King James II, had abdicated the throne in favor of Mary II. As this succession took place, there was no shortage of voices celebrating the new queen for pulling "England back from a slide into Catholic tyranny and onto the path of the Godly Reformation."[107]

Dominique Bouhours dedicated his biography of Saint Francis Xavier (published in 1682) to Queen Ann of Austria who, after twenty years of barrenness, was able to conceive, thanks to the intercession of Xavier, an heir to the throne of France in the person of Louis XIV. Thus, Dryden argues, by choosing Francis Xavier as her celestial patron, Queen Mary of Modena was following on the footsteps of the Austrian queen. Dryden's dedication of the English translation of the same book to Queen Mary of Modena, in July 1688, was a toast to the English Catholic queen, who had also been struggling with giving birth and had now benefited from the same miraculous intervention. On June 10, 1688, she had given birth to a son, James Edward, a Catholic heir to the English throne.

King Charles II (1630–1685) had named Dryden poet laureate in 1668 and royal historian in 1670, yet his intention in dedicating this book to Queen Modena seemed clearly missionary:

> Some may even be ingenious enough to freely admit that in order to propagate the faith among infidels and heathens, miraculous operations are necessary today in these ignorant regions, as when the Christian doctrine was first implanted by our blessed Savior and his Apostles.[108]

This birth, for a while at least, seemed to ensure Catholic succession to the throne. At the same time, in mid-July 1688, Jacob Tonson, a London bookseller, advertised Dryden's translation of *The Life of Saint Francis Xavier* from the Jesuit grammarian and rhetorician Dominique Bouhours. Mary of Modena herself would have commissioned this translation in early 1688, for she had already had a series of pregnancies with varying misfortunes; if the children were not stillborn, they had all died young. The translation was therefore commissioned to soften the birth of an heir who would ensure the succession of the Catholic Stuarts. The public was aware of Mary of Modena's medical history and was not very happy about the appearance of a Catholic heir who appeared to be in good health.[109]

Dryden had maintained a certain anti-Jesuitism despite his conversion to Catholicism.[110] Indeed, even the most moderate in England were convinced that "the Papacy was a threat to liberty, property and religion, namely parliamentary monarchy, common law, low taxation and Protestantism."[111] Against this parliamentary monarchy, he opposed the singular Hispanicization of the British monarchy. For Spain represented a form of state Catholicism, an enemy of England and of its interests in the world.

Dryden praised Xavier as a great and holy missionary. In directing these words to Mary II, he was celebrating a saint beyond geographical and religious boundaries. The queen herself had chosen the Apostle of India as her patron, "in a country where the doctrine of the Holy Church is doubted, and religious addresses ridiculed."[112] In dedicating *The Life of Saint Francis Xavier* to the queen, Dryden drew a parallel with Anne of Austria, the mother of the French king, Louis XIV. She was said to have been expecting a child for twenty years and was only able to conceive Louis XIV after a prayer to Saint Francis Xavier.[113]

If, through the intercession of Xavier, Queen Ann could conceive, if Mary II had finally given birth to a son, and if, through the same saint, nations with civilizations comparable to the greatest in Europe, India and Japan, could be converted to Christ, it would not be England that would remain closed to the light. A Stuart had already brought it back to Catholicism. What a grace for the whole nation to count on a queen devoted, even secretly, to the Catholic faith.

Dryden thus dreamed of the day when divine providence, through Xavier's intercession, would reestablish his Church in England, even though it must still go through trials and afflictions. Speaking of the biography itself, Dryden anticipated a modern, rationalist critique:

> I have no doubt that it will suffer censure from those who teach the people that miracles have ceased. However, there are, I suppose, a number of clear-headed Protestants, and even of the most learned among them, who, convinced by the concordant testimonies of the last age, by the suffrages of whole nations in India and Japan, and by the severe examinations which have been made before the act of canonization, will not dispute the truth of most of the facts here related.[114]

Dryden, in his dedication to the queen, had only anticipated what the author of the book, Dominique Bouhours, emphasized in the body of the text: The number of Christians increased with the reputation of the saint.[115] Witnesses of his miracles in Cincheo were converted en masse, in all, "about sixty people, some Ethiopians, others Indians, all idolaters or Mohammedans."[116] The theology of the first Jesuit missionaries was thus also a theology of the masses. The "Douctrina" of Francis Xavier was itself a catechism, as was the catechism of Peter Canisius in Germany, or of Coucto among the "gentiles" of the Kongo kingdom. During the lifetime of Saint Ignatius, a certain François Le Picart (d. 1556) preached on purgatory and hell while contrasting the pains of these places with the infinite goodness of God.[117]

RURAL MISSIONS IN THE NINETEENTH AND TWENTIETH CENTURIES

"Even today," an old missionary asked, "is the black man capable of affection? You will see him pause for a moment, hesitate, perhaps, before answering."[118] It was in 1912 that Father Davister did this analysis of Africa as a mission land. For this Jesuit missionary, any missionary who arrived on the dark continent was shrouded in thick darkness from the start. It seemed to him impossible "to civilize this savage who is said to be a brute," "this barely human heart."[119] Davister could not resist the easy, ready-made diagnosis of "the black man's innate laziness," "his almost virtuous lies," "his greed for other people's property." He recognized, however, that underneath all these vices, the African's eye, accustomed to probing consciences, was looking for a feeling that could powerfully aid the missionary work of moral uplift: affection. Davister admitted that the love and gentleness that are characteristic of the Christian religion were able to "strengthen the good dispositions of some, to implant in the hearts of others that beautiful and strong affection, one of the most beautiful fruits of the Gospel."[120]

That this Belgian missionary could have such a view of Africa in the middle of the twentieth century is not unusual in missionary archives. And yet, his description stands in sharp contrast to the time of Saint Ignatius, when there was a vibrant history of Christianity in Africa. This early African Christianity was the object of singular attention by the early Jesuits. It even allowed Ignatius, through letters and instructions, to offer his most elaborate version of a Catholic missiology in the sixteenth century. In contrast to Davister's description, African Christianity in the early Middle Ages was polite, diplomatic, and intercultural, involving trade between Portuguese kings and their African colleagues of similar rank.

The New Mission

In the time of Ignatius, some African kings asked for missionaries to be sent from Europe. It is true that some historiography has insisted on the self-interested nature of these requests. It argues that, in the face of the wars that opposed them among themselves and with the Muslims, these leaders would have approached Portugal or Spain for pure political calculation, that is, to obtain military support in exchange for converting to Christianity. Their form of Christianity would therefore have been a façade, without deep adherence in the hearts of the believers. The existence of proven cases in favor of this thesis would be reductionist, however, if it were not complemented by two important factors: the diplomatic subtleties that led African rulers to create conditions for religious competition in their territories, and the expressions of religious adherence present in many of their letters.

Twenty years after Davister's observation, in 1932, the mission had indeed borne fruit in Africa. Its priority was the promotion of an Indigenous African clergy. The idea of founding a seminary for Indigenous priests had been dear to the missionaries since their arrival. Already in 1896, three years after the arrival of the first Jesuits in the Belgian Congo, Father Liagre, who had previously been a professor of rhetoric at the College of Namur, taught the rudiments of Latin to five particularly gifted young men, with a view to the priesthood. Although this first attempt was not successful, it did show hope: Christianity was growing, and the missionaries needed to be assisted in the apostolate by native priests.[121]

In the Congo, the mission was organized around the farm-chapels. The catechumens were grouped together in farms on which they lived together as in a village. They farmed and raised livestock for their survival, sold products to the mission, and thus learned the art of cultivating the land and doing business. From the point of view of evangelization itself, a catechist taught the first elements of social life every day to change habits. In the Central Mission, under the watchful eye of the missionary, a more careful instruction, a more complete education was offered to the young Africans.[122] After the boys and girls had received this good education from the priests and sisters, they were married among themselves, young. They could thus, it was thought, gain in morals and increase the population at the same time as the love of work. The young couple had an apostolic role to play; through them, faith and civilization were to spread to some new corners of the territory.

The results were spectacular. There were eighty farm-chapels in 1900; six years later, in 1906, there were four hundred. The surroundings of the city of Kisantu were transformed. The thick forest, patiently cleared, was replaced by beautiful cassava plantations. Great works of watering and irrigation had been done. The flora was enriched by imports from India and America. Brother Gillet began his "acclimatization" garden, now famous throughout Africa.[123] As a result of these missionary efforts, the Vicar Apostolic of Kwango observed that between 1935 and 1938, the number of Catholics had not stopped increasing. Religious fervor was measured mainly by the frequent reception of the sacraments of the Eucharist and penance. Available figures show that each Christian in the Kwango received communion, on average, at least fourteen times a year.[124]

At about the same time, in 1879, a caravan of eleven Belgian, English, and German priests and brothers, led by Father Depelchin, who had come from Bengal, set out via Kimberley for the highlands south of the Zambezi. They left on April 15 and arrived on September 2 at the Kraal of Bulawayo at the home of Lo-Bengula, king of the Matabele. Since the fall of the Monomotapa empire four centuries earlier, the Matabele had become the true masters of the Zambezi region. They were a conquering people who colonized their Mashona and Makalaka neighbors, degenerate descendants of the Monomotapa empire. Curiously, Lo-Bengula welcomed the European traders, hunters, and missionaries who asked to settle near him.[125] They divided themselves into four groups. One remained in observation in Matabeleland. Two priests and two brothers left for the northeast, where they founded a station among the Oumgoumis, another Zulu people closer to the Portuguese lands, and whose king, Umzila, was Lo-Bengula's brother-in-law. Another band went to try their luck on the upper Zambezi, among the Barotsés. When the news came that the Jesuits were in the Zambezi region, the prelate of Mozambique, whose mission was short of priests, invited them to establish a mission there.[126]

For about ten years, the Jesuit missionaries in Matabeleland maintained a simple presence with the king, who used them when necessary. However, any apostolate remained forbidden. The Mashonas whom the Matabelelanders had defeated were treated as slaves, unworthy of any instruction. The Jesuits' wait was painful. However, it was necessary to maintain this position for fear that the mission territory would be abandoned to the Protestants alone. In 1887, the king finally authorized the agricultural and industrial education of the Blacks. A year later, in 1888, under the leadership of Father Prestage, sixty children were studying, learning prayers, singing hymns: "he built, forged, cared for, catechized." But there was a sudden interruption. All the whites, including the missionaries, were ordered to disappear. A serious conflict had just broken out with England.

If these apostolic initiatives led to the growth of membership in the church, they also later gave reasons to some observers to decry certain Jesuit activism, to the detriment, the critique argued, of true evangelism.

CONTEMPORARY JESUIT MISSIONARY EVANGELISM

One of the major crises facing the Society of Jesus since the end of Vatican II has been the growing gap between what the delegates of the 31st and 32nd General Congregations (GC) called ministries that are properly priestly, and therefore "spiritual," and other ministries that are more secular. Pope Paul VI expressed concern about this at GC 32. Pope John Paul I took up this theme in the speech he never gave to the Society's procurators meeting in Rome in 1978. And it was at the heart of the tensions between the pontificate of John Paul II and the generalate of Pedro Arrupe. The tension between these ministries and Jesuit identity was sometimes so sharp that some historians of Christianity have denounced a certain NGOization of the Jesuits to the detriment of evangelism—a Bible-centered and sacramental evangelization.

Rather than getting distracted in the semantic labyrinth of the term *evangelical*, let us briefly summarize what some contemporary inspirers say about "Evangelicalism." David Bebbington presents it as a religious movement that emphasizes conversion, a personal relationship with Christ, a dose of activism that includes missions to non-Christians, the centrality of the Bible, and a crucicentrism.[127] Mark A. Noll situates contemporary Pentecostalism within this global evangelical movement. In the nineteenth century, John and Charles Wesley, for example, presented themselves as heirs of a spirituality that emphasized personal sanctification and the work of the Holy Spirit. Later, in his years at Oxford in the 1750s, Thomas Haweis asserted that true holiness lay in the acceptance of becoming a new creature by professing faith in Jesus under the work of the Holy Spirit.[128] The believer was then to grow in holiness through regular meditation on the Holy Scriptures, self-examination, conversation with other believers, and devout attendance at the Holy Eucharist.[129]

Historians have recently offered four movements that presided over the origins of Evangelicalism. The first is British Puritanism. Calvinistic in essence and stemming from a radical Protestantism that rejected the religious compromises made during the reign of Elizabeth I (ca. 1558–1563), Puritanism began as one of the "Dissenting" movements, going so far as to reject the trappings of Anglo-Catholicism. Puritanism, however, was unique in that its adherents not only believed in the personal salvation of the individual, but later some of its leaders, such as Thomas Chalmers, believed in a form of theocracy, in which the state would be built on Christian ideals.[130] Chalmers believed that religion had such great social power that it could give identity to any institution, including the political power embodied in the modern state.

The second movement that influenced the evangelical movement was Scottish Presbyterianism, also descended from Calvinism and English Puritanism. Rejecting the notion of a state religion, it believed in Tradition and in the strength of institutions. The Lord's Supper occupied an important place in the lives of believers.

A third movement was Anglicanism itself, especially under the label High Church Anglicanism. It was unique in that it encouraged the organization of lay volunteer groups with an apostolic focus. One of the earliest groups, founded in 1698, could have taken its name from the Formula of the Society's Institute: The Society for the Promotion of Christian Knowledge (SPCK). It carried out its mission of promoting the faith through youth education and publications. The Society for the Propagation of the Gospel, founded in 1701, supported missions among non-Christians.[131]

The New Mission

The last movement that gave rise to contemporary Evangelicalism is Continental Pietism, which is also found in the Netherlands, Switzerland, and Germany. Philipp Jakob Spener (1635–1705) was its initiator. Spener wanted to renew Presbyterianism from within by stimulating the spiritual and devotional life of the laity around small communities of Christian life (*collegia pietatis*). The members of these communities prayed and read the Bible together. In this way, Spener intended to make the common priesthood of the faithful, which was also ministerial among Protestants, a reality.[132]

It would be surprising to associate certain aspects of those movements with the most papist of Catholic religious orders: the Jesuits. Yet, if their pioneers and their rather Calvinist origins had been kept anonymous, they could also have been attributed to some Jesuit initiatives. Beginning with Ignatius, the early Jesuits used the *Spiritual Exercises* as a tool for radical conversion and as the basis for their missions. The *Exercises* were used to recruit missionaries and were used by them both to reform the church from within, that is, in its head and members, and to convert non-Catholics. Based on the meditation of the life of Christ contained in the Gospels, the *Exercises* are in essence biblical and christocentric. They give a special place to self-examination, but also to all kinds of devotions in which the sanctification of the individual solicits all the operations of his being and positions him for a radical response to the call of God. It was from them that several works of mercy and charity associated with the Jesuit missions were developed.

In a second phase, the Jesuit mission developed under Catholic rulers who aspired to the creation and perpetuation of a universal Catholic commonwealth. In practice, too, the Jesuit missions contributed to social and political transformation, ranging from education, reform of a small region such as Azpeitia, investment in the politics of nations and the no lesser Guaraní Republic.

Furthermore, in the missions toward non-Catholics, the Society knew how to combine a proclamation effort with an extraordinary capacity of adaptation. This adaptation was done through a policy of accommodation, and therefore, of progressive integration of certain elements of non-Christian cultures into Christian practices. It also involved, however, the witness of life. The virtue and holiness of the missionaries converted the peoples as much as, if not more than, all the other strategies they adopted and that have been the subject of recent studies. Indeed, recovering this spiritual, devotional, witnessing side of mission has been the purpose of this chapter.

A TESTIMONY IN THE JESUIT GUARANI REPUBLIC

Father Marcial de Lorenzana applied himself to the catechizing of the faithful and of those who were preparing to embrace the Christian faith. It was, for him, the most laborious office that the missions had. He spent the whole day at this work, without resting, either to prepare some for confession or to prepare others for baptism. Seeing the love with which Father Marcial came to them, and having experienced his rectitude and purity, all, great and small, came to love him deeply. Even those who had previously fled from other priests changed their fear into confidence. They followed him wherever he went, going in troops to meet him.[133]

Born in 1560 of a noble family in the Spanish city of León, many called Father Marcial "the apostle of the Indians of Paraná." He studied at the University of Alcalá and was a disciple of Francisco Suarez, one of the greatest Jesuit theologians of all times. The literary exercises did not, however, dry up his devotions. On the contrary, through frequent confession and communion, he prepared himself for greater undertakings in the service of God.[134]

Lorenzana had not asked to go to India. His poor health dissuaded him from such long and dangerous journeys. Father Diego de Zuñiga, Procurator of the Province of Peru, who was going to Rome to ask Father General Claudio Acquaviva for subjects for the conversion of the Indians, noted Lorenzana's many virtues, his letters, and his modesty. He asked Father General to have Lorenzana among his missionaries.

His obedience remained Lorenzana's guide. He accepted the new mission with zeal. He trusted that Our Lord, who ordered him to undertake something so arduous and difficult, would give him the means and strength to go.[135] The Lord began to reward him for this confidence not only in the growth of his spirit, but also in his physical health. He miraculously gave him perfect health, without the intervention of doctors or medicines, having only his faith.[136]

Before going to his new mission, Lorenzana left for Seville, where he was ordained in 1591.

In the Jesuit reductions in Paraguay where Lorenzana was to work, music played an important role in the conversion of the masses. It was Manuel de Nóbrega, sent to Brazil by Saint Ignatius in 1549, who is the author of the famous quote, slightly modified by Hollywood in Roland Joffé's 1986 film, *The Mission*: "Give me an orchestra of musicians and I will convert all the Indians for Christ."[137] As early as January 1550, João de Azpilcueta Navarro used indigenous melodies with Portuguese and Tupi Christian texts to catechize the young natives.[138] In the same register, argues John K. Thornton, Kongolese Christianity incorporated African concepts into Christian theology. This synthesis would have influenced the Brazilian Christianity that is now world famous.[139]

Linda Heywood has shown that in areas such as São Paulo, for example, the fact that the first Blacks to arrive in the region came not from Africa but from Portugal meant that many of the cultural adaptations that had already taken place in Portugal, Kongo, and Angola came with the slaves to Brazil.[140] In the 1690s, an Italian visitor to Bahia estimated the city's mulatto population at between 8,000 and 10,000; whites numbered only 20,000, and enslaved Africans 50,000. This presence of Africans and Luso-Africans guaranteed a dominant African element in the emerging Brazilian popular culture.[141] The growth of an Afro-Catholic Brazilian (folk) religion with an Angolan flavor accelerated from 1701, when the Catholic churches of Angola and Brazil were administratively linked with the extension of the suffragan diocese of Bahia to include not only Rio de Janeiro and Pernambuco, but also Angola and São Tomé.[142]

Moreover, Heywood shows that between 1509 and 1542, before the arrival of the Jesuits, Kongo was already a very fertile land for the mission. The Kongolese king, Afonso, had created a state Catholicism, with numerous confraternities in which the Portuguese, Kongolese, and other emigrant populations practiced an inculturated Christianity.[143] Its language was Creole, its religious practices syncretic, in a cultural mix that affected clothing, food, music, and social practices. Thus, in 1620, in preparation for the canonization of Saint Francis Xavier, the Jesuit-sponsored Luanda carnival showcased the dynamism of this inculturation process. The ceremony struck a balance between the military parade, the caricature of political figures, and the incorporation of local African cultural motifs. The procession represented a complete syncretism between the pagan rituals of the Mediterranean pantheon, the Christian rituals of the Iberian church, and the Mbundu and Kongo rituals.[144] There were, in fact, catechisms in the Jesuit missions written in Latin, Portuguese, and Kongo Kimbundu.[145] Their authors were intercontinental, intercultural actors, and intellectual and spiritual agents of this first globalization.

CONCLUSION

In his dedication to the biography of Francis Xavier mentioned above, Dryden had highlighted the miracle as an important element of Xavier's missionary outreach. Since the mid-seventeenth century, miracles, as well as the emotion and even the language of holiness and virtue, had become less salient in the historiography of the Jesuit missions. Centuries of scientific rationalism had had a profound impact on the humanities, sociology, and history. This rationalism had thus sidelined the paranormal, the emotional and spiritual manifestations of the religious, and the discourse of miracles in the historical debate.

The new face of world Christianity, the one represented by villager Joseph in this chapter, invites us to revisit this way of writing the history of Christianity. Here it was, therefore, a question of taking its new forms of religious expression seriously and making them the subject of history.

In this chapter, we see that the effectiveness of the missionary activity of the first Jesuits was not only a matter of humanistic and rationalist accommodation. Although the merits of the latter missionary strategy have been well established, we have sought to emphasize the crucial role played by the perception by non-Christians of the more successful Jesuits. Often, they saw them primarily as living saints. Where modern rationalism established reason as the criterion for crosscultural encounters par excellence, this chapter shows that virtue and sanctity could have had equal value. Sanctity and virtue appealed far beyond cultures and religions and even seemed to be the primary instrument of cross-cultural dialogue.

The new approach to the history of the Society not only allows us to go beyond historical rationalism, but also to resituate virtue and holiness at the heart of the Society's ministries. The example of the first patriarchs of Ethiopia—their science combined with their virtue—helped redefine the ecclesiastical function after the Council of Trent. Their style was more popular, focused on humble service among the humblest. For a religious order that shied away from ecclesiastical dignities, this simplicity in the exercise of authority and service became characteristic of the Jesuit bishop.

Moreover, the chapter highlights that the language of virtue and holiness is accessible to all social and religious classes. The noblest people—kings and queens—sought in the first Companions not only missionaries capable of science and sacrifice; they also valued models of virtue, miracle workers, and reconcilers for their peoples. Likewise, the death of missionaries aroused great devotion among the masses and became an important tool for their evangelization. There were cases, as in Ethiopia, in which the power of their intercession could act on the forces of nature and augur better harvests to eradicate famine.

Because all history of the Society is institutional, we end this chapter recalling that the first miracle of Ignatius's canonization was the very birth of the Society, its approval, and its expansion. The success of this missionary expansion was the miracle par excellence of Xavier as of many other saintly confessors of the Society. To speak of the mission is therefore to take seriously the providential character of its spirit and its success, for this is how the missionaries themselves lived it.

4

THE SUPPRESSION AND THE RESTORATION

In 1786, at St. Mary's Church, Philadelphia, the Reverend Robert Molyneux, "very stately in appearance," ascended the pulpit to pay his last tribute to a Jesuit friend, the Reverend Ferdinand Farmer. The Society of Jesus had been suppressed by Pope Clement XIV more than ten years earlier. A spirit of solidarity could not bind the survivors more strongly. Each loss of one of them reminded the Jesuits that the organization they had joined was being slain or, rather, that it was in survival mode. Even thousands of miles away from Rome and the Bourbon kings who controlled the colonial empires, and even in the United States, it had become impossible to recruit new novices for the Society. This forced many of its best sons to join other religious groups or to secularize.

Every eulogy, a sermon in this case, felt like a farewell to one of the most powerful religious orders the Catholic Church has ever known. Yet, although the enemies of the Society of Jesus treated it primarily as a human creation, for Jesuits like Molyneux, the words of Saint Ignatius were truer than ever: The Society of Jesus had not been created by human means; it could only survive by divine means. For Molyneux and the generations of Jesuits who followed him, hope amid this tragedy meant trusting in divine means and experiencing each loss as a loss for a greater purpose.

107

Molyneux found the inspiration for his sermon in another believer in troubled times: the heart of the righteous, says the Psalmist, "are firm, secure in the LORD. Their hearts are steady, they will not be afraid; in the end they will look in triumph on their foes. They have distributed freely, they have given to the poor; their righteousness endures forever" (Psalm 112:7–9). Throughout the 1780s in the United States of America, the enemy was not just the hostile land of Protestant settlers, it was the grim reality of a beloved daughter, the Society, sacrificed at the altar of dark interests by the Father to whom she pledged unconditional love and loyalty. The enemy was also the loss of Jesuit identity as originally understood. The hope, meanwhile, was to reshape that same identity amid new and often hostile realities.

To Molyneux, Father Farmer was not just any Jesuit. He was a "venerable brother and kind friend," revered for his piety and zeal for ministry. Father Farmer had been a mentor to Molyneux. That he felt orphaned by his sudden departure was only fitting: "He is gone too soon," Molyneux mourned, "for us who still needed his fatherly counsel and salutary instruction, but not too soon for himself, who had no other desire on earth than to serve his heavenly Master, under whose banners he had enlisted."[1] The hope and consolation of those who remained was that Farmer had lived all his life for a higher purpose, and that he now enjoyed "the sweet consolation of finding the end of all his views and wishes immutably accomplished" in the glory of Almighty God.[2]

Farmer had been born of reputable parents in Germany on October 13, 1720, and had been initiated into piety and liberal learning, studying philosophy and physics before being called for a higher purpose, to be "a nourisher and physician of souls."[3] He entered the Jesuits on September 26, 1742, at the Landsperge novitiate, and offered himself as a candidate for the foreign missions. He made his solemn profession on February 2, 1761. Initially sent to China, his disappointment was blissful for Lancaster and Philadelphia, where he finally landed to fulfill his ministries. Of him, Dr. Carroll says, "He did much good until his death on August 17, 1786."[4] Not only was Farmer admitted to the Philadelphia Philosophical Society, but he was also appointed to the Board of Trustees of his university.[5]

A century after the sermon was delivered, in 1878, the Reverend Joseph M. Finotti, the author of a famous biography of Saint Peter Claver,[6] had seventy-five copies of the sermon reprinted at his own expense for private distribution. It was not only that Molyneux's oratorical powers were well known in his day, but it was the symbolic significance of this sermon that made it so important to posterity.

To pay tribute to Farmer's life and work was, for Molyneux, a way of showing his regard and affection for his memory, "and of dropping the tear of mourning on his grave." More interestingly, Molyneux urged his audience not to "indulge in unreasonable grief or be sad, like those who are without hope." Instead, all were to take his living example as a "surviving guide through the paths of virtue in which he has directed you; they shall be as the North Star, by which you may safely steer yourselves to the harbor of eternal bliss, which we hope he himself has arrived at."[7] And while all should remember his tireless work for the poor and unlettered, all should also remember the higher purpose of Farmer's entire life and work: "There is still a treasure hidden in heaven, unseen and unknown to the world, but most precious before God."[8] This was the origin, the goal, and the end toward which, at every stage of his life, Farmer's mind and heart had been uniformly directed.

Concluding his sermon, Molyneux went through the Gospel of Matthew, bringing his audience before the Lord who welcomed Farmer into his kingdom: "Well done, good and faithful servant, because you have been faithful in a few things, I will establish you in many things. Enter into the joy of the Lord." Farmer was now in the joy of the Lord. It was up to the living, the survivors, to follow on the steps of virtue that he had set for them by his example.[9]

If there is one reason why the history of the Society is of interest to its own members, it is its immolation. It was after the Restoration that the generals became more conscious of encouraging studies on the history of the Society, and it was after the Restoration that the Historical Institute was created and the publication of the *Monumenta* was decided. This essay does not intend to offer all the details and intrigues of this history. It is content to read this history in the light of a simple thesis: the problem of the Society was primarily in its response to a double call: the call of the pope symbolized by the fourth vow and the call of the temporal kings. From these two relationships came its privileges, but also its setbacks. It also happened that the Society was out of step with the signs of the times, either because it lagged behind progress or because it was too far ahead. Each progress, each failure was often linked to a leader. In short, to the alleged evil in its seed were added, at the height of its glory, the enemies of progress, its quarrel with the Jansenists, and the institutional fragility of the Lavalette Affair. All of these gave an alibi to the Society's opponents and prepared the ground for a ruthless political plot that led to its suppression by Pope Clement XIV.

THE SUPPRESSION

Anyone who carefully analyzes the remote causes of the suppression of the Society is called to return to the context of its emergence and the arguments developed by both its most enthusiastic admirers and those who opposed its Institute. First, the Society, from its inception, was linked to the papacy by a special vow. This closeness to the Roman Pontiff was a point that attracted many favors in its history from the popes. Paul III (r. 1534–1549) approved the Institute and delegated to the Superior General the power to send Jesuits to mission. Julius III (r. 1550–1555), his successor, approved the *Constitutions* and other special privileges. He also founded the Germanic College and entrusted it to the Society. Gregory XIII (r. 1572–1585) gave the College a solid foundation and provided the building of the Roman College, hence its present name: Gregorian University.

However, these favors and this special relationship also earned the Society the epithet of "papists" or "popish." The enemies of the papacy or those who, in the name of nationalism, resisted its universal claims, thus automatically became the enemies of the Society. The same was true of the enemies of the church itself. The weakening of the church, for many politicians, had to begin with the decapitation of the Society.

Moreover, from the very beginning of the order, voices were raised, including among the popes, and thereby undermining the special vow about certain aspects of the new Institute that seemed presumptuous to them and earned the Society suspicions of an insatiable desire for power that its enemies would later exploit. Pope Paul IV (r. 1555–1559) wanted to change the name of the Institute. The lifelong nature of the office of the Superior General and its immense powers were questioned. Furthermore, the fact that they did not hold General Chapters at specific times like other congregations, or the absence of a choir, a regime of penances, and the fact that priestly ordination occurred prior to definitive incorporation were other contentious issues.

Popes could also "abuse" this special vow. Already, two imminent heirs of Saint Ignatius had different opinions on the meaning of the special vow to obey the pope: Nadal seemed to embrace the "papist" epithet in an absolute sense; Laínez had to rectify this absolutist interpretation, affirming that "although those of the Society are papists, they are and can [only] be so in cases not contrary to the will of God and the common good."[10] Moreover, in almost every generation there have been popes who have used their authority and interfered directly in the ordinary government of the Society. One of its greatest benefactors, Gregory XIII, practically imposed the choice of Everard Mercurian as General—officially, to avoid the election of a third successive Spaniard, and unofficially, because the election of the designated Vicar General, Juan de Polanco, a *converso*, as General had become almost impossible because, across Spain and Europe, purity laws targeting Jews, *conversos,* and *Moriscos* were being implemented. Pope Innocent III did the same when, worried that the Society was becoming morally lax, he imposed on the General Congregation the election of Tirso González, a fanatic of *probabiliorism,* as General. And in 1981, John Paul II dismissed the Vicar General chosen by Pedro Arrupe, and appointed in his place two personal delegates, Paolo Dezza and Giuseppe Pittau.

These examples show that the special vow could be a double-edged sword for the Society, especially since its enemies had observed the seriousness with which the Jesuits lived it. Such fidelity to the vow, coupled with the fact that the popes fluctuated in their esteem for the Society and thus did not guarantee its protection in times of crisis, was exploited by philosophers and proponents of the republic in the immediate causes of the suppression. Loyalty to this vow often put the Society at odds with the nationalists. There were also nationalists within the Society, itself, who were not only political but ideological, with a Christian, often Jansenist background.

TOWARD THE EFFECTIVE SUPPRESSION OF THE SOCIETY

In France, at the time of Claudio Acquaviva, there were divisions between Gallican Jesuits, royalists favorable to Henry II, and the "internationalists" or ultramontanes. It was a division that reflected the schism at the heart of French political life and church-state relations. In 1589, there was an assassination attempt on Henry III by Jacques Clément (known as Clément Jacob in some sources). In the aftermath, Henry IV asked the Jesuits to swear an oath of loyalty to him during a confrontation he was having with the pope. The French Jesuits saw this as a lesser evil despite Acquaviva's reprimands that such a compromise was unacceptable.

In 1610, Henry IV was assassinated. For the enemies of the Society, François Ravaillac, the main suspect, had been inspired by the tyrannicidal or regicidal theories of the Spanish Jesuit (a foreigner) Juan de Mariana (1536–1624), author of *De rege et regis institutione,* which was published in 1599, the day after the death of Philip II. In Spain, this book served as a manual for the education of the new king, Philip III. The Jesuits in Clermont feared the repercussions such an accusation would have on an already debilitating relationship for the Society in France. They disobeyed Acquaviva and took an oath of loyalty to the king on February 22, 1611.

A historian and theologian, de Mariana was, along with Francisco Suarez and Pedro de Ribadaneira, one of the most prominent Jesuit writers of the Spanish Golden Age. Mariana, like de Ribadaneira in his *Princeps Christianus adversus Nicholaus Machiavelum* (1595), inscribed the legitimacy of all political power in its management of public affairs for the common good. What is more, de Mariana suggested that it was legitimate to eliminate any king who acted against this principle.

Resistance to tyrannical leaders had been part of Western literature since Cicero. It had spread in the Middle Ages and was the subject of another publication in Spain four years earlier, in Juan de Roa Dávila's *De regnorum justicia* (1591). In chapter 6 of his book, de Mariana explicitly mentioned the assassination of Henry III in France. Although this attack was deplorable and unworthy of praise, the author argued, it remained a lesson for all tyrants that their impious and unjust acts could not go unpunished. He went so far as to enumerate the crimes committed by the king and spoke in a rather enthusiastic tone about the act of Clement Jacob.[11]

De Mariana was not the only Jesuit intellectual to venture into the political realm in the seventeenth century. In *Controversies*, Robert Bellarmine argued that the church was "neither a democracy nor an aristocracy, but a monarchy tempered by an aristocratic element."[12] He also recognized the indirect power of the pope over the temporal. However, the Supreme Pontiff could not depose kings nor interfere directly in the elaboration or annulment of laws unless the salvation of souls depended absolutely on his intervention.[13] For Francisco Suarez, civil power was regarded as "a common good that is imposed on all, on citizens and rulers alike. An absolute power, legitimate in its source as the monarchy, can therefore become tyrannical if it is exercised against it. And from then on are justified the revolt and the tyrannicide."[14] He also recognized the power of the pope to advise the king and to consent to his deposition when the latter acted against the vital interests of the kingdom, especially for what touched the spiritual good of the people. Suarez saw this interventionism as a necessity to prevent schisms and heresies.[15]

PRESSURE, CORRUPTION, ANTI-JESUIT PROPAGANDA

In 1640, Robert le Coq, one of the workers/employees in the fathers' community, returned from Quebec in a serious state of illness. He caused as much horror as compassion to all those who had enough courage to consider the ulcers with which his limbs were covered. No Huron would have believed that a body so full of misery could return to health. Judging him dead, some slanderers publicly claimed that this young Frenchman had told them in confidence that the Jesuits were the sole authors and causes of the illnesses that year after year were depopulating the country. He had discovered the mysteries and the most hidden secrets of the Jesuits' "witchcraft." Some said that the Jesuits were feeding a snake in a secluded place in their house, which was causing the illness. Others said that it was a kind of toad, all marked with the pox. Still others said that the disease was a demon that the Jesuits had hidden in the barrel of a harquebus. A thousand similar fables were told, and all of this was believed to be true, since it was said to have come from the mouth of a Frenchman. The latter, before dying, would have done the good work of warning the Hurons of the black magic of the Jesuits. These were the most powerful weapons against them, the peremptory reason that made them all criminals. The neighboring nations were soon informed. Everyone, even the children, were imbued with it. Thus, the fathers, wherever they went, carried with them a surety of their own death.[16]

On June 26 of the same year (1640), the niece of Peter, the first Christian converted by the Jesuits, died despite the wishes and prayers of the fathers for her recovery. This was the first shock for the family. It was followed sometime later by the death of Peter's wife, then his daughter and brother-in-law. Several slanderous tongues thought they had a new subject to throw the cat at the legs of the Jesuits. They alleged that the affliction had only entered the hut since the solemn baptism of Peter.[17]

This story of a generalized conspiracy, and others like it against the Society, followed an assembly, a sort of popular parliament, which had presided over a trial against the Jesuits, not in eighteenth-century Paris, but among the Hurons in the seventeenth century.[18] Clearly, it did not take the advent of the Republic of Philosophers to perceive the "black robes" as a political threat that needed to be urgently extirpated. The key elements of repression were already present in North America.

Those who spread these slanders and propaganda did not believe them themselves. Nevertheless, they spoke in such expressive terms that those who listened to them did not doubt them. As a result, women and children started looking upon the Jesuits as people who brought them bad luck. Those who loved the Jesuits and used to speak in their favor gradually lost their voices completely amid the propaganda. Even when they were forced to speak, they resorted to excuses and justified themselves as best they could, but not in a clear-cut manner.[19] Those who intervened on their behalf made it clear to the Jesuits that the best they could hope for was to be expelled from the country and sent back to Quebec.[20]

On August 20, 1772, a year before the suppression of the Society, José Moñino, ambassador of Carlos III of Spain to the Holy See, delivered his *Latin Note* to Pope Clement XIV. The note, with eighteen articles, served as a blueprint for the brief of suppression of the Society. The first article of Moñino's note asked the pope not to give a specific cause for the suppression. His Holiness was simply to allude to some "aggravating and urgent causes" on the part of the Jesuits. These causes required drastic measures to restore prudent governance of the universal church. In article 2, the Jesuits were strictly forbidden to defend themselves or even to speak of this suppression under penalty of excommunication. The Catholic princes were thus to ensure that the same silence was observed in all the territories under their dominion.[21]

Continuing his work of presenting the Society under the most sinister auspices, Moñino did not hesitate to present the novices and young scholastics as young captives of a system of manipulation well mastered by the Jesuits. The suppression of the order would free these young people and return them to their families. Such a historical tartuffery could no longer be repeated, for the colleges where the Jesuits recruited their young members were taken away from the Jesuits. Those of the priests who wished to join other religious orders or dioceses or to become laypeople could do so. The dioceses and congregations that would receive the Jesuits would not lack the means to care for the new recruits. The former Jesuit properties would be sold and the money put to the good care of the former Jesuits. If the bishops would not allow them to preach or confess, the Jesuits would continue to teach in colleges whose charge had been taken away from them. Their superior general was to lose all authority over the members, perpetually (art. 17). At the time of the publication of the *Note*, he and his assistants were to be imprisoned in separate places, without any contact between them.

Among Moñino's sources was a slanderous pamphlet of Jansenist origin that alluded to the chronic disobedience of the Jesuits, especially toward Popes Paul IV and Clement XIII. Finally, it was on January 6, 1773, that Pope Clement XIV received a draft of this plan to extinguish the Jesuits. Immediately after handing the text to the pope, the Spanish troops were also withdrawn from the borders of the Papal States. In an audience on January 24, Moñino asked the pope to change the bull to a brief and thus limit the number of people to be consulted. The pope then sent Carlos III the final draft. And he instructed Carlos to circulate it among the other Bourbon kings of France, Portugal, and Naples, as well as to Maria Theresa of Austria.

In sum, the extinction of the Society was the result of political and religious pressures, mingled with corruption at the highest levels in the face of an increasingly impotent church. Finally, it was the result of an anti-Jesuit campaign supported by the French Parliament and the illustrious wing of the despotic Bourbon governments. The latter were sympathetic to the Jansenist cause. They were supported by a clandestine and satirical anti-Jesuit literature that went unanswered by the Society itself. Isaac Disraeli summed up the situation most eloquently in 1811, when he stated, "Motherly Rome stretched out her withered hands in grief over her child and champion, while she herself united in one sacrifice for peace—and the Jesuits were immolated."[22]

THE QUARREL WITH THE JANSENISTS

A century after the death of Saint Ignatius, the Society was confronted with an enemy that ended up being the greatest threat it had ever known. It has already been noted that the Parliament of Paris was the institution that expelled the Society in 1595. At the beginning of the eighteenth century, this same Parliament consisted of influential Jansenists who were quick to blame the Society, and not without good reason, for their troubles with the Vatican.

The conflict was thus more than a century old. By the 1640s, in the face of a society losing its way, the church seemed to be absorbed by the state, its cult of the king, and secularism. Jean du Vergier de Hauranne, abbot of Saint-Cyran (1581–1643) and friend of Jansenius, was spiritual director of the abbey of Port-Royal. Du Vergier proposed a return to the purity of the Scriptures, the church fathers, and the sacraments. He called for greater penance and devotion to the Eucharist. These Jansenists found an ally in Gallicanism, which hardened itself against the Vatican and, in addition to its nationalistic emphasis, called for a return to the simplicity (Episcopalian, we would say) of the origins.

In 1700, the conflict reached the university. The Sorbonne condemned the Jesuits' proposals in China on the question of rites, which it described in these terms: (1) Before Christ, the Chinese already believed in the true God; (2) they had offered sacrifices on the altar of the oldest temple in the universe; (3) their experience of God can serve as an example to Christians; (4) their ethics are as pure as the Christian religion; (5) their spiritualities, rituals, priesthood, love of neighbor are the expression of a perfect religion; and (6) they are, of all the nations, God's favorite. These propositions were in direct contradiction with Bossuet's classification of races, for whom all non-Christian nations were idolatrous and backward.[23]

In 1701, certainly in reaction to this anti-Jesuitism in the academic world, the French Jesuits founded the journal *Mémoires de Trévoux*. Initially, they intended to promote the arts, science, and history. But not for long, because the journal became an instrument to defend religion against its enemies, not only Protestants, but also Jansenists who had become powerful in the Parliament, and against a new form of materialism of which the encyclopedist Baron d'Holbach was one of the promoters. On July 13, 1708, the Vatican intervened, as requested by the Jesuits. In the brief *Universi Dominici Gregis*, Clement XI condemned Quesnel's moral reflections. This brief was initially opposed by Cardinal de Noailles and some bishops who thought that it infringed on Gallican liberties. This is why, at the instigation of the king, on September 8, 1713, the pope promulgated the bull *Unigenitus Dei Filius*, written by a commission of Dominicans and Jesuits. It condemned one hundred and one propositions taken from Quesnel's book.[24]

By 1730, *Unigenitus* had become law in France, sealing a short-lived alliance between the king and Rome, much to the dismay of the Parliament, which soon retaliated. Taking advantage of an incident over the sacraments—some bishops, with the king's approval, required a certificate (confession bill) from dying Christians before receiving the last rites—Parliament voted against this condition in 1740. The king's resistance lasted for a time until the beginning of the Seven Years' War (1756–1763). He needed the vote of Parliament to finance the war.[25]

From 1751 to 1772, Jean d'Alembert and Jean Didérot published a total of seventeen volumes, one of which, in 1765, was *Sur la destruction des jésuites par un auteur désintéressé* (On the destruction of the Jesuits by an indifferent author) by d'Alembert. While this literature was being published and propagated, monarchists—those who promoted greater autonomy for monarchies from Rome, a secular state rid of what they considered the obscurantism of religion, and a stronger national church—were coming to power throughout Europe. The prime ministers of these monarchies were of a certain competence and very skillful in propaganda: Sebastian de Carvalho (Marquis of Pombal) in Lisbon; the Duke of Choiseul in Paris; the Count of Aranda in Madrid; Tanuci in Naples; and du Tillot in Parma. According to Philippe Lécrivain, all these leaders were "more or less imbued with Jansenist ideas and French philosophers, distrustful of Rome and hostile to the Society."[26] And unlike Charles de Montesquieu, who had found in the Jesuit reductions of Paraguay the spirit of a republic,[27] these politicians faced an armed opposition there that they believed was led by Jesuits. They accused the Jesuits of being driven by a thirst for absolute power. These leaders were determined to end it all. Some saw behind this relentlessness a Masonic front against the Society. This thesis is challenged by recent historiography. The Italian socialist historian Carlo Francovich and the Spaniard José Antonio Ferrer Benimeli, the latter a Jesuit, have shown that the great adversaries of the Society, including Carlos III, were also fervent anti-Masons.[28]

THE LAVALETTE AFFAIR AND THE SUPPRESSION IN FRANCE

In 1755, the British patrol captured Antoine Lavalette (1708–1767) and two ships coming from Martinique, near Bordeaux. They were carrying the equivalent of 600,000 pounds of merchandise that was intended to pay his debts in France. Superior and procurator of the Martinique mission, Lavalette wanted to save the mission from bankruptcy and became involved in business with French investors. A year later, in 1756, a second shipment belonging to him was once again captured. The losses were enormous. As a result, Lavalette found himself unable to pay the 5.3 million pounds he owed his creditors. The Jesuit Province of France had to intervene. Unable to pay these debts, it turned to the Province of England, which, by paying about 800,000 pounds, found itself close to bankruptcy.[29]

A creditor in Nantes obtained from the courts a mortgage on all the Society's assets in France in exchange for payment of Lavalette's debt. Meanwhile, an attempt on the life of Louis XV, orchestrated by Robert François Damiens, failed. Damiens had acted alone. But Jansenist circles were quick to associate him with the Jesuits, while the Duke of Choiseul was appointed to head the government. By the conclusion of Lavalette's trial, the whole Society was on trial.[30]

According to Clément Charles François de Laverdy de Nizeret, one of the judges for the prosecution, "it was the security of the king's person, the public peace, the preservation of religion and the education of youth" that were at stake in this trial.[31] De Laverdy reiterated that the Society, in its present form, was irreformable. What is more, it would never have been approved or recognized in France. It was therefore urgent, he concluded, that its *Constitutions* and all the founding bulls of its Institute be examined. In the meantime, for the good of the nation and of religion, the Parliament was to forbid any recruitment to the Society. All Jesuit colleges and seminaries in France were to be closed immediately. The Jesuits, he said, who were under the orders of a foreign Superior General, could not be entrusted with the education of French youth. *Ad intra*, they were a direct threat to Gallicanism and thus, to the French bishops. Furthermore, their expansion throughout the world was a serious threat to the stability of the empire.[32]

On August 6, 1762, Parliament effectively suppressed the Society in France, leaving 3,500 Jesuits in the street.[33] In 1764, a royal decree confirmed this sentence. All correspondence between the French Jesuits and the Superior General were forbidden. Instead, the Jesuits had to obey the local bishops. In 1767, they were definitively expelled from France and forced to denounce the *Constitutions*. They were forbidden to wear the habit and to live in the communities. All had to cut off relations with the Superior General and with other Jesuits, their properties were confiscated, and their libraries dispersed. Moñino's *Note* was followed to the letter. On December 1, 1764, the suppression was final. Although weakened by intense pressure from the Bourbon courts, Clement XIII signed the bull *Apostolicum* in 1765 in support of the Society. The Jesuits could still survive in France, at least until 1767.

THE SUPPRESSION IN PORTUGAL

In Portugal, the suppression was orchestrated by the will of one man: Sebastian Carvalho e Melo (1699–1782), who became the Marquis of Pombal in 1770. Before becoming Prime Minister of Portugal, he had been ambassador to London (1738), Vienna (1745), and Secretary of State (1755). It was in this last position that he witnessed the Lisbon earthquake (magnitude 8.75) on November 1, 1755, the Feast of All Saints.

Together with the ravages of the fire, the event covered the inhabitants with mourning and consternation. On this occasion, Carvalho gave proof of serenity and fearlessness. While the royal family fled the city, Carvalho remained in Lisbon to rebuild both the city and his popularity. The Jesuits, however, made their way through the rubble to rescue victims from death. Their seven houses were devastated.[34] According to estimates, between 10,000 and 100,000 people lost their lives; 85 percent of the houses were destroyed, including the royal palace and its library and archives.[35]

This event increased, for a relatively short time, the credit and popularity of the Jesuits. Sometime later, between 1756 and 1757, a mutiny broke out in Porto, and Carvalho tried to attribute its cause to the Jesuits. But this plot failed. The story of this event was that among the various and extravagant projects that the minister had implemented, there was the creation of the Upper Douro Wine Company, which, according to another account, was known as the General Company of Pernambuco and Paraiba, two cities in Brazil. Of this company, established in Porto, Carvalho was declared Protector, a title that earned him an exorbitant profit. All the harvesters were obliged, under very severe sanctions, to sell their wines to the same company at a fixed price, and the company then shipped them at a very high price.[36]

The city was exposed to the great famine that followed and to the very severe judicial acts of the new governor, Francisco de Almada e Mendoça. The bishop tried to mollify the spirits of the monarch and his minister, but in vain. He also distributed twenty thousand crusaders among his poor. The cause of the popular movement that had brought so much misfortune and bloodshed to the city of Porto was well known to all. But Carvalho was determined to implicate the Jesuits and make them look like the perpetrators. To this end, he discreetly recommended to the commissioner who was going to investigate the case that he should spare no effort to find out if these religious had any part in the mutiny. The commissioner made a long and careful examination to accomplish his task, but he found no evidence or the slightest hint of guilt against the Jesuits. This hardly prevented Carvalho from publishing that the Jesuits had been the leaders of the uproar, and that therefore they were responsible for the capital executions that had been carried out as punishment for it. However, His Majesty, in an act of excessive clemency and in order not to discredit the Society of Jesus, to whose saints he was devoted, would have ordered that everything that contributed to the dishonor of the Jesuits be deleted from the trial.[37]

The terror of November 1 in Lisbon became, for the members of the church, including the Jesuits, a perfect pretext to prick the conscience of the faithful and demand contrition and penance. It was like a divine punishment, and Lisbon was the new Sodom. The idea that the wrath of God had destroyed Lisbon served as a constant in sermons, pamphlets, treatises, and moralizing poems, not only in Portugal, but throughout Europe.[38] By such an obvious lie and in taking advantage of the superstitious character of the Portuguese, Minister Carvalho intended to make the Jesuits unpopular. For a time, his efforts in Portugal to deal a decisive blow to the sons of Ignatius failed. So, he transferred the plot to the Americas.

Since 1750, the reductions of Paraguay had passed under Portuguese control. Under the impulse of Carvalho, the government decided to dismantle them so as to exploit the gold resources that it said were there. The Jesuits were fiercely opposed to this, even though Portugal needed it for its economy. In 1757, Carvalho published a pamphlet about "The New Republic" that the Jesuits had created among the Guaranis and how they were at war with the Catholic kings of Spain and Portugal. The story that the Superior General of the Society had been made king under the name of Nicholas I was considered true. The news reached Europe sometime between 1754 and 1755 and was reported in both the *Historical and Political Mercury* and the *Amsterdam Gazette*. It also reached Naples, as did the book in which the story was told, presenting the so-called Jesuit state in a rather critical way. At the time, it was difficult to say who was really behind this story, which was surely false. As Voltaire said, "It is true that King Nicholas does not exist; but it is certainly true that the Jesuits are kings in their missions."[39]

Pope Benedict XIV sent Cardinal Francisco de Saldanha de Gama (1713–1776) as a visitor. Without visiting any Jesuit community, he wrote a report against the Society, which Carvalho promptly disseminated. After being elected Superior General of the Society in May 1758, Lorenzo Ricci wrote to Pope Clement XIII on July 6, 1758, to contest the report. The latter believed the Jesuits. But on the night of September 3, there was an assassination attempt against the king. The Tavora family, one of whose sons was suspected and executed on January 12, 1759, had ties to the Jesuits. In fact, a dozen Companions were executed with the suspect, including Fr. Gabriel Malagrida, a former missionary in Brazil. Carvalho asked the pope to expel the Jesuits. The pope refused. Diplomatic relations with the Holy See were broken off until the death of the pope in 1769. Carvalho, however, managed to convince the king that it was in the interest of his own safety to expel the Jesuits. The decree of expulsion was signed on September 30, 1759. About 1,100 Jesuits were expelled from Portugal and its empire, 127 of them from the Province of Goa alone. After a long journey around the world, the expellees finally ended up in the seaport of Civitavecchia, in one of the territories of the Papal States.

SUPPRESSION IN SPAIN

The Bourbon kings had lobbied the popes for the creation of a national church in Spain, where the Inquisition had passed into the hands of the Jansenists. Conservative Catholics also had a grievance against the Society, which they suspected of sedition and independence in Latin America where they allegedly had large investments. In 1759, Charles Bourbon of Naples became king in Madrid. Choiseul of France, also a Bourbon, proposed an alliance that would include the kingdoms of France, Spain, and Naples to resist British hegemony. He also wanted to take advantage of this alliance to put an end to the Jesuits by uniting all the great Catholic kingdoms of Europe against them.

From March 23 to 26, 1766, the populace took to the streets of Madrid to protest the high cost of living. Leopoldo di Gregorio was replaced as head of government by the Count of Aranda, while Manuel de Roda was appointed Minister of Justice. They accused the Society of conspiring against the king by manipulating the starving poor. On February 27, 1767, Charles III signed the decree of expulsion of the six thousand Jesuits from his kingdom. They arrived in Genoa, Bologna, and Ferrara in June, where José Pignatelli received them. On November 4, 1769, the masses asked in vain for the reestablishment of the Jesuits. In fact, without realizing it, and to the great pleasure of the enemies of the Society, the masses had just confirmed that they had indeed been in league with the Jesuits.

NAPLES AND ROME

In Naples, Ferdinand IV inherited the throne from his father, Charles III. He was, however, very young to reign. Bernardo Tanucci, an illustrious sovereigntist, assumed the regency. He was an enemy of the Society and forced the young king to sign the decree of expulsion on October 31, 1767, which was put into effect in Parma on April 22, 1768.

The conclave elected Lorenzo Ganganelli as Pope Clement XIV on July 21, 1769. He had promised, if elected, to abolish the

Society. This he did on July 21, 1773, with the bull *Dominus ac Redemptor Noster.*

The archbishop of Paris rejected the decision, Spain found it insufficient, and the court of Naples forbade its promulgation. As for Pombal, he had a *Te Deum* sung in all the churches and offered fireworks to the people over three nights. In Austria, Maria Theresa agreed completely with the pope, while Poland and Switzerland put up temporary resistance.[40] The brief reached Peking, but the Chinese emperor K'ien Long disliked Pombal and refused to publish it. Fearing for the French missions in China, Louis XVI supported the emperor there.

On September 22, 1773, Father General Lorenzo Ricci and his assistants were arrested and locked up in the Castle of St. Angelo. After the death of Clement XIV on September 22, 1774, Pius VI was elected in 1775. He released Ricci, who died a few months later on November 24, 1775. There is no lack of historians who think that Ricci was not the right Superior General for the Society in these times of crisis. He was passive and sorely lacked experience of government.

PROPAGANDA, TRUTH, AND REALITY

Propaganda could be unfounded, not false. But left to its own devices, it produced a catastrophe for a well-established institution like the Society of Jesus. Despite attacks and a growing anti-Jesuitism more determined than ever to do battle with it, the Society, in the middle of the eighteenth century, still looked like a solid organization resplendent in its vast network of colleges throughout the world, as well as in its missionary exploits unparalleled in the history of Christianity. In 1749, the *Catalogus Provinciarum, Domorum, Collegiorum, Residentiarum, Seminariorum et Missionum Societatis Iesu* counted a total of 22,589 Jesuits worldwide. The German Assistancy and its ten provinces, the largest, had 8,749 Jesuits, 81 seminaries, 207 colleges, 24 houses of probation, 80 communities, and 160 missions. Spain and its twelve provinces had 196 colleges, 33 seminaries, 12 houses of probation, 57 communities, and 20 missions for a total of 5,114 members. Italy, France, and Portugal had 3,622, 3,350, and 1,754 Jesuits respectively. At the time of the suppression, the Society had 728 schools throughout the world, with more than 250,000 students, making it the largest educational organization that had ever existed.[41] The projected strength, however, rested on a very fragile foundation.

At the purely institutional level, the Society, which for two centuries had succeeded in imposing itself in all aspects of the political, religious, and social life of Europe and beyond, had never mounted an effective defense against adversaries as sophisticated as they were powerful. From the mid-eighteenth century onward, the society that it helped transform seemed to have taken the Society over. With skillful propaganda, the most powerful intellectual and political leaders in Europe turned against her. This merciless propaganda against her Institute eventually sowed doubt among the populace. So easily manipulated, they were fed daily by macabre myths cleverly propagated by politicians trained in modern means of communication. They associated the name of the Society with all the social ills that plagued their societies, from the slightest sexual scandal to the devastation of a pandemic or an earthquake. When the Black Death ravaged the Jesuit ranks in the 1730s, the enemies were merciless and saw it as God's punishment for them. One of her most prominent sons in France and rector of the royal seminary, Jean-Baptiste Gérard, was accused of having an affair with Madame Cathérine Cadière. The propaganda claimed that he had bewitched his alleged victim and induced her to have an abortion. Under the influence of this campaign, Madame Cadière's brothers, all religious, diocesan, Dominican, or Carmelite, took a stand in favor of their sister. After investigation, Gérard was found innocent. But the damage had already been done, aggravating the reputation of the Society at its lowest point in public opinion.

Moreover, the Society was facing financial difficulties. Benefactors were becoming rare. Communes wanted to have their share of the profits in its patrimony. Bursars and procurators, stressed by the blow of the order's expansion, were making high-risk investments. Others borrowed money from individuals. Among these treasurers was Lavalette, the man through whom the machinery that had taken centuries to build reached the point of no return against the Society.

The stage was thus set for the perfect explosion of the Lavalette Affair. The Jansenist Parliament of Paris was ready for its revenge. Its Jansenist members, or those among them who were sympathizers, had survived their own persecution, which they attributed to the Jesuits. It was their turn to deal the Jesuits the fatal blow, without giving their enemy the slightest chance of survival. The Christian temporal kings to whose call the Society had so often responded enthusiastically, and the papacy to which it had become so intimately attached, were armed with swords for the supreme sacrifice. Abandoned and homeless, members of the Society were imprisoned, others deported to what it had so often mistaken for Babylon, to the land of heresy, to the Prussia of Catherine.

THE EXILE

The suppression was brutal in France, Spain, Portugal, and Italy. Elsewhere, as in China, the Jesuits remained safe from persecution. In Canada, the last presuppression Jesuit was Jean-Joseph Casot (1728–1800).[42] Since the status of the Catholic Church was not recognized in Great Britain and its colonies, the governments of London, Wales, and the British colonies of Maryland and Pennsylvania considered the suppression of the Jesuits primarily an ecclesiastical matter and did not issue the papal writ. The majority of Jesuits in North America therefore continued their pastoral work, although some chose to do so as secular priests.[43] Immediately after the suppression in France in 1762, Jesuits of English origin established colleges in the Austrian Netherlands and in Bruges, including the Grand and Petit Collège Anglais. The one in Bruges remained open until 1773.

François Charles de Velbruck (1719–1784), bishop of Liège, allowed the Jesuits to remain in his diocese on condition that they adopt the habit and customs of secular priests. He allowed them, under these new conditions, to continue all their ministries as before the suppression. In the field of education, the English exiles even took advantage of the suppression to innovate. Whereas the *Ratio Studiorum* prohibited the study of science by students before the age of eighteen, the new English colleges, on the contrary, adapted the *Ratio* to the English academy model, which allowed students from the age of six to be introduced to belles-lettres, history, geography, arithmetic, geometry, and astronomy. They also learned treatises on general and particular physics as well as general and applied mathematics. As one priest wrote, students "will be made sensitive by experiments; to which various machines and instruments gathered at great expense will be put to use and which form a cabinet destined for this use."[44]

In France, on July 19, 1790, Pierre de Clorivière, a former Jesuit, created the Congregation of the Heart of Jesus. His bishop, Cortois de Pressigny, approved. Its first novices took vows at Montmartre in 1791, as did the first Jesuits. Two other congregations of the same kind were the Society of the Heart of Jesus and the Society of the Faith of Jesus, the latter created by Nicolas Paccaniri in 1797. All made the Exercises and vowed to live according to the spirit of Saint Ignatius and to obey the pope. These congregations spread to Belgium, Austria, and the Paccanirists to Rome, the Netherlands, Great Britain, Switzerland, and Austria.

In Russia, Catherine II refused to promulgate the papal brief. Moreover, the heretic queen asked that Stanislas Czerniewicz, Gabriel Lenkiewicz, and Joseph Kutenbry become her advisors. The tradition had a hard skin. The Jesuits seemed unable to escape from the court life! Moreover, it was the essence of the Society itself that refused to compromise when, on November 29, 1773, Czerniewicz informed the Queen that he and his companions intended to obey the papal brief.

Respectful of the conscience of her new subjects, Catherine wrote to the provincial of the Jesuits in Russia, Casimir Sobolewski, to express her disagreement. She also asked Bishop Stanislas Siestzrencewicz to allow the Jesuits to open a novitiate. The novitiate was opened on June 30, 1779. The restoration was underway. Pius VI protested. Catherine turned a deaf ear and allowed a General Congregation to be held on Russian soil in 1782. This one elected Czerniewicz as the new Superior General of the Society. It was Catherine herself, not the pope, who approved the new General and gave him the mandate to reorganize the structures of the Society. A second General Congregation met between September and October 1785 and elected Gabriel Lenkiewicz as the new Superior General.

THE CATHOLIC KINGDOMS

In the meantime, the revolution that was raging in Europe was worrying the courts in Paris, Lisbon, and Madrid. These courts immediately began to become aware of the void created by the immolation of the Society. Ferdinand of Parma wrote to his uncle Charles III of Spain informing him that he would like to recall the Jesuits to Parma. And in 1792, he asked the Jesuits to resume the direction of their colleges. Seeing that most of the Italian Jesuits had grown old and tired, Ferdinand appealed to Father Lenkiewicz on July 23, 1793, telling him that the suppression of the Society had done incalculable harm to the church and the monarchy and that he needed them. Lenkiewicz sent him three Jesuits. Ferdinand also appealed to Pius VI. The pope did not oppose the project but asked that he proceed with caution. Four years later, on September 17, 1797, Pius VI also recognized that the suppression of the Society had left the church defenseless in the face of the revolution. If Charles IV did not want Jesuits in Spain, the pope wrote, he should at least inform the pope that he would not object to the pope sending them elsewhere.

Father François-Xavier Kareu was elected General in February 1799. Six months later, on August 29, Pius VI died. The Dean of Cardinals, Jean-Francois Albani, and his influential Secretary of State, Ercole Consalvi, thought it was time. Thanks to the revolution, they had discovered the true face of the Jansenists and concluded that without the Jesuits, the church would remain defenseless in the face of the new challenges.

On March 14, 1800, Barnabas Chiaramonti, a Benedictine, was elected to the See of Saint Peter. Following in the footsteps of his predecessor, he took the name of Pius VII. He quickly moved into action. On March 14, 1801, he issued the brief *Catholicae Fidei*, reestablishing the Society in Russia, with Kareu as Superior General. Kareu died a year later and was replaced by Gabriel Gruber, then by Thaddée Bzrozowski, elected on September 2, 1805.

At that time, there were 265 Jesuits in Russia. On July 30, 1804, Pius VII issued another brief, *Per Alias*, reestablishing the Society in the Kingdom of the Two Sicilies. In this brief he referred to the Formula of the Institute and the special vocation of the Society for the education of the young. Joseph Pignatelli was then the provincial of Naples. In 1805, Pierre de Clorivière joined Gruber and the Society in Russia.

On August 7, 1814, Pope Pius VII, surrounded by almost all the cardinals in Rome, issued the bull, *Sollicitudo Omnium Ecclesiarum*. It was a solemn occasion. There were also some of the 428 surviving Jesuits still in Italy. They were deaf, dumb, lame, apoplectic. Some, like Manuel Luengo, did not hide their emotion and relief.[45] In 1815, it was the turn of the 460 Spanish survivors to receive the good news: the Society had been reestablished in Spain.[46]

After the canonical reestablishment of the Society, Pius VII asked Brzozowski to return to Rome as Superior General of the Society. But Tsar Alexander I did not allow him to leave Russia. The pope had to appoint a Vicar General in Rome, Petrucci, with full power to direct the Society until 1820. A serious incident occurred during this General Congregation.

One of the delegates, Luigi Rezzi, with the support of the Cardinal Vicar General of Rome, Anibale Della Genga and the future pope, Leo XII, questioned the legitimacy of the forty years of exile of the Society in Russia and even of the General Congregation itself. The cardinal therefore forbade the entry into Rome of certain delegates until the question of the legitimacy of their eligibility had been completely settled. He gave full powers to Petrucci, who had supported Rizzi, acting contrary to the provisions of the *Constitutions* regarding the General Congregation. The cardinal's letter to the Congregation questioned the right of the Congregation to meet and potentially questioned the validity of the vote of most of its members. A group of Jesuits around the French Jean-Louis de Rozaven thus went to see the cardinal Secretary of State Ercole Consalvi, who convinced the pope to give reason to Rozaven and his group. He issued a decree reconvening the congregation and recognizing the validity of the votes of all participants. With Luis Fortis elected, Rizzi was excluded from the general congregation and ordered to leave Rome.[47]

AFTER THE RESTORATION

In 1852, Most Reverend Jan Roothaan, Superior General of the Jesuits, wrote to Antonio Morey, the Vice Provincial of Spain, concerning the need to renew the spiritual commitment of the members serving in the missions of Cuba, the Philippines, Puerto Rico, and Tarragona:

> It seems to me also that the time has come for us to be a little more demanding with those who have been living in dispersion for so long. Therefore, all those who still have the true spirit and love of the Society must show it by allowing themselves to be completely governed by their superiors, either by abandoning everything to go and take up the post that will be entrusted to them, or by joining together to form the various residences or missions in the best possible way, or finally by contributing according to their strength and means to the general good, in the way they think most opportune.[48]

Anyone who might find himself eager to govern himself solely by the way he understands it, Roothaan continued, must be given letters of dismissal. A few years earlier, on December 15, 1846, Father Roothaan had written to Father Pierre Colom, as the latter was struggling with religious discipline. The Superior General urged Colom to discipline himself and be a good religious, faithful to his religious promises. The latter should apply himself "to the interior life, in the exercise of virtue, especially humility and obedience, and that [he] will persevere until death in the Company."[49]

Roothaan's message reflected the broader spiritual needs of the Society after its restoration. Aged, sometimes sickly members, as well as reduced well-trained Jesuits, affected the quality of formation and, with it, religious discipline. In addition to these challenges, the expansion of missions and a context of continuous persecutions dispersed the energies and weakened the spirit. This fragile situation after the Society's restoration required major reforms to secure its preservation in good state.

The Suppression and the Restoration

The forty years of suppression had certainly created a vacuum in leadership that the new generation was to seal. Following a time of transition with the first two superiors general, there followed a tendency to groom younger Jesuits to provide the Society with younger and efficient leaders, some of whom, like Roothaan, became the true restorers of the order. They renewed the spiritual life of the Jesuits, adjusted their training to the Society's modern needs, and rekindled the spirit of missions, while dealing with renewed opposition and persecutions from governments.

Superiors General were literally groomed. The best case was Luigi Fortis (r. 1820–1829), who, during his entire tenure as Superior General, groomed his successor Roothaan. Marc Lindeijer recently discovered that Roothaan had been merely a professor of rhetoric to a dozen scholastics in the juniorate when Fortis picked him to run a major college in Turin. From there on, almost a weekly correspondence between the Superior General and his protégé helped test Roothaan's skills, develop his talents, and improve his ability to lead.[50] Roothaan succeeded Fortis after the latter's death in 1829.

Fortis had worked to rebuild the Society, despite the difficult circumstances. By the time of his death, the number of Jesuits had grown from 1,300 in 1820 to 2,100 in 1829. Yet, Roothaan was the one considered to be the second founder of the Society, the first after its restoration. A Dutchman, he was elected the twenty-first Superior General of the Society at only forty-three years of age and while serving as Provincial of Italy. The General Congregation that elected him gave Roothaan the mandate to restore the structures of the old Society, improve the spiritual formation of its members, and reform its curriculum,[51] after Pope Leo XII had returned the Roman College to the Society in 1824. The same pope also entrusted the German College to the Jesuits and confirmed the privileges of the Society in a bull.

Under Roothaan the number of Jesuits reached 5,209, and the Society underwent a great missionary expansion in Asia, Africa, Australia, and America. Implementing the Congregation's mandate, the Superior General published three important documents on "The Love of the Society and its Institute" (1830), "To Arouse and Promote the Desire for Missions in Foreign Lands" (1833), and on "The Use of the Spiritual Exercises of St. Ignatius"

(1834), of which, in 1835, he published a *versio litteralis* and a *versio vulgata*. In the meantime, in 1832, he published a new edition of the *Ratio Studiorum* and innovated by including the teaching of church history and canon law in theology; studies of mathematics, physics, and chemistry in philosophy; and gave a greater place to the study of vernacular languages.

Roothaan's successor, Father Peter Jan Beckx, entered the Society at the age of twenty-four, on October 29, 1819. He was professed on the Feast of Saint Ignatius, 1830, and was elected Superior General on July 2, 1853.[52] Roothaan, then Superior General, put great trust in Beckx's wisdom and counsel. He had the opportunity to know him intimately and to appreciate him during his occasional visits to Rome. From 1830 to 1849, Father Beckx was entrusted by Roothaan with very delicate and important missions in Lombardy, Bavaria, and Hungary.

On October 10, 1850, Beckx was appointed the rector of the Scholasticate at Leuven, where he displayed eminent qualities and great care of the community members. In February 1852, he was charged by Roothaan with a new and important mission in Vienna as chief negotiator. On September 8 of the same year, Beckx was named Provincial of Austria. In June 1853, he was obliged to go to Rome to attend, as Provincial, the General Congregation convened by order of Father Roothaan. The latter died on June 22 and on July 2, Father Beckx was elected on the first ballot as Superior General of the Society.[53]

During his novitiate, Father Beckx had read carefully Father Acquaviva's "Instructions for Confessors of Kings." The book had been put into his hands by his Master of Novices, who foresaw the future usefulness of such reading. Beckx died March 4, 1887, having been Superior General for nearly thirty-four years.[54]

Beckx's tenure—longer than that of any of his predecessors— was at the same time one of the most prosperous and full of trials. The membership of the Society more than doubled. Many of the ancient provinces were reestablished in Ireland, France, Portugal, Spain, and America. New missions were created and existing ones were extended, as was the education of youth—a work so dear to the Society.[55] Numerous letters addressed to the Society remain as monuments of Beckx's wisdom, piety, and watchful zeal. Lastly, a legion of new models and protectors was obtained by the canonization or beatification of more than eighty Jesuits, of whom all except three were missionaries or martyrs. Such are in larger outline the fruits of his productive government. But these were gathered through many difficulties and at the cost of many sufferings.[56]

At the very beginning of Beckx's tenure, a persecution raised against the members of the Society in Spain, groundless accusations of political intrigue made against them in Naples, and the spoliation of those at Fribourg prepared the Society for more sorrowful trials. In 1859 and 1860, Beckx saw his religious expelled from nearly the whole of the Italian peninsula. In 1866, they were banished from the Province of Venice and, in 1868, from Spain, following similar expulsions in 1820, 1823, and 1835.[57] In 1871, the Jesuits were massacred in Paris, as they had been in Syria in 1860. In 1873, they were proscribed in Germany on the inauguration of the Kulturkampf and finally, in 1880, forcibly ejected from their houses and colleges in France and all her colonies.[58]

Beckx spent more than ten years displaced, living in the ancient convent of San Girolamo at Fiesole, whence he continued to govern the Society, until the advanced age of ninety warned him that it was more prudent to lay the burden on younger shoulders. A General Congregation was then convoked at Fiesole on September 24, 1883, which elected as Vicar General, with right of succession, Very Reverend Father Anderledy, to whom, six months later, Father Beckx committed entirely the government of the Society. The remaining years of his life were spent in Rome. According to his wishes, Beckx spent his last days in the quiet and solitude of San Andrea, near the tomb of Saint Stanislaus and amid the cherished memories of the old novitiate of the Society.

Born on June 3, 1819, Anton M. Anderledy entered the Society on October 5, 1838, and made his profession on March 26, 1855. On September 24, 1883, by the authority of the pope and the consent of the Superior General, he was elected Vicar General with right of succession. And by a circular dated from Fiesole on January 20, 1884, Father Beckx informed the Society that he had granted to Father Anderledy all the faculties that it was in his power to give. From there on, all members of the Society might have recourse to him in their necessities, as Anderledy's precepts and letters were to have all the authority and force they would have had if issued or signed by the Superior General himself.[59]

A "useful book," *Renovation Reading*, published by *The Woodstock College Press*, summarizes the work of the superiors general of the restored Society of Jesus. The book contains translations of their important letters, beginning with the time of Saint Ignatius. Among those, we have Roothaan's letters on the "Desire of Foreign Missions," "The Centennial Year," "The Spiritual Exercises," and "The Devotion to the Sacred Heart." His successor, Peter Jan Beckx, emphasized "The Observance of Vows" and raised the profile of the Jesuit saints Peter Canisius and Jan Berchmans, whose exemplary lives served to inspire the zeal for souls among the members. He also wrote on obedience and other virtues.[60] By the turn of the century, the foundations of the new Society were set, although the political challenges had not diminished. The new century in the history of Christianity, however, was American. This American wind also blew in the Society.

THE AMERICAN JESUITS' CENTURY

A small Catholic community had been present in the United States since the 1630s. In April 1779, the Diocese of Baltimore was created, the first in the United States, with John Carroll (1735–1815), a former Jesuit, at its head. In his charge, he had to balance several centrifugal interests. Carroll had to build a diocesan church with the tools of a suppressed Society whose members still dreamed of its restoration. He also had to manage the Catholic minority in the context of a hostile Protestant majority.

Moreover, the restoration of the Society and its consolidation in the United States corresponded with the birth of a state that embraced the republican ideas that were partly behind its suppression. The founding fathers of the American nation had in fact embraced the French ideas of Liberty-Equality-Fraternity, as well as a clearer separation between church and state that guaranteed religious freedom. Yet, the new nation was also the ideal home for a religious order that, by its very nature, was always in tension between different and often competing worldviews. The United

States' multiculturalism and its respect for liberties was the ideal place for the Society of Jesus to feel at home.

While George Washington was sympathetic to Catholics, he also knew that the Protestant majority in the country did not look kindly on the development of Catholicism on American soil. This was not only because of the age-old struggles between Catholics and Protestants in Europe, but also because of the new church with the Jesuits in charge. Charles Carroll of Carrollton articulated this deep fear to his namesake, Charles Carroll of Indianapolis, concerning the parliamentary debate that later led to the suppression of the Society:

> I cannot but concur with the opinion of Parliament: judging dangerous to the state a body of men who implicitly believe in the dictates of a Superior, & are inclined to the execution of his orders with a blind impetuosity of will & an eagerness to obey without the least inquiry or examination….No one has more esteem for the Jesuits than I do; I revere their virtue, I esteem their instruction, I respect the apostolic labors of the individuals, but I am compelled to acknowledge that their institute & plan of government are subject to great abuses.[61]

Carroll's fear of the Jesuits was based on centuries of stereotypes, that is, on a misperception that, because of their exemplary vow of obedience, the Jesuits were, in fact, a totalizing order and therefore antithetical to democratic values. He was afraid of their alleged lack of freedom among the members who blindly submit without inquiry or examination. If obedience seemed to him something proper to premodern obscurantism, he nonetheless admired the virtue of the Jesuits, their science, and their work. In short, the Jesuits were terrifyingly ambiguous men of science and virtue who, nevertheless, appeared to obey their leader as if the latter were a divinely chosen monarch. And monarchy was completely un-American.

Not all American early patriots shared this fear about the Jesuits. John Carroll, the former Jesuit and bishop, used his personal connections with George Washington to secure a vote on religious freedom in the Constitution of 1784. His cousin, Charles Carroll, was the only Catholic to sign the Declaration of Independence. Advised by a former confrere, Charles Plowden, Bishop Carroll's task was to keep the American church in communion with Rome and to convince the American Protestant majority of the limits of Roman control over the American church. In this role, the new nation offered a political system in which the universal and the local could coexist, a system that guaranteed freedom of religion to the Jesuits.

Only when one part of the American society attempted to claim monopoly or predominance over the system did it become a threat to the very existence of the Jesuits in that nation. Washington was the first to acknowledge the Jesuits' delicate situation. In a March 1790 letter to Bishop Carroll, Washington called him "citizen" and acknowledged the "patriotic" contribution of Catholics during the revolution that led to the creation of the American nation and system of government. In view of the growing American Nativism, he hoped that other "citizens" would not forget this contribution, nor the help received from Catholic France in support of their new republic. As he spoke to Carroll, Washington also knew that he was speaking to a former Jesuit, still Jesuit at heart. He expressed his wish to see the Jesuits thrive in the United States:

> And may the members of your Company in America, animated only by the pure spirit of Christianity, and always conducting themselves as the faithful subjects of our free government, enjoy every temporal and spiritual felicity.[62]

Among the fellow citizens that Washington had in mind because of their suspicion of the Society may have been his own successor as president, John Adams. A year after the Society's restoration, on May 6, 1816, Adams wrote to Thomas Jefferson and expressed his disgust for the "latest resurrection of the Jesuits." He explained his fear over the pretext of the Russian exile of the order, with a superior general residing in Russia and corresponding with American Jesuits who were "more numerous than anyone knows."[63] Among Adams's sources was Blaise Pascal and four volumes of the history of the Society, the author of which is not identified. From this research of rather unfriendly sources, Adams concluded by asserting his belief that the Jesuits were incompatible with the American way of life. And yet, faithful to the laws of the nation, he admitted the right of the Jesuits to exist in the United States:

> If ever a congregation of men deserved eternal perdition on earth and in hell…it is this Company of Loiola. Our system of religious freedom must, however, offer them an asylum. But if they do not subject the purity of our elections to a severe test, it will be a wonder.[64]

Adams's concerns over Russian and Roman influence went beyond the Jesuits. His views represented the broader question posed by American citizens and leaders concerning the suitability of Roman Catholicism with the American way of life. As they settled in Maryland, Catholics were seen as backward and distrusted.[65]

Bishop Carroll had to reassure its Protestant majority and adapt to a secular, republican nation suspicious of Rome. The American Jesuit project, like the Catholic one, was to prove the compatibility of Roman Catholicism with America. It was an agenda of continuous reforms and adaptation. In this effort to consolidate the local church, Carroll founded Georgetown Academy in 1789, the first Catholic school in the United States, which was also considered "a nursery for future clergymen."[66] Giovanni Grassi (1775–1849), another former Jesuit, reformed Georgetown's curriculum, strengthening the teaching of languages as well as science and astronomy: "he built an earthquake counter, calculated an eclipse, calculated the altitude of the sun, wrote dialogues and made drawings to illustrate geometry and astronomy, and imported books and other scientific instruments from Europe."[67]

Grassi had arrived in the United States in 1810. Carroll appointed him Superior of the Jesuit mission in Maryland in 1814 (with the approval of Tadeusz Brzozowski, the Superior General of the Jesuits in Russia), in addition to his position as president of Georgetown. The college was in dire financial straits at the time.[68] Enrollment was low and tuition revenue did not cover operating expenses. There were thirty-one new students in 1810, including seven Jesuit novices, and a deficit of $3,000. In a desperate situation, Eduardo Desperamus (1732–1812), Father Brzozowski's assistant, urged a "speedy and efficient remedy" for the Society's credit. The number of enrollments increased from 31 in 1810 to 119 in 1817. Grassi adapted the educational system to the religious freedom and democratic political system of America. He also lobbied parents and alumni, including Congressman William Gaston (1778–1834), Georgetown's first student and only Catholic member of Congress, to advocate for his school and the church.[69]

The results of the efforts of Carroll and his collaborators were not long in coming for the consolidation of the Catholic Church in the United States. In 1789, Catholics numbered about 30,000; they were 318,000 in 1830; 660,000 in 1840; 1,600,000 in 1850; and 4,500,000 in 1870. But with the great migrations of the nineteenth century, especially from Germany, Ireland, and Italy, the church began a process of profound transformation.[70] The American church took the form of an immigrant church, with a strong Irish and Germanic flavor.[71] The lower east side of New York had its own Italian Catholic community, shepherded by the Jesuits.[72] Some immigrant priests found the spirit of Republicanism antithetical to true Catholicism. Others, however, reacted more favorably to the republican egalitarianism of nineteenth-century culture.[73] The lines were thus drawn for American Catholicism in the nineteenth and twentieth centuries, and the Jesuits were on both sides of the fence.

Moreover, with few priests in the United States in the early years, lay administrators organized to build and maintain churches. Their growing influence also led to tensions with the hierarchy. The development of lay committees—the trustees, who, in imitation of the Protestant churches, saw themselves governing parish life—came to encroach on the rights of parish priests and even bishops.[74] Trusteeism went so far as to appoint parish priests by these trustees against the will of the bishops. Once again, traditionalists argued that trusteeism was antithetical to true Catholicism, and that it was a surrender of the church's historical vision to the corrosive tendencies of popular democracy.[75]

American colleges were opened in Louvain and Rome to train ultramontane priests, that is, priests unquestioningly loyal to the pope. Their number grew from 1,820 in 1850 to 3,780 in 1870. This led to an important influx of religious congregations.[76] Between 1832 and 1869, ten provincial councils and synods were held in Baltimore. The entire episcopate of the United States met there. The National Council of 1866, where a huge campaign for the Catholic school was launched, was a triumph: its opening, on October 7, with the entry into the cathedral of a procession of archbishops, thirty-seven bishops, two abbots, and more than a thousand priests, caused a sensation.[77]

During the same period, in the 1820s, John C. Calhoun, Secretary of War for President James Monroe, worked with the Maryland Jesuits and with the Sulpician and former president of Georgetown College, Bishop Louis Valentine du Bourg of Louisiana, to gain the government's support for the mission among the Indians. As a result of du Bourg's effort, Monroe's government agreed to support the mission financially and to provide it with a building to accommodate the priests and brothers. Yet, the civilization of the Indian Osages relied primarily on the virtue and holiness of the missionaries. More than the "doubtful and tedious process of books," the civilization of the Indians, du Bourg wrote to Calhoun on February 15, 1823, should commence with "familiar conversations, striking representations and by the pious lives of their spiritual leaders. Men, dis-enthralled from all family cares, abstracted from every earthly enjoyment, inured to fatigue and self-denial, living in the flesh as if strangers to all sensual inclination."[78]

Toward the end of the century, between 1884 and 1889, a question was at the forefront: In a changing American society, to what extent should the church conform? Some American Catholics (liberals), including those in the hierarchy, advocated adapting Roman Catholicism to the American context; others (conservatives), more faithful to Rome, argued that the church of God, the embodiment of truth, stood outside of history and was not, and should not be, affected by societal changes. It could not simply conform to the world. For liberal Catholics, the United States was unique and required flexibility in a country in which the Catholic Church was a minority. For conservatives, adapting Roman Catholicism to American society was a form of Americanism that, in its extreme form, could lead to an American schism and dilute fundamental Catholic beliefs.[79] This American debate also became the debate within the Society in the second half of the twentieth century. In a changing, postconciliar, postcolonial society, to what extent could the Society adapt without the risk of schism?

Among American Jesuits, the line between liberals and conservatives existed as well. Father Rudolph J. Meyer, twice provincial of Missouri between 1871 and 1919, never permitted changes in the application of the *Ratio Studiorum* in Jesuit schools. In contrast, one of his successors, Alexander J. Burrower, completely adhered to the project of bringing Jesuit schools in the United States "into harmony with outside academic standards, believing it could be done without sacrifice of anything essential in Jesuit educational ideals and methods."[80] Another provincial, John P. Frieden, had among his council members "the ablest men of business and professional skills, regardless of their religious affiliations."[81]

Therefore, if the nineteenth and twentieth centuries were American centuries for Roman Catholicism and for the Jesuits, it was because of America's pluralism and protection of it, including within religious corporations. Where the state and the church could easily align in sixteenth- or seventeenth-century Spain or Portugal to create a church free from the Jews or the Moors, such an alignment was impossible in the United States. Difference of religious opinions from the same congregation often created a doublemindedness in a context of cultural monopoly. In a pluralistic society, though, it remains just that, difference of nations, opinions, religions, or cultures, which were already acknowledged in the Jesuit Formula of 1539.

In the United States, old competitions among religious orders and within the same religious corporations were greatly exacerbated by tensions between the European and American wings of the church. As a result, any idea of a monolithic church or religious corporation in the United States seemed not only "fundamentally flawed and reductionist"[82] but also quasi-impossible. Like all Americans, Jesuits and students from Jesuit schools and their parents fought on both sides of the Civil War. In their missions, hundreds of Osage Indians, for example, joined the Union in the first year of the conflict, and many others joined the Confederate later.[83] The church in the United States, including the Society of Jesus, was also a church of immigrants. And immigrant children grew through the ranks of the Society's leadership. Of the nine provincials of Missouri from 1871 to 1919, five arrived in the United States as immigrants, and most of them had studied in Europe.[84]

For instance, different nationalities ran different Jesuit schools in different states in the United States. They also enrolled students with diverse cultural, economic, and cultural backgrounds:

> St. Louis University was run by Belgians; French expatriates launched institutions in Alabama, Kentucky, and New York; and Woodstock College, the Order's national seminary in Maryland, was the creation of exiled Neapolitans. German Jesuits, deported by Bismarck's Kulturkampf, founded five schools across the northeast from New York to the Mississippi River. In the Far West, Italians and other immigrant priests operated colleges in Santa Clara, San Francisco, Denver, Spokane, and Seattle.[85]

Because of this diversity, "the typical Jesuit college fostered shared cultural values."[86] Furthermore, "a more diversified course of studies emerged in the United States that prized professional development and research."[87] When challenged by their European superiors to remain faithful to the Society's traditional approach toward education, American Jesuits "pointed to their distinctive curriculum as a contribution to Society. While succumbing to greater specialization, the Society had retained the holistic and formative feature that had always been central to its pedagogical system."[88]

Jesuit distinctiveness in the United States, one might say, consisted in its cultural and ideological pluralism and its ability to accommodate opposites. It reconciled the universal and different locals in a single nation. And, as part of a minority religion, it adjusted to the laws of the new nation while borrowing from and competing with Protestant neighbors. It was a microcosm of global Catholicism in its own right. This view of the distinctiveness of American Jesuits might depart, even if slightly, from recent historiography on American Jesuits. In his *American Jesuits and the World*, John McGreevy emphasizes the fact that the hundreds of Jesuits moving from Europe to the United States and from the United States to the world sought to expand Catholicism and its uniformity. And yet, "these same Jesuits became central to the nationalist imagination"[89] as they threatened nationalist projects across the globe. The increased persecution and anticlericalism that followed in Protestant-dominated nations, McGreevy argues, led to the segregation of Catholic communities in the nineteenth century. The more confessional the Jesuits became, the more global they became.[90]

Introducing their book *Passionate Uncertainty*, Peter McDonough and Eugene C. Bianchi challenge this vision. They analyze the current demographic and institutional shifts within global Catholicism, and thus within the Jesuit order, to observe that "Catholicism is a paradoxical holdout" in which the Jesuits are "caught" in its "crosscurrents," leaving the Jesuits "searching for corporate purpose."[91] The uncertainty of the Jesuits is described in terms of "lack of conviction about once solid moral verities" and "outreach polarization between defenders of a return to the old code and advocates of reform."[92] The claim of the Jesuits to be countercultural has neither increased their numbers nor "contributed to the coherence of the Society. But it has kept the order from extinction by way of assimilation, and a semblance of distinctiveness has been maintained."[93] The author of *Men Astutely Trained* is simply rehearsing a thesis he defended a decade earlier, when he showed how the rise of the laity had thrown the Jesuits and the clerical state into turmoil. For instance, McDonough then argued, "Jesuits worked themselves out of a leadership role in education by training generations of laypeople who eventually surpassed them and whose offspring, with wider options available, no longer sought the expertise of Jesuits in such numbers."[94]

McDonough's thesis basically repeats what is traditionally said about the causes of the suppression of the Jesuits in the eighteenth century—that Pascal, Diderot, and other philosophers whom the Jesuits had trained, the argument goes, had outperformed them. The children of Jesuit modernism basically killed the father/mother for not being modern or, in this case, rationalist enough. "The crushing blow was the Enlightenment," William Bangert argues, "personified in Locke, Diderot, Hume, and Voltaire—Voltaire and Diderot were Jesuit educated." All of them, Peter Gay confirms, were part of "modern paganism," which, as Raymond A. Schroth noted, "swelled to flood tide the waters that swept away the old order."[95] And, as Schroth concludes, "overly reliant on the Greek and Roman classics in their humanities classes, the Jesuits did not teach their students to write their own vernacular languages well. Pupils untrained to write a good letter were ill-prepared to defend the faith."[96]

Schroth's thesis is not only Protestant-oriented, suggesting that the translation into the vernacular—as Protestants did—could have saved the Jesuits from suppression, but it also questions the efficacy of the Jesuits as a counterreformation movement when they pushed back against the Protestants in the sixteenth and seventeenth centuries. Additionally, Schroth hints to a valid argument for the sake of this book. Maybe, he suggests, too much erudition might have forgotten about the defense of faith.

The concept of "defense of faith" enshrined in the Formula of the Institute and repeated in different forms during the last General Congregations of the Jesuits might not actually help depart from erudition. It can simply be primarily intellectual, a *disputatio*, recycling the counterreformation thesis imbedded in Jesuit historiography. It further reinforces the rationalizing paradigm and logically leads to the conclusion that the Jesuits might have been suppressed for their lack of philosophy, reason, and argument. Fathers of the modern mind, they had become obscurantists.

Even in its suppression, it is the rationalist thesis that seems to prevail. However, the history of the suppression of the Jesuits studied in this chapter is the most likely either to support the rationalist thesis, as Schroth does, or to expose its limits. Concerning the limits of Jesuit rationalism, if the Society had been suppressed because it failed to adjust to the Enlightenment, it might well be because the Society was something else, not necessarily uniform, but beyond the established paradigms. The Society was and has always been a river in between a world beyond reason. This world is Jesuit mysticism and its intellectual and sociopolitical incarnations in this world. As the Rationalists rejected the unseen and unverifiable aspects of Jesuit mysticism, so did the Jansenists and the Indians who, respectively, rejected what they perceived as the Jesuits' abject secularity and the lack of miraculous performances in their ministries.

The trials of suppression took place in the middle of that transition, and those with greater political power won the battle to enforce their own logic. As fortunes were reversed with the failures of the revolutions and the old regime regained steam, so did the prospect of the restoration of the Society. The restoration was not a mere return of the medieval or prerevolutionary era; it was postrevolutionary. And rather than being a simple reaction, the restoration was an alternative to the excesses of the revolutions, welcomed by some, and unwelcomed by others.

Thus resulted the ambiguous reaction of the founding fathers of the United States and the raison d'être of the American century in the church and its future. The multiculturalism of the United States and its ability to accommodate the opposites, the universal and the local, made it home to a pluralistic and diverse Society not unlike that already noted in the above-mentioned quotation from "Jesuit Schools in the U.S.A."[97] and the nationalities listed in the Jesuit Formula of 1539. That medieval vision was implemented in the nineteenth-century United States. Therefore, only in the United States and similar pluralistic societies, such as the African ones, could the ambiguities of the Society coexist without breaking apart the church or the Society. The Society thrives in pluralistic societies and shrinks in places where monolithic systems dominate or are in the process of being created.

If the Society helped create the world of Diderot and Voltaire, and if the same world of philosophers rejected her to death, it was not because the Society was by its very nature anti-philosophy or anti-science or anti-reason. It was, instead, because the philosophical system of Enlightenment thought was in the process of becoming total with Reason, as they understood it, as the only goddess acceptable. Recent historiographies have effectively confirmed the strength of the Jesuits in science and astronomy. If they were suppressed, it was because, like Galileo, the Jesuits claimed that they could be ambiguous, both scientists and believers at the same time. The same thing that condemned Galileo at a time of ecclesiastical monopoly and intolerance now suppressed the Jesuits at a time of the monopoly and paradoxical intolerance of Reason.

At this point, what had been the strength of the Society across cultures had become a liability. Their language of faith, mysticism, and holiness was mere obscurantism for Enlightened philosophers and governments. They did not lack science, or reason, or accommodation. Their mysticism had become the problem. In fact, once the pious Jansenists had helped the philosophers suppress the Jesuits, the same system turned on them with the same ferocity. Emboldened by the Synod of Pistoia (1791), the Jansenists were condemned by Pope Pius VI three years later (1794).[98] In this condemnation, as in the suppression of the Jesuits, it was a matter not only of the adequacy, or lack of it, between the claim to universalism by the Ultramontanes and the defense of national churches by the Gallicans and their Jansenists allies, but also a struggle between faith as a lived experience and Reason. In the choice between totalitarianism and liberalism, despite the latter's shortcomings, many American Jesuits, including John LaFarge, in the mid-twentieth century, with its inclinations toward fascism, chose liberalism. It was, one might say, a matter of the survival of their order.

5

HABEMUS PAPAM!

"So," my grandmother shouted when her granddaughter handed her the phone, "*Habemus Papam!*" She was celebrating, as were many newspapers around the world, the election of Jorge Bergoglio, SJ, as the new Roman Pontiff. This was not the first time my grandmother had addressed her grandson, now a Jesuit priest, in Latin. I was barely seven years old when, working as a domestic catechist, she taught me the Latin version of the Lord's Prayer: *Pater Noster*! She did not understand all the declensions of Cicero herself, but was convinced that, one day, I would grasp the meaning of the Lord's Prayer on my own. In gratitude for this beautiful lesson, and mindful of the presence of the Gregorian choir that had sung the *Kyrie*, I resolved, at my first Mass after ordination, to pray the *Pater Noster* in Latin. All sang in unison, showing as much devotion as they did with the entrance hymn and the Gloria, all performed in the Ewondo language.

Here, in this very Catholic region of central Cameroon, the region of uncle Joseph, Latin, like English, French, or Ewondo, does not cause division. The languages are skillfully linked in the same celebration. In fact, they add to the rich religious experience of the community.

After her Latin greeting, *Habemus papam*, my grandmother told me that she had learned that the new pope was Black: "What country, what nationality was he from?" She had gotten the information about the pontiff's supposedly Black identity from another

147

grandson who teaches at the local Catholic school. The latter would have communicated it himself to the granddaughter, who owned the telephone. It was she who finally brought the great news to her grandmother before passing the phone to her. In this chain of information and misinformation, the grandmother and her grandchildren were living globalization in their own way.

The rumors that shaped their understanding of the identity of the new pope had had even more weight during this conclave, as the names of African cardinals were circulating in the media as being *papabile*: Tuckson, Arinze, Monsengwo, and even our local Tumi, son of Cameroon. In a village in which we only vote for the people we know—what a democracy!—the vote of the grandmother and other villagers at the conclave was therefore clear: the pope had to be Black.

The villagers were not totally wrong about their appreciation of the identity of the new pope. Bergoglio, who came all the way from Argentina, was "black" in his own way. He is a Jesuit; and the history of the Jesuits is varnished with all sorts of rumors, legends, and conspiracies. These "stories" were able to establish, as historical truth, that the Superior General of the Jesuits, who was often dressed in black and whose office is just a few leagues from that of the one and only true pope, was a "black pope." This legend had a thick skin. Its latest victim was Father Pedro Arrupe, the Superior General who, in 1973, had appointed Bergoglio as provincial of the Jesuits in Argentina, and whose charisma soon came into competition with that of the popular "white pope," John Paul II. If the Superior General of the Jesuits could be a black pope, even more so a Jesuit pope dressed in white, the first in the history of Roman Catholicism.

Arrupe and Bergoglio represent the face of the new Society of Jesus, the one that arose from the Second Vatican Council. It is the church of the aggiornamento, the church of the crisis of religious life in the West, the church of liberation theology, and finally, the church of the South: Latin America, Africa, and Asia.

At the time of Bergoglio's birth, all these regions were part of the nonaligned bloc. They were regarded, and still are, as underdeveloped and/or developing countries. Their economic and technological backwardness had once placed them in the column of peoples to be civilized and evangelized. Today, through this election, the church of the missions has simply become the church. It is in the context of this transition from a missionary church to the center of Christianity that the contemporary African Society was conceived. It is in the context of these demographic shifts that we must also understand that there are two "black popes" in Rome, Bergoglio, but also the first South American to be Superior General of the Jesuits, Arturo Sosa. The latter, it is well known, would not use the concept of "black pope" even for a joke.[1] Both are from Latin America, that is, beyond the color of their skin, they are black! —soldiers of a certain theology of liberation.

FROM THE 31ST GENERAL CONGREGATION TO THE ELECTION OF KOLVENBACH

Pope Pius XI (r. 1922–1939) found in Superior General Wladimir Ledochowski a privileged interlocutor. Concomitantly, Pietro Tacchi Venturi (1861–1956) served as an intermediary between the Jesuits and the Mussolini government and was one of the architects of the 1929 Concordat known as the Lateran Accords. Pius XI, assisted by another Jesuit, John LaFarge, wrote an encyclical against racism that never saw the light of day. His successor, Pius XII, found in Jean-Baptiste Janssens a Jesuit Superior General who was not especially enthused by the Jesuit progressivism that was emerging in France during World War II. During his term as the head of the Jesuit order, prominent theologians were sidelined. Janssens remained equally discreet during the tribulations of Pierre Teilhard de Chardin. Such ideological closeness was certainly lacking in Paul VI and later in John Paul II in their respective relationships with Pedro Arrupe.

Paul VI and Arrupe

When Father Janssens died on October 5, 1964, the 31st General Congregation of the Jesuits elected Pedro Arrupe as his successor on May 6, 1965. Celebrated amid the Second Vatican Council and, like the council and for the first time in the history of the Society, this General Congregation was held in two sessions.

After his election, Arrupe made his first trip to Africa and then to the Middle East. When the cardinals gathered in conclave elected Paul VI to the See of Saint Peter, there was great hope among Jesuits that this former student of the Gregorian University would at least continue the détente that had characterized several pontificates, including the latest of John XXIII. One could even hope for better relations with the Society. Promises kept, some thought; total incomprehension, others concluded.

The Jesuits immediately realized that Paul VI came to the papacy with a rather militaristic understanding of their order. He also understood the council in terms less progressive than that of Arrupe and the general congregation that had elected him. If both personalities remained on the same page about their African policy, the initial very enthusiastic tone did not deceive all Jesuits. To the delegates of the 31st General Congregation, the pope's first speech was militant and full of uncomfortable superlatives. The Society and its members were presented as "soldiers of Christ," "army," and "squadron" of the Holy See. The Society would help the Vatican in the "battle," mainly against atheism, which it would seek out in its own "strongholds," until the "final victory." As a true general of this army, the pope reminded the delegates insistently of the fourth vow and the intimacy that bound the Institute and its members to the person of the pope.

For the first time in history, the pope received all the delegates in the Sistine Chapel, where he warned them in a serious tone that the necessary postconciliar aggiornamento should not change either the spirit or the norms of the Institute. Therefore, he said, the Society should be itself, and not fall into (a harsh word for Jesuits) "laxity." This was the eternal Jansenist accusation against the Jesuits![2]

In 1966, the draft of the speech Arrupe received from the Secretary of State, Agostino Casaroli (1914–1998), was more explicit about the main problems the pope wanted the Society to reflect on: (1) a poor interior life and a complacent observance of its rules could neither protect nor promote the order; (2) the abandonment of external discipline and the complacency of superiors to remedy it; (3) the doctrinal crisis and the practice of religious obedience; and (4) a certain secularizing mentality and lack of appreciation of specifically religious values. To each of these evils, the pope also offered insight into the damage they would do to the church and the people of God and offered solutions fresh from *Perfectae caritatis*, *Lumen gentium*, and *Presbyterorum ordinis*. As a good diplomat, he was already bringing the Society into line on what the interpretation of the council and the Society's loyalty to the Apostolic See should be.

The increasing rift between the Vatican and the Jesuit curia grew in the context of an emerging crisis in Spain. In 1966, some *postulata* from Spain had asked for a report on the state of the Society. A group of Jesuits present at the Congress and Days on the Spiritual Exercises at Loyola (August 7, 1966) also sent a letter to the delegates of the 31st General Congregation in which they decried the alarming number of dismissals among the Jesuits. Their analysis of the situation of the Jesuits could not be more similar to that of the Vatican. According to these restless Spanish Jesuits, the cause of these departures was the degradation of community life and prayer life, the growing and unannounced criticism of any opinion of the superior, the reigning worldliness, the disorientation of young Jesuits, especially in houses of formation, that seriously marred the image of the Society. All this was also due to the lack of authority and personality of the superiors who, wanting to please, knelt before the young people and gave in to their slightest wishes, while marginalizing the priests with some experience. The authors of this letter concluded that they were willing to make any sacrifice so that "our Society could return to its former glory."[3]

Urbano Valero narrates that three years later in 1969, when he was provincial of Castile, a professor from the Jesuit-run Comillas Pontifical University who had taught him and with whom he maintained cordial relations asked him if he did not think that Arrupe was leading the Society to its destruction. The professor added that something was being prepared with the support of the provincial of Toledo, Luis González, which would soon become known.[4] Priests had gathered with González's approval and, in a letter dated February 8, 1969, they offered a litany of evils facing the Society. To remedy them, they proposed the creation of reformed Jesuit communities directly under the supervision of the Superior General. To maintain the original spirit of the order, these communities would have the right to admit their own novices and to train scholastics until their final incorporation into the Society. This was the Vera Compañía, a "Parallel Society, a Society of the Future."[5] A copy of the letter was sent to the pope, who soon alerted Spain's Conference of Catholic Bishops.

In 1970, the president of Spain's Conference of Catholic Bishops, Casimiro Morcillo, also archbishop of Madrid, included the situation of the Society in Spain in the agenda of their assembly. The pope had drawn his attention to its alarming situation based on information he had received from respectable Jesuits in Spain. On November 17, he had asked the Spanish bishops for their opinion on this reform project. The archbishop seemed to suggest that the creation of a province specific to this group could advance the reform of the Society. Forty-eight bishops out of seventy voted in favor. Cardinal Vincente Enrique y Tarancón told Father Valero that the bishops wanted to clean up the Society and were thinking of the Carmelite model of Teresa of Jesus in the sixteenth century. Archbishop Morcillo supported the initiative.[6]

Cardinal Tarancón, who was primate of Spain, vice-president of the Conference, and archbishop of Toledo, intervened and asked the pope to help preserve the unity of the Society in Spain. The implications of a Jesuit schism, he believed, would be unforeseeable for the unity of the church. Only later, in 1994, did he admit that about one hundred Jesuits were behind the affair and that this same group was opposed to the Council. These tensions between the Society and the Holy See and within the Society itself had not been diffused at the time of the 32nd General Congregation (GC).[7]

The 32nd General Congregation

The tension remained constant until GC 32. As a result, the pope asked Cardinal Villot to oversee the process. Speaking on behalf of the pope (April 18, 1972), Villot confirmed the date of the GC and informed Arrupe of the Holy Father's wish that "all tendencies" be represented in the congregation to maintain the spirit and rules of the Society. On February 15, 1973, the Holy See again expressed its unease about the crisis in the Society. But on July 2, Villot informed Arrupe that the Holy See believed in the Society and its ability to overcome this crisis for which the Vatican held Arrupe personally responsible.[8]

On April 8, 1973, when he convened the congregation, Arrupe was received by the pope. In a handwritten note, the pope told Arrupe to understand the importance of this congregation for the survival of the Society and for the impact on religious life in general and on the church. He added, however, that he believed in the Society and in its capacity for reform. At the opening of the Congregation, the pope directly questioned the Jesuits on their own identity and what was becoming of it: "Where do you come from? Who are you? Where are you going?"[9] He was concerned about some of the *postulata* pertaining to the possible extension of the fourth vow to all Jesuits, including the Jesuit brothers. On December 3, 1974, Cardinal Villot reiterated that the Society should not deviate from the nature of its Institute in its efforts toward aggiornamento, and that the Holy See would not approve any reform of the vows as inscribed in the Formula.

The Crisis of 1981–1983

On August 6, 1978, Pope Paul VI died. John Paul II was elected two months later, after the brief pontificate of John Paul I. Some cardinals surrounding the new pontiff, including Agostino Casaroli and Giovanni Benelli, had closely followed the Spanish question and the tense relations between Paul VI and Arrupe, including GC 32. Now they had become influential around John Paul II, who had appointed Casaroli to succeed Villot as Secretary of State.

Things were not close to improving between Arrupe and the new pope. Since the 1970s, Latin America had become a cold war battleground in which the church, through liberation theology, was heavily involved. The Society of Jesus played too ambiguous a role for the liking of John Paul II, whose Polish origins did not allow for any ambiguity in the face of communism. From his description of the positions of John Paul II and Arrupe, Kolvenbach states,

> John Paul II affirmed that the struggle for justice is not sufficient if it focuses primarily on unjust structures; it must also be at the service of charity and conditioned by it....Arrupe, on the other hand, emphasizes first of all that not all charity is in itself authentic. Charity can be false and superficial and, as such, can constitute a

camouflaged injustice when one gives to a person by benevolence what is due to him by right.[10]

It should also be remembered that when Arrupe was elected in 1965, Europeans found his government very Americanized. He himself had been to the United States, and three out of four of his assistants *ad providentiam* were Americans (2) or residents of the United States (1). Among them was Vincent O'Keefe, the former president of Fordham University. While Americanism might not have had the same connotation as it did in the eighteenth or nineteenth centuries, from the 1940s it had become synonymous with Protestant liberalism and moral laxity. In some places, including Chad, Americanism was also the symbol of the loss of European political and religious monopoly in some regions. There was obviously a new king in town thanks to his mastery of mass communication and a religious and moral agenda that, for some in the Vatican, was more than suspicious.

Arrupe had sensed that the pope was distant, and on September 21, 1979, when he was received by John Paul II, the pope told him bluntly that he was fully aware of the state of the Society and that it was disorienting the people of God and causing great concern at the level of the hierarchy. He urged the Superior General to do everything possible to help the Jesuits rediscover their vocation. The pope was also taking up the spirit of the speech his predecessor wanted to give to the Society's procurators gathered in Rome on November 30, 1978. This speech, according to Vincent O'Keefe, was written by Paolo Dezza.[11]

Arrupe was already frustrated by these repeated rebukes, and then another surprise came from across the Atlantic. John McNeil, an American Jesuit, published his book *The Church and Homosexuality*, in which the author spoke of his own personal journey. This was too much for the Vatican. On January 3, 1980, Arrupe was received by the pope and realized that communication was not going well with the Holy Father. On leaving, Arrupe informed his assistants *ad providentiam*—Jean-Yves Calvez, Permananda Divarkar, Cecil McGarry, and Vincent O'Keefe—of his desire to resign his office. They agreed that fatigue, illness, and age were the reasons for his decision. As he informed the pope of his wish to convene a General Congregation, Arrupe was told that his resignation was not opportune.

When Arrupe suffered a brain hemorrhage on August 7, 1981, it became clear that he could not fully recover. The designated vicar was O'Keefe. On October 6, John Paul II informed the vicar that he could not convene a GC for the election of the general until he had personally approved it, and that he had decided to appoint his own delegate to carry out the tasks the Society reserved for the vicar general in such circumstances. He chose Paolo Dezza as Vicar, with Giuseppe Pittau, then Provincial of Japan, as his assistant.

GC 33 convened on September 1, 1983, and the pope, rather than receiving the delegates at Castel Gandolfo as originally planned, made his intervention at the Jesuit Roman Curia in the very aula of the General Congregation. He concelebrated the Eucharist with the delegates before delivering his speech. Eleven days later, on September 3, 1983, Peter Hans Kolvenbach was elected as the twenty-ninth Superior General of the Society. It was a vote in favor of a return to normalization of relations with the Holy See.[12]

Kolvenbach succeeded in normalizing relations with the Holy See. Above all, he carried out a work of aggiornamento of the Society. Arrupe was the ideological new founder, the one who knew how to rearticulate for the Society the faith-justice tension for modern times. Kolvenbach, however, was the last Roothaan, the one who, in the spirit of aggiornamento advocated by the Second Vatican Council, went back to the sources of the Society to update it in the postconciliar context.

For Kolvenbach, and following Arrupe, being a Jesuit involved a certain mysticism. It was a journey "From La Storta"[13] by which the Jesuit knew how to be crazy for Christ,[14] and from there to be with and for others.[15] He restructured the entire formation of the Society,[16] always maintaining a tension between mysticism and action, and with an extraordinary capacity to interpret the signs of the times. He took it upon himself to clarify but also to encourage and renew the intellectual apostolate of the Jesuits.[17] In a context of vocational crisis, especially in the West, Kolvenbach elaborated on the importance of collaborators in the mission of the Society,[18] both among Ignatian families and with other congregations and Christian and non-Christian confessions.[19] Having resigned as

Superior General in 2008, he retired as a librarian in Beirut where he passed away on November 26, 2016.

ADOLFO NICOLÁS AND THE DIALOGUE OF CULTURES

It was Sunday, January 20, 2008, in the Church of the Gesù in Rome. Father Adolfo Nicolás stood up and, after reading the Gospel, he closed the lectionary and began what he called a "simple homily":

The newspapers and magazines of the last few days have taken up a lot of clichés: the black Pope, the white Pope, the power, the meetings, the discussions….But all this is superficial, unreal! It feeds those who love politics, but not us. Isaiah says: to serve pleases God. It is service that counts. Serving the Church, serving the world, serving people, serving the Gospel.[20]

If this homily showed that the conspiracy of the parallel pontiff—which makes the Jesuits themselves so uncomfortable—was far from disappearing from the imagination of a certain public, it also set the tone of a short generalate, but one that is so important for understanding the mission of the Society in the world today. The new Superior General was full of humor, disarmingly simple. He also knew how to go straight to the point, without ambiguity.

In this short homily, he already redefined the new frontiers of the mission, namely, the poor, the excluded, and the marginalized, who were steadily increasing in this globalized world. The new frontier of the Society's mission was among all those who found themselves in disadvantaged situations: "all these are, perhaps for us, the new nations, the nations that need prophets, the message of God."[21] It was these same poor who should define the terms of collaboration. Non-Jesuits, on the one hand, would be their collaborators if they shared the Jesuit perspective on the poor, "if they have the same heart that Jesus gave us." Jesuits, on the other hand, were to be collaborators of others if the latter had a much bigger heart.[22]

Nicolás spoke of a globalized world that he knew well. He was formed in the mold of this world. He also understood its Jesuit perspective from the inside and knew how to speak about it with depth. Born in 1936 in Villamuriel de Cerrato, Spain, he made his novitiate there from 1953 to 1955. He then studied philosophy in Alcalá de Henares and theology in Tokyo from 1964 to 1968. He was ordained a priest in Tokyo in 1967. Between 1968 and 1971, Nicolás did his doctoral studies in theology at the Gregorian University in Rome. His thesis was on the theology of progress. At the end of his thesis, he was sent to Sophia University in Tokyo to teach systematic theology. He then directed the Pastoral Institute in Manila, Philippines, from 1978 to 1984. Back in Japan, he became rector of the Jesuit Student House in Tokyo in 1991 and superior of the Jesuit Province of Japan in 1993.[23]

It was in this capacity as Major Superior of Japan that Nicolás took part in the 34th General Congregation. Together with General Kolvenbach and other experienced Jesuits, he was part of the *Coetius praevius officialis*, the committee in charge of the immediate preparation of the said congregation. His peer delegates from other provinces and regions of the world later elected him Secretary General of the General Congregation.[24] This role gave him first-hand experience in managing such a complex gathering. Above all, it allowed him to develop his ability to find consensus in the preparation and approval of complex documents.

At the end of his term as provincial of Japan, Nicolás worked as a pastor in a poor immigrant parish in Tokyo, ministering to Filipinos and other Asian migrants in Japan. In 2004, he was appointed moderator of the Jesuit Conference of East Asia and Oceania, with the task of coordinating the work of Jesuit provinces and regions from Myanmar to East Timor, and from Australia to Japan. It was in this capacity that he participated in the 35th General Congregation. Once again, a member of his *Coetius praevius officialis*, he was then elected as Superior General of the Jesuits, a task he carried out until 2016,[25] thereby spending his last three years in office under a Jesuit pontiff, a first in history.

Nicolás resigned to retire to the Philippines. He died there on May 20, 2020, at the age of eighty-four. His extraordinary journey is an indication of how a Superior General is prepared in the new Society. Arrupe, Kolvenbach, and Nicolás were Europeans by birth, Asians by culture, where they worked as missionaries. They also had great experience of government in their places of mission, with some knowledge of the central government of the Society that they served as provincial, rector of a major house, or through their participation in the General Congregations of the order.

Elected at the age of seventy-two, Nicolás brought to his office a global vision of the Society. He committed the Jesuits to using their universality to carry out a profound dialogue of cultures. His starting point was Asia, where he had worked. The characteristic of Asian spiritualities, he repeated, is to seek the way, the path to a more spiritual life that seemed detached from this-worldly concerns. The Westerners, his ancestors, who had served as missionaries in Asian lands had, however, insisted on the search for objective truth, the rationalism that had become their main philosophical concern since the Middle Ages. In trying to impose this model not only on the Asians but also on the Africans, the missionaries had not always preached the totality of Christ, who is not only the Way, but also the Truth and the Life. It was this last element that Nicolás discovered as essential to African spirituality. This was also Africa's main contribution to the Society and to humanity:

> The world needs Africa, and the Society needs Africa…. It is not only because we have more vocations; it is the very series and cumulative effect of all its traditions, values, people's lives, ability to overcome conflicts and difficulties and so on. It is an immense treasure that the world cannot do without.[26]

Our global world, Nicolás thought, needs all three, that is, the Way, the Truth, and the Life. And in a context of demographic shifts within the church and the Society, Nicolás reflected further on Africa, whose values he presented as necessary for the church and the Society. Edward W. Blyden had spoken in his time of Africa as a spiritual reserve of humanity.[27] Pope Benedict XVI, so close to the Jesuits and to Nicolás, confirmed this when he spoke of Africa as the spiritual lung of humanity.[28] For Nicolás, part of this spiritual reserve was the ability of Africans to cope with and overcome difficulties with grace. The African spirituality of life finds a parallel in the ancient tradition of the Society to pray for a good death and to journey with those who are on the threshold of death. Writing in the middle of the COVID-19 pandemic, Sosa also recalled Africa's life-giving-and-strengthening spirituality.

THE JESUIT ETHOS IN THE FACE OF THE PANDEMIC

In John's Gospel, the question "How is this possible?" is a turning point in Jesus's nighttime conversation with Nicodemus. It is also symbolic of the necessary condition for the passage from the old to the new. In the loneliness of a struggling soul, darkness is often the only companion and communication with God often the only way out. Africans eat at night; they travel at night; and they converse a great deal at night, either to tell the story of their people or to strategize about their future, or simply to deliberate on the most burning issues facing the people and challenging their hopes: issues of war, health, death.

On December 30, 1918, writing from Ginahabar, India, the Belgian Jesuit Van den Driessche expressed relief and satisfaction at the conclusion of the armistice ending World War I. However, he also informed his provincial that the Spanish flu had claimed many of his Christian friends. For almost two months, he wrote, there were sick and dying people everywhere. Because of the difficulty of communication, the medicines arrived very late and were insufficient, given the large number of sick people. Many people had died without receiving the last rites.[29]

From Lemfu, Kongo, Father Joseph Opdebeek observed the same devastating impact of the pandemic on the population. It had entered the country through explorers, since the first to be affected in Europe were postal workers. The spread of the pandemic in Kongo then followed the railroad, and its impact was compounded by a severe drought that caused famine and death among the African population.[30] An estimated 1.9 to 2.3 million Africans died of the Spanish flu, including about 300,000 in the Belgian Congo alone and 100,000 in Ghana. In the city of Kinshasa alone, Father Opdebeek writes, twenty to thirty black men died each day. And although some Europeans were infected, none of them died. In the Union of South Africa alone, between 250,000 and 350,000 people, out of a population of 6.1 million in 1918, had died from the pandemic.[31]

Most disturbing to the missionaries was the impression among African Christians that they might have caused the tragedy. They had worked hard to build farms and bridges,[32] create new villages,[33] and establish seminaries.[34] By the turn of the century, Kongo missionaries had come to believe that mission was no longer limited to the chapel or the school; it extended to the hospital.[35] Moreover, "the soul could not be healthy if its vehicle, the body, was damaged."[36] Now, in the middle of the pandemic, they had to face the distrust of the people they intended to help, leading one missionary to wonder if Africans were heartless.[37] This feeling was not new. In Kimwenza (Kongo) in 1902, during the trypano-somiasis epidemic, Father De Vos witnessed the death of many of his new converts. He felt betrayed as they ran away from him. It was a harrowing experience for him to bury children every day whom he had barely christianized and who represented hope for the future. He ran around the country consoling and encouraging the survivors. At the end of the long and painful road, exhausted, he often found only ruins. Those he was looking for among the living were dead, or they had fled to the railroad for fear of the solitude. The missionary continued this life for eight years, going at fixed hours to visit the chapels of the dying farms, as if they were still full of life, always caring with the same devotion for the poor sick whom he knew he could not cure.[38]

The first half of the twentieth century was the scene of a series of tragedies, from the Russian flu (1890s) to the Spanish flu (1920s) and, in its midst, the First World War (1914–1918). Yet, as Elizabeth Outka has recently demonstrated, most of the literature of the interwar period focused on the war and less on the flu, which is estimated to have claimed between 50 and 100 million victims. In the final chapter of the book "Spiritualism, Zombies, and the Return of the Dead," Outka analyzes how the pandemic was experienced in popular culture, particularly among those concerned with resurrection. Instead of being a source of solace, she argues, these images represented "bodily states ranging from delirium to hallucinations; a sense of living death; emotional representations of loss, fear, and guilt; and the biological realities of viral replication."[39]

The prevalence of death by virus, viral death, created an environment for the emergence of a religiosity of spiritualism, zombies, and the belief in the return of the dead. This religiosity focused on ectoplasm and spirit photography, "providing physical evidence of a loved one's presence in a way that helps to negate the unique burden of the pandemic, namely, helplessness."[40] Zombies, spiritualism, and the return of the dead had an obvious eschatological purpose. There was also an Ignatian connection in the concept of "threatening consolation." Also, African religiosity would feel comfortable with it because of its voodoo background and the cohabitation between the living and the dead in African traditional religiosity.

Speaking of eschatology, the Jesuit theologian Karl Rahner defines it as the doctrine on the last things. It is also the doctrine about the human person insofar as he/she is a being open to the absolute future of God.[41] Eschatology is therefore fundamentally a doctrine of hope, of fulfillment. Catholics understand the resurrection of the body as the fulfillment of the concrete person in their corporality, the ultimate validation by God of their temporality, the becoming-God-of-humans.[42] The viral nature of the "last things" as described by Outka, and its connection with zombieism and spiritualism, raises the question of this ultimate hope, not fear, of the divinization of humans that Christian resurrection implies.

The fact that the pandemic was viral accentuated the emptiness caused by the absence of the body amid the overflow of bodies found after the war. To this emptiness should also be added the powerlessness of doctors to cure the disease. In addition, the doctors had to face the growing suspicion of the friends and family members of the victims, who also found it difficult to understand this new form of bodily presence with their deceased. According to Outka, both zombieism and spiritualism were intended to address the same issue, namely, the sense of helplessness and guilt felt by medical personnel and the general public during the pandemic.[43] On the one hand, "the dead arrived in living rooms, stood just behind the shoulders of family members, walked from battlefields to villages, rose from cemeteries to enter domestic spaces." On the other hand, and in this context of despair, "spiritualism created life-giving doctor figures who counterbalanced the anguish of those who were unable to stop the spread of the virus. While the

161

zombies provided an outlet for repressed fury at the doctors who had failed to contain the destruction…one denied the threat by declaring that his victims were living happily; the other materialized an invisible threat but then safely repressed it."[44]

Outka uniquely employs the concept of "threatening consolation," a cathartic experience provoked by the emergence of zombie figures and their cinematic representations. Zombies "are uncontrolled, reanimated corpses that hunt humans and hunger for their flesh."[45] They often seem to have no compassion for a victim doctor who, the sicker they are, the more like a zombie they become. How, then, can the zombie be a source of consolation?

Ignatius of Loyola made a distinction between consolation and desolation. Consolation, he said, inflames the heart with joy, with much love and desire, moving it to more good and empathy.[46] In a sense, eschatological fulfillment is the ultimate consolation. The experience of desolation simply does the opposite, saddening the heart and making it lukewarm and less desirous of giving greater love and service.[47] Both consolation and desolation are deeply connected to the body. On the one hand, all Ignatian prayer assumes that the body is an essential part, the necessary link of the one who prays with the world around him or her. The body, says Maurice Giuliani, cannot be ignored without creating a deeper rupture between the one who prays and God.[48] In the same way, in moments of desolation, the one who makes the Spiritual Exercises is invited to a greater penitence. The body is the place of the deteriorating manifestations of desolation and the necessary condition for penance, its remedy.[49]

Consolation also appears in Ignatius's letters as bringing "comfort" to a struggling soul.[50] Teresa Rejadell, a Benedictine nun from the convent of Santa Clara in Barcelona, was struggling with scruples and asked Ignatius for advice. In response, Ignatius gave her a detailed description of the "enemy of human nature" that attacks delicate souls, causing confusion and persuading them to have a poor humility and an excessive fear of God.[51] God, on the contrary, "gives interior consolation." And "with this divine consolation, every trial is a pleasure, every toil is a rest." Consolation and desolation, however, are never separate.[52]

The terrifying nature of the mysterious presence of zombies and the spiritualism that convinces doctors that all is well are two sides of the same spiritual experience of God and godlessness, emptiness and fullness, despair and hope. In Ignatius, both consolation and desolation are the reality of an awakening soul, the constant struggle of the human person's spiritual journey toward God and eternity—eternity being, according to Karl Rahner, more a "mode of spiritual freedom exercised in time" than pure timelessness. It is the validation of a life resolutely turned toward God, love, and service in absolute obedience to the higher law. Eternity is the ultimate "last thing," the fulfillment of human existence. Here, a "person truly discovers his true self in an authentic act of self-realization if he radically risks himself for another,"[53] if the person loses his or her life for a greater purpose.

THE JESUIT ETHOS IN THE FACE OF PERSECUTION AND SUFFERING

In 1875, a man approached Father Vito Carrozzini (1839–1877) and asked him, "Are you the local Catholic priest?" "I am," Carrozzini replied. "Can I do something for you?" "From what I heard," the man said, "you insulted me and my family this morning in your sermon." "Sir," the priest replied, "I don't have the pleasure of knowing you or your family, not even your name." "Yet you have insulted me," replied the other, and as he said this, he struck him two heavy punches in the face and gave him two vigorous kicks. "Thank you, sir," the priest groaned, and without another word, he withdrew, offering everything to God.[54]

The fact that Father Carrozzini thanked his attacker reflects a very Ignatian grace—to be asked, of course—in responding to humiliation and opprobrium. It was a way to identify with the suffering Christ whom Carrozzini had vowed to serve. Moreover, Vito was a man of deep faith, a man of prayer. He had lived his religious life with great zeal even though "sufferings and trials of all kinds came his way." Yet he considered these daily privations his daily bread, with "the salvation of souls as his great goal; prayer, and especially the Holy Sacrifice of the Mass, his strength and support."[55] He died a few years later, in 1877, at the age of thirty-nine, after having spent twenty years in the service of his Lord and Savior.

The initial question, "Are you the local Catholic priest?," and the resulting aggression reflected the growing tensions between Catholics and Protestants in America in the late nineteenth century. The number of Catholic converts was growing, and they were increasingly seen as a threat to the dominant religion.[56] From being a minority religion in the United States at the turn of the century, Catholics became the largest Christian denomination by the 1850s, with 1.5 million members. That number doubled to 3 million a decade later.[57]

The cost of the crisis on the Jesuits was high, and, as part of their coping strategy, some Jesuits disguised themselves and assumed pseudonyms to escape death. Historians have often pointed out that these religious tensions, including among the Jesuits themselves, were related to the issue of slavery, its morality, and its biblical justification.[58] A competing literature on Jesuits and slavery had emerged by the turn of the nineteenth century. From Joseph M. Finotti's exaltation of Saint Peter Claver's work on behalf of Black slaves,[59] to John R. Slattery's biography of Claver the Apostle to the Negroes,[60] Jesuits seemed to have shown a strong interest in Blacks well into the twentieth century.

A 1937 editorial in the newsletter *Jesuit Missions* was a clear manifestation of the growing Jesuit concern for the cause of people of color in the United States. The Jesuit newsletter recognized that the Indians had been pushed in many cases onto reservations that had little fertile soil, even if there was much natural beauty. In such an environment, the Indians could hardly live, let alone improve their living conditions.[61] In the same vein, the Jesuits expressed "the urgent need to take their condition to heart and to provide them with the light of the true teaching of Jesus Christ."[62]

This Jesuit program for Blacks and Indians unfortunately went hand in hand with the practice of holding and trading slaves.[63] Understandably, scholars have long thought that Protestants were more likely to be abolitionists while Catholics were less likely to oppose slavery. The press and recent research on Georgetown University have reinforced this view. It also explains the joyous reaction of the American public when Pope Gregory XVI condemned the slave trade.[64] On the ground, however, there is evidence that the Jesuits had great sympathy for the Blacks, and that this sympathy had not always won them friends among the larger public. Working in Puerto Rico, Father Carrozzini gave "clear evidence of his zeal for the salvation of souls by the persevering care he took of the Negroes of the city."[65]

Moreover, the sacramental system of the Catholics proved very attractive during social tragedies. The story of the 1918 pandemic sheds new light on the interfaith reality of dealing with a disturbing, unpredictable, and invisible pandemic. As young people in the prime of life were confined to beds "racked with fever and choked with coughs," Catholic chaplains and their sacraments became rays of hope amid tragedy, not only for dying Catholics, but for all the dying sick and the nurses and doctors who cared for them and feared for their own lives:

> We found time for the Protestants who were clamoring for the priest and prepared many for a good death.... We were walking, so to speak, hand in hand with death, at the gates of eternity, but we felt that for the Catholic soldiers, at least, death was only the angel of God waiting for the signal to crown these young knights with the garland of victory. For some, the viaticum was their first communion, for others, it was the Master who arrived just in time to welcome them into the beatific vision. And their graces became graces for all those around them. Doctors and nurses marveled at the effects of the sacraments and, with mixed feelings of admiration and reverence, welcomed God's priest into their ward, knowing that his presence meant peace of mind and calm of soul for their feverish patients.[66]

The Protestant and Jewish nurses and doctors were the first to notice the added value of the Catholic priests who served as chaplains in the camp. They appreciated their courage during the pandemic and saw them as "heroes" on the battlefield. They represented and witnessed a religion that could overcome death:

> They realized that God was there, bringing light to the eyes of the dying and igniting hope in the breasts of the

dying; that Christ was still with his Church, continuing to do good—the comfort and even the joy of the afflicted, the sick and the dying. But they were not as keenly aware of this as we priests are.[67]

THE POETRY OF GRIEF IN AFRICA: THE WAY OF THE CROSS OF ENGELBERT MVENG

While the COVID-19 pandemic was raging, a Jesuit on mission lost his mother. He was unable to travel because of health restrictions. He could not be present to accompany her in her final days. In the tradition of his people, there is usually a ceremony nine days after the burial of the deceased. Her name is called. The food she loved is prepared and shared among children, grandchildren, and friends. She is expected to respond to the call, and the food is given to her through incantations and songs. This ceremony is a necessary step for the deceased to truly rest, instead of wandering around villages and houses, restless and without direction. This moment also gives the living a respite, assured that all the rituals have been respected, and that the deceased is welcomed among the ancestors. In this village, every old man and child understands the power of performance and ritual. Widows are dressed in black.

According to the late Cameroonian Jesuit Engelbert Mveng, the dark color was not synonymous with black. The symbolism of blackness was thus preserved. For black is not dark. The white, underlining his poetry, was a symbol of death; the black symbolized suffering; and red conveyed life. It was the combination of the three that represented African life, both historically and anthropologically. The purpose of Mveng's poetry, however, was to overcome death, historical trauma, and the consciousness of being miserable. There was a spiritual perspective in this poetry. His Stations of the Cross, *Si Quelqu'un…* ("If Someone") is drawn from the Bible. In his first station, Mveng takes up Jesus's invitation that anyone who wants to be his disciple must take up his cross and follow him (see Mark 8:34).[68]

The main artistic characteristics of *Si Quelqu'un…* are drawn from traditional Bamun art. The Bamun are a people of the Grassfields of Cameroon of which Mveng had a particular admiration. They are also a people of the mountains. And Cameroon, for Mveng, is first a mountain that stands at the top of the Atlantic Ocean, like a giant and fiery watchtower of the Atlantic coast of Africa. Its grandeur is therefore the symbol of an Africa that is always challenged, tested, but also an Africa that refuses to die. This mountain is the birthplace of the new Africa, freed from the chains of slavery, colonialism, and oppression, whose independence can force even the admiration of the colonists.[69]

Mveng's poetry is therefore not a romanticized poetry. It is a poetry rooted in history, which recognizes history and its overwhelming memory, but also a poetry raised by Christ who embraced it by taking human flesh, and restored it in his passion, death, and resurrection.

In this first station, Mveng opens with a universal forgiveness granted by Africa to all its tormentors: "You have taught me to forgive," opening on a litany of beatitudes. It is above all the perfect response that Africa gives to the tragedies of world history, "to the Jews in the crematoria, to the Negroes crushed by Apartheid." On all these victims and their executioners, "let the ocean of God's mercy come." In the second station, Jesus takes up his cross, made of the three most precious woods of Africa: iroko, okoume, and ebony. And this Suffering Jesus now has the face of a "brother" carrying with him the suffering of Africa but also the "wood of total life and forgiveness." The cross of Jesus becomes the sign of hope and patience for people who carry the hope of humanity because they have learned to be patient in times of trials.

Thus, Jesus could still fall in the third station, but the African poet sees this fall primarily as another friendly gesture. By falling, Jesus proves that only he can understand those who are constantly falling under the weight of their own sins and fatigue, or under the blows of a ruthless conqueror and oppressor. In this Jesus, the suffering African finds his strength, the strength of love made vulnerable and understanding. This love is confirmed by the Son's encounter with his mother in the fourth station. Mary is African. She bears on her flesh the marks of her race and her tragic history. She is there above all as a mother, to meet a son tired of the humiliation and opprobrium of the passion, to put her arm around his wounded shoulder and to encourage him to continue to advance in the procession of humanity in search of salvation. In the voice of Mary, Mveng hears the voice of all African mothers, the cry of those whose children are gone for good, sometimes without saying goodbye. In her, the orphans of Africa have found a loving and caring mother.

Some children of Africa had gone to America as slaves. Others left as adventurers to discover America before Columbus and contribute to its greatness.[70] Some came from the African Gulf, near Cameroon,[71] for the Cameroonians had traditionally served as middlemen between the Europeans and the African hinterland.[72] And still others, hungry,[73] left for the north to cross the Mediterranean in a spirit of discovery,[74] sometimes in search of dreamed opportunities, and to fight for the liberation of Europe from fascism.[75]

These realities described by the poetry of Mveng did not end with his tragic death in 1995. And if he invites us to higher ground and forgiveness for a reconciled humanity, it remains that he was himself a contemporary of a theology that believed that this reconciliation will be complete only if all humanity is freed from the forces of oppression and misery. Mveng was thus a son and an actor of liberation theology, a movement that continues to challenge the Society of Jesus today. Since Arrupe, the Society's relationship to the poor has not changed.

FROM JORGE BERGOGLIO TO ARTURO SOSA: THE LAST BLACK POPES

Jorge Bergoglio and Arturo Sosa are both sons of Arrupe. As we have seen, it was Arrupe who appointed Bergoglio provincial of Argentina in 1973 amid the conflict in Argentina in which the Society was divided on the practical steps it had to take during the crisis. The General Congregation that elected his successor, Kolvenbach, also saw the participation of a young delegate from the province of Venezuela: Arturo Sosa. The emotion with which the delegates lived this congregation is known, especially their homage and farewell to Arrupe, which only increased the emotional attachment of this generation of Jesuits to his person. When he became Superior General in 2016, Sosa even seemed to interpret the situation of the world in the light of Arrupe's experience and vision, while paying tribute to Adolfo Nicolás, his immediate predecessor:

> Reflecting on the discovery of the energy of the atomic bomb, Sosa told Jesuits in Nagasaki on Aug. 2, 2019, Arrupe noted how powerful forces have declared themselves masters of the world, eliminating God, and treating other humans as "objects," instruments for their own good, "the ultimate perversion of the human person."… Among the students who listened to him in the auditorium of the Areneros School in Madrid, Adolfo Nicolás later declared that he had come across a great missionary, "a man of fire."[76]

Sosa thus placed his Generalate, and the general line of the Society's mission, in the continuity of Arrupe, the reception of the Second Vatican Council, and the responses to the societal challenges that emerged from it. It is the context of the defense of faith and the struggle for justice that this implies. Sosa recognizes himself in figures such as Dom Helder Cámara, Oscar Arnulfo Romero, Rutilio Grande, Frans van der Lugt, Christophe Munzihirwa, A.T. Thomas, Richard Fernando, Thomas Gafney, and so on. Following these inspiring figures, he called for an "Ignatian Year" "to allow ourselves to be moved once again by Ignatius of Loyola, wounded in Pamplona in 1521 and transformed by God's action in Manresa to become the pilgrim who began this journey that we too have chosen to travel in the service of Jesus Christ and his Church."[77] As if to mark the importance of the event, Sosa even allowed himself a confession:

> I have just celebrated 53 years since I entered the novitiate of the Society of Jesus in Los Teques, Venezuela. My vocation, my formation and my apostolic mission in the Society of Jesus have been nourished and marked by what we call "the social apostolate."… The Society of Jesus—we read in the Formula of the Institute of 1550—was "founded first and foremost to

concern itself principally with the defense and propagation of the faith and for the benefit of souls in Christian life and doctrine."[78]

Sosa's vocation, his charisma, was formed in the heart of the social action of the Gumilla Center of Caracas and his progress within the governance of the Society. These moments of his vocation were also marked by prolific intellectual activity in which his political analysis of his native Venezuela was gradually combined with an internal look at the identity of the Society.

Sosa knows something about politics, perhaps even more than any of his predecessors as Superior General. He is a political scientist by training. And if he has remained mostly silent on political issues since his election even though Venezuela, like many countries in the world where Jesuits work, is experiencing serious political and economic crises, it is perhaps because he had already said it all before entering Borgo Santo Spirito 4, the Jesuit headquarters in Rome.

The Early Sosa

The early Sosa did not miss any opportunity in Venezuelan political life to express his opinion. Born in 1948, Sosa grew up, until the early 1980s, in the shadow of the birth of Venezuelan democracy. It was also, and above all, a prosperous country, rich in its enormous oil resources. In 1978, Sosa commemorated the twentieth anniversary of the Bourgeois Revolution of January 23, 1958, the year of the advent of democracy. His diagnosis was clear. For him, the historical importance of January 23, 1958, lay in the fact that it was a dense moment in which the different possibilities of the country's historical and political future came together: Would it continue the militaristic path traced by the military dictatorship, or would it opt for a bourgeois democracy of the Western style around civil political forces such as Democratic Action (AD), the Committee of Independent Electoral Political Organization (COPEI), or the Democratic Republican Union (URD), or align with its communist alternative, the Communist Party of Venezuela (PCV)?

Twenty years after this democratic revolution, it seemed to Sosa that the second option had prevailed. The internal pact between the main political parties, the rather prosperous economic situation, and the determination of the United States to support the so-called democratic regimes in Latin America favored this option. This project led to the marginalization of the Venezuelan Communist Party until the division of the AD to form the MIR (Revolutionary Left Movement) on April 8, 1960.[79] Together with the Venezuelan Communist Party, these two parties formed the Venezuelan Liberation Front, which had an armed wing that was defeated by the national armed forces supported by the United States.

Bourgeois democracy had created a middle class that became its main support. Without trembling, Sosa explained his position. "The social pact born on January 23," he said, "has become a system in our country. Any proposal for change must start from this reality." As for the revolutionary action, "it cannot be satisfied with planning the conquest of the government; a strategy of action is necessary that affects all the levels, that supports the current state of things and that provokes a new convergence and relation of the economic and social forces, and that will bring about the gestation of the new order to which we aspire."[80] In short, it was the status quo and hoping for better days. This expectation was under the control of the United States, especially with the Reagan administration, which saw a concordance of interests with Venezuela. Sosa was extraordinarily lucid in his analysis. The United States, Sosa acknowledged, is a powerful, modern, and innovative country. It is therefore "natural" that Latin America has become the "backyard" of the United States. It is thanks to the unique relationship that Reagan's country has with Venezuela that this country has modernized itself "overcoming our ancestral handicaps and the weight of Iberian colonization."[81] Sosa even had a sense of humor:

> We are Venezuelans who eat *hallacas* and *arepas*; we dance to the sound of the *cuatro* and applaud "Un Solo Pueblo," but we end up having the same perspective, the same goals and the same path to achieve them as Yankees who eat hot dogs and drink Coca-Cola, enchanted by rock music.[82]

Sosa is therefore a realistic intellectual who understands perfectly well the irresistible Americanization of his country and is worried about it, for the doctrine of national security was becoming a form of deepening the oppression of the masses by an elite whose interests converged on both sides of the border. As an alternative, Sosa thinks of a "decisive struggle" "in the form of a social project," but without saying more.[83]

The Later Sosa

Toward the 1990s, a different Sosa, who sometimes seemed disenchanted, appeared. He also became suddenly less prolific. The decade of the 1980s had seen an impoverishment of the masses and a political shift in Venezuela to the left. Already in 1978, under the government of Carlos Andrés Pérez, Venezuelan economists were alarmed by the burden of the foreign debt, which at that time amounted to $2,950 million.[84] As a symbol of the country's troubles, the price of a bag of cement suddenly rose to 70 percent of its 1973 price.[85] The immense oil revenues enriched the ruling class and left millions of Venezuelans in great misery.[86] All of this took place under the shadow of the Puebla Conference. Considering this meeting, the base communities of Venezuela expressed their concern:

> On our continent, it is a fact that cries out to the sky the hunger, the lack of work, health, housing, education, rest that affect the great majority....A problem that destroys thousands of human lives and disrupts all social coexistence on our continent is the growing violation of human rights in more or less all countries and in a persistent and systematic way.[87]

At the heart of this crisis is the Gumilla Center. The researchers who work there analyze and make proposals. They also go to the neighborhoods to tell the "stories of the neighborhoods,"[88] the daily life of the poor masses, their means of transportation, and their diet. In these neighborhoods also swarmed religious movements, sometimes with deadly practices like the sect that saw the mysterious death of nine hundred followers in Guyana.[89]

Sosa worked in the Gumilla Center; he was one of its leaders. Faced with the deep social crisis that exasperated Venezuelans,

Sosa took them back to January 23, 1958, the day that had marked the turning point in the country's political history. Unfortunately, twenty-five years later, he observed, its leaders would prefer to see this date cloned in a distant past, without any impact on their present. The "owner," "producer," and "employer" state has reduced to nothing a civil society made up of people without autonomy or real social strength. This political and economic system has shown its limits. The populations have lost all confidence in it. Without supporting a change of the said system, Sosa believes that the latter has the capacity to renew itself by making a "leap toward the little people."[90]

Carlos Andrés Pérez and his allies knew the revolution was inevitable. While they presented the crisis from a purely economic perspective, Sosa was convinced that the root of the crisis was political. With the elections approaching, he feared that the people would not have a clear alternative because of the indefinite nature of Venezuelan democracy. The people seemed to be called to a plebiscite without alternative, where military authoritarianism, although a costly step backward, seemed increasingly likely. The apathy of the electorate was another concern. The 1984 legislative elections saw an unprecedented rate of absenteeism, reflecting a system that was running out of steam. Sosa saw a national political life evolving "in a critical situation that has exceeded the capacity of its current leaders and the organizations that have dominated decision-making. The horizon is not clear and new alternatives must emerge."[91] A year later, in 1985, and in the face of a threatened democracy in which workers were hounded and beaten, Sosa proposed solidarity among the workers as a political alternative:

> In Venezuela, democracy is in danger because it is very dangerous to try to exercise it….The only thing that remains for the workers under legal protection is the solidarity of their comrades and the conviction that the path they have taken is the one that can avoid the situation of this democracy in danger.[92]

To democratize Venezuela, Sosa argued, it was necessary to organize the workers beyond the partisan fractions, for without independent and strong unions, there can be no democracy.[93] It was also necessary to democratize the vote through a reform of the electoral code, to mobilize civil society, and to promote freedom of expression.[94] This "social state" (which could be called democratic) would imply that civil society "has the power over the state that party leaders have in the current system."[95] On February 4, 1992, a first coup attempt against Carlos Andrés Pérez seemed to prove Sosa right. The regime was at risk of prolonging the democratic crisis in Venezuela and plunging it into the regression of militarism.

It must also be said that there was a decline in the number of political publications by Sosa. His editorial line had not changed. But, as usual, he offered an excellent analysis of the political and economic situation of the country, center-right, with a more social leaning from the 1980s. This analysis sometimes lacked bold alternative proposals. This was probably the step that the priest in him refused to take. However, he showed little reserve in criticizing regimes (or rather the Regime) and its leaders. He did not fail to blame Carlos Pérez for his setbacks. After the coup attempt, Sosa wrote, President Perez "is alive and in office. However, from a political point of view, there was a 'death' of the president."[96] Pérez suffocated the Venezuelans economically, asking them each time for the "sacrifice necessary for the success of the adjustment measures." But these promises never had a return in investment. On the contrary:

> The sacrifice turned into a wider gap of social injustice. While the people have become alarmingly impoverished, a few small minorities have grown rich without contributing even a small part of their earnings to the revenues of a state that is incapable of guaranteeing its people the minimum necessary for survival and of respecting the basis of the constitutional agreement on which the Republic is founded.[97]

Later, in 2011, Sosa offered a harsh critique of the regime of Hugo Chavez, who was campaigning for reelection despite a very advanced cancer:

> The scenario of Chávez's re-election puts democracy to the test in several respects. If it is interpreted as an

opportunity to increase the identification of the leader with the government, the state and the country, increasing personalism and the subordination of the institutions to his will, signed as the will of the people, Venezuelan society moves away from the path of democratic legitimacy. This leads to a dictatorial personalism that imposes its own vision, stifling the space for the expression of other points of view.[98]

Since then, and with his election as Superior General of the Society in 2016, the facts have changed little economically and politically in Venezuela. Sosa knows this. Yet he remains silent. Is it the silence of the prophet who cried out in the desert when there was still time to correct the course of events? The silence of the political scientist who has already said what he had to say and thinks that the proposals he made years ago are still relevant? Or the prudent posture of a Superior General of the Society of Jesus who has understood that the priority of his mandate is the internal renewal of the Society? Probably a little of all of these. It is worth noting, however, that since joining the Society, Sosa has been a member of a religious order that is still searching for its identity and mission in the world today.

THE VIEW OF THE SOCIETY

To understand Sosa's view of the Society and its mission in today's world, it is necessary to recall that

the worsening structural crisis of the Venezuelan economy and the accelerated loss of legitimacy of the political system have led people to turn to the Church as an institution capable of fostering the search for common paths that will make it possible to peacefully overcome the enormous deficiencies of the current state of affairs. Assuming this social responsibility from the very identity of the Church, however, requires the boldness that comes from the Christian freedom to run the risks of committing oneself to the defense of the Common Good, in the midst of actors obsessed with preserving their privileges or defending their particular interests to the detriment of public interests.[99]

During the years of crisis, the church's base throughout Latin America had become increasingly dominated by the populace. The common people were its most active and committed members in pastoral work. Basic ecclesial movements were multiplying in poor neighborhoods. Even vocations to the religious life came from the disadvantaged sectors of society. The preferential option for the poor was therefore essential for the church's survival. It had to embrace the theology of liberation.[100]

The Society had followed the same evolution. During these same decades, Sosa participated in the 33rd and 34th General Congregations of the Jesuits and rose through the ranks of its governance. Thus, at times, he looked back on the Society's situation. In 1983, when Sosa participated in the 33rd General Congregation as one of the delegates of the Venezuelan Province, he took advantage of this experience to speak about the Society in its current state. Legends, he then said, have surrounded the history of the Jesuits, and that remains the case today. Some see them as uncompromising defenders of conservatism, others as rebels, others as people of discernment, and still others as cynics who would use any means to get what they want. The reality, however, is more complex. It can only be understood in the context of the Second Vatican Council, which saw the election of Paul VI as pope and Pedro Arrupe as Superior General of the Jesuits.[101]

In this changing world, the Society had to adapt without losing its own identity or breaking the unity within the church. Within the Society itself there were different currents and degrees of assimilation and interpretation of the challenges of the council that led to successes, but also to failures. Thus, the Jesuits were sometimes divided among themselves or in conflict with other sectors of the church and other interests that were affected by their societal positions.[102]

The end of Arrupe's Generalate and the intervention of the pope in the ordinary government of the Society must be interpreted in this context. While many saw this papal intervention as a confirmation of the suspicions of "deviation" and "rebellion" of the Jesuits in their postconciliar actions, within the Society the measure was received with sadness and gravity. However, the reset requested by John Paul II was undertaken. In February 1982, all provincial superiors were called to a meeting in Rome where the pope communicated his intentions and wishes. Each province of the Society then conducted its own self-examination, and when John Paul II learned of the results of the review process, he authorized the convocation of the 31st General Congregation for September 1983.[103] Reflecting later on the 34th General Congregation, Sosa would sum up this postconciliar situation in more social terms: "In a radically unjust world, the raison d'être of the Society of Jesus is the proclamation of the faith for which the struggle for justice is an absolute requirement."[104]

In this context, there are situations that are more critical than others and that require immediate attention: "the marginalization of Africa, a continent that includes the thirty poorest countries in the world, as well as ethnic conflicts, massive migrations and the difficulties of replacing colonial and semi-colonial structures."[105] The same is true of women, whose rights are violated in many cultures around the world. The Society has a role to play in humanizing humanity. It is a question of its identity and mission, of a realistic recognition of the role and responsibility of Jesuits in their encounter with other cultures. For, at times, "we have alienated rather than evangelized; we have allied ourselves with oppressive elites within cultures, or we have remained a 'foreign presence.' However, we have also made progress in the process of inculturation, and today we recognize ourselves as a multicultural body eager to take advantage of the variety that this variety brings us."[106]

CONCLUSION

When Bergoglio, a Jesuit, was elected pope, most Jesuits experienced the moment with surprise, even shock. They were waiting, like all other Christians, to find out what would be "Jesuit" in a pope who could not escape the labels traditionally attached to the name of the Society. As he left the balcony, the whole world, including the Society, was moved by his humility and simplicity. The pope asked for prayers before he gave his blessing. The tone was set.

The pontificate immediately took a social turn toward the poorest and the marginalized. The pope went to Lampedusa to share the Eucharist with African refugee survivors of the Mediterranean shipwrecks. He invited the rich countries to be more hospitable while the rhetoric around immigration was getting more radical among populist governments. He visited prisoners and washed their feet on Holy Thursday. He began the reform of the Vatican, choosing at first to stay in a simpler and more modest apartment, as he did as archbishop of Buenos Aires. He appointed cardinals from the poorest regions of the world, from Mali, Central Africa, Rwanda, the Democratic Republic of Congo, to name only the Africans. He also firmly tackled the crisis of abuse in the church, preaching mercy to those Christians who have remained distant from ecclesial communion, and he convened a synod on synodality. In short, he indicated that it was necessary to return the church to the poor. He is a son of Arrupe, a Jesuit who can now reconcile in his person the white pope and the black pope. My grandmother was right. From Africa, *Habemus papam*!

Bergoglio, extraordinarily, is also close to the powerful of this world, who are also children of Abraham. He received Donald Trump, as he received Barack Obama before him and Joe Biden after him. He wanted to be a bridge, a father who consoled the leader of the free world who was grieving a beloved son he lost to cancer. He embraced him as a son who felt unloved, rejected by his own people who condemned him for the abortion he never performed, the prohibition of which he could not impose on the rest of the country without violating the sacred law of separation between church and state, a law without which there would never have been a Catholic Church in the United States. It was the great victory of a former Jesuit, John Carroll, who used his friendship with George Washington to pass the Religious Freedom Act, which allowed Catholics to enjoy the protection of the American Constitution. Without that law, there would never have been a John F. Kennedy, or a Joseph R. Biden, a Nancy Pelosi, or a John Boehner, the full image of the podium at the U.S. Congress when Pope Francis was received there on September 24, 2015: the pope was a Jesuit and a Catholic, giving a speech to the Congress, surrounded by the Catholic vice president and a Catholic congressional leader in tears. James Madison would never have anticipated this. And yet! There are the new Madisons who cry out against this pope and his style, as if the church he leads has become too powerful and intolerant of the gray areas that are the reality of the very complexity of our societies. *"Habemus papam,"* my grandmother cried. It was her pope, our pope!

Bergoglio's career and ministry are contemporaneous with the last three Superiors General of the Society. He enjoyed a closeness with Arrupe that could be less with Arrupe's successor, the very reserved Kolvenbach. He was born in the same year as Nicolás and was Kolvenbach's pope for the last three years of the latter's Generalate (2013–2016). There is no need to go back to Arrupe. Much has been written and said about him. I would like to recall an observation from this chapter: Kolvenbach not only normalized the Society's relations with the Holy See, he also carried out its aggiornamento. He was the one who resituated the Society in its intellectual tradition, reformed the formation of its members, and worked to modernize its government.

Kolvenbach's successor, Adolfo Nicolás, a European by birth and a missionary outside Europe like Arrupe and Kolvenbach, also returned to these three areas. A mystic, Nicolás asked the Jesuits to go deep. He reorganized the governance of the Society, creating new secretariats in the curia and insisting on networking. It was under his Generalate that a better structuring of the conferences of provincials could be achieved.

Aware of the demographic changes in both the church and in the Society, Nicolás Africanized and Indianized. Thus, he created branches of the Jesuit Historical Institute with headquarters in Rome, Nairobi, and Goa. In the context of the new evangelization, he understood that the "older" evangelization, led by the West as opposed to the "new," had its greatness and its misery, and that it was the duty of the Africans and Indians themselves to write their own history. The "black pope" was no longer black simply by virtue of his cassock; he was black at heart and acted accordingly. Having been elected at the advanced age of seventy-two, Nicolás resigned for health reasons and returned to the Philippines as a missionary, where, as we have noted, he passed away on May 20, 2020.

Sosa finally completes the picture of the generals of the liberation. He is a political scientist, from the global southern region of the church and the Society. He understands well the political issues of the day, but he also seems to have concluded that what the Society needs most is a spiritual renewal that is in consonance with globalization and that addresses its crises: ecology, the poor, and the youth, without whom there are no vocations to religious life. Like his three predecessors, a certain Ignatian mysticism is essential to the Society today as the source of its own renewal and mission.

CONCLUSION

In 1979, a survey was conducted to get young Jesuits to decide on the future of their order. The question was what they thought would be characteristic of the Jesuit of the third millennium. The resulting reflections were published in 1980 by the Roman magazine *Centrum Ignatianum Spiritualitatis* (CIS). Loïc de Cannière, a student in Munich, dreamed of a Society of Jesus that would be smaller in membership, but more fraternal, social in its apostolic orientation, and Ignatian in its outlook.[1] A young Bolivian Jesuit saw in this future Society "communities open to people, where no one of the neighborhood would feel an outsider or unwanted… in this context a neighbor will not think twice about asking us to take care of his babies while he and his wife go to see a movie."[2] Above all, he foresaw a Bolivian missionary Society that would send Jesuits outside of Bolivia. The Frontier Society, which had once been at the receiving end of the missions, would thus gradually occupy the center, with its strengths and weaknesses. It would also enrich this center with a spirituality of the poor, which is marked by the expansion of the Charismatic Renewal in Latin America[3] and in Africa, as evidenced by the story of Joseph, an African villager in this book.

In 1984, at the time of his death on March 30, the Jesuit theologian Karl Rahner left on his table an English translation of a text he had written about "Jesuits and the Charismatic Renewal." This text served as a spiritual testament. Rahner had reservations about the movement, which he found at times uncultured and lacking discernment. To him, the Renewal seemed too simplistic and dreamy to be taken seriously as a great reform movement. This observation applied even more to the Jesuits, Rahner recognized, because they were above all institutionalists, champions of the hierarchical church, of the pope, of authority, of the sacraments, of dogmas and morals. This is their ethos, he concluded, of which they should not be ashamed.[4]

However, Rahner added, the figure of Ignatius of Loyola and his project go beyond this institutional character. Ignatius was above all a mystic, a man guided by the Spirit to reform the (hierarchical and institutional) church from within. In this sense, Rahner observed, there is a great affinity between the spirituality of Saint Ignatius and the Charismatic Renewal movement. That the Jesuits departed from this mystagogy—the existence of the sacred in our lives and around us—was not surprising to Rahner, for it is the Jesuits, he argued, who had contributed to modern rationalism, which did not accept the Ignatian maxim that the Holy Spirit could communicate directly to the human soul, and that the church does indeed mediate between God and us![5]

The passage from this Ignatian mysticism to institutionalized rationalism has been the focus in this book. The mediating church of which Rahner spoke, and of which the Jesuit Institute is a part, struggles, because of the aggressive rationalism that surrounds it, to navigate the immediacy that is so prevalent in contemporary Christianity. Therefore, as Rahner concluded, "it is well to learn from the charismatic movement, and put it into practice, what we should have learned, long ago, from Ignatius." For the Jesuits to embrace this movement, no doubt with discernment, is to reclaim their own spirituality.[6]

On the eve of the third millennium, everything seemed to indicate that the Jesuits were regaining awareness of the deeply spiritual dimension of their organization. There were even signs that they wanted to see their approach to history marked by this spirituality. Ignacio Iglesias, for example, speaking about the Jesuits' service in the frontiers, started from the fact that Ignatius's wound in Pamplona had the merit, above all, of turning him resolutely toward God. It was this inward movement that opened his horizons to the dimensions of the new world that was his. In a sense, this spiritual approach to reality affects all the structures of the Society. The spirit is what drives the Jesuits and sets them in motion: "At the deepest level," Iglesias writes, "it was because this desire to be with Christ in human need was so strong that Ignatius did not want to restrict the life of a Jesuit with structures that would limit his availability and the speed with which he could respond."[7] From this perspective, "history is seen as suffused with God and is read as a call."[8]

Around this concept of frontier, social history and spiritual history meet and embrace each other. From there, one recognizes that the first Jesuits were neither professionals nor neoliberal corporatists. Their ministries stemmed from their experience of God and were oriented toward helping souls by showing them the way to God. It was the Jesuits, moreover, who applied the theological and trinitarian concept of "mission" to the ministry of evangelization to non-Christians.[9] In their missionary practice, John O'Malley reminds us, the Jesuits did develop strategies of accommodation. But, in an unprecedented way, O'Malley adds another word to the concept of accommodation. He speaks of "discerning accommodation," "which was both a set of spiritual sensibilities and an actual way of proceeding verified in practice from the earliest days of Ignatius's conversion."[10]

It was this discerning attitude of Ignatius and the early Jesuits that marked the initial expansion of the order and its ministries. As early as 1548, in Messina, the educational apostolate that began to define them, and by which they are best known today, was seen as an unexpected development that took the original apostolic plan by surprise. Ignatius called this unexpected event several names to define the providential character of the Society. The first Jesuits, as coined in the *Constitutions* of the order, shared the conviction that this institution was founded by divine means and could only be maintained by the same (*Const.* 840). In their missionary and apostolic drive, crossing oceans and sometimes facing violent and untimely deaths, the first Jesuits remained eminently spiritual. Their Society, like a mustard seed, was "little," made up of fragile men, and harbored nests of nationalities and cultures on its branches only because its members were rooted in God and driven, they believed, by the same fire and called to the same cause.

The providential character of the Jesuit order sometimes took the form of paradoxes in history. The first of these paradoxes was undoubtedly the French soldiers, enemies of Ignatius, who carried him from the battlefield to the castle of Loyola. Ignatius owed his life to his enemies in this world. He remembered this and never again doubted that God could sometimes use contrary ways to direct the course of history toward sublime ends. Without the French enemy of the battle of Pamplona, Ignatius and his cannon-ball might never have deserved to be footnotes in history books. They would have remained unknown, like all the other casualties of that battle. Without this enemy, there would have been no Society of Jesus.

Another paradox was the missionary impulse that accompanied the order from its origins. The prototypes of modern intellectuals that were the first Jesuits also shone with a certain spiritual radicalism, a mysticism in the daily conduct of their lives and a "zeal" for the mission. It is this zeal, this spiritual fire, that explains why bright, normal young people, students at the most prestigious universities of the European renaissance, left everything behind to follow a lame beggar man who was intellectually less equipped to begin with. In this self-surrender, they went to the discovery of unknown lands and peoples, animated by a spirit of adventurism, which they justified by a desire to save souls. In this way, they committed themselves to the service of the poorest as well as the rich. By their lives, the first Jesuits associated the intellectual project of the order, despite its elitist deviations, with a project of formation of a virtuous and holy modern being. Some made themselves slaves among slaves, brokers among brokers, humble ecclesiastics, but above all ecclesial, in a spirit of reforming the church in its head and members.

As chapter 3 indicates, it was this holiness, more than any other strategy, that was the determining factor in their missionary success. It was this that was celebrated at the time of the canonizations, sometimes protected by enemies such as those Muslim Arabs of North Africa who, for fear of offending God by persecuting such pious people, took care to protect them. These virtuous Jesuits were also, paradoxically, taken under suspicion by an inquisitive church that was averse to spiritualist movements.

The time of the suppression of the Jesuits is known for another paradox. Historians speak of this event as an immolation. The sacrifice of Abraham was finally carried out, but by a Sarah caught in the whirlpools of political intrigues and massive propaganda built, for two centuries, against a loyal daughter. The pope, to whom the Jesuits vowed loyalty, served as the hand that carried the sword of suppression. In this divided Christian world, in which the Jesuits were rightly or wrongly portrayed as the agents of the Counter-Reformation, they found refuge not only in Catherine II of Prussia but also in England and Protestant America. This America considerably influenced the last century of the history of Christianity, and therefore also that of the Jesuits.

The respect for religious liberty and cultural pluralism, which was natural to the new American nation, served as an ideal refuge for a paradoxical, multicultural, global organization like the Society. Rather than accommodating Eastern cultures whose religious or cultural rituals created conflicts of interpretation in the West, which was one of the leading causes of the suppression of the Jesuits, in the United States the Jesuits had to adapt to the ideals of the multicultural and multireligious Republic. Members of a group suppressed by its Roman mother, yet among the leaders of a minority and nascent Roman Catholic Church in the United States, the Jesuits built bridges between the church and modernism. Their educational institutions became places of experimentation for ecumenism, effective collaboration with the laity, and new approaches to pedagogy beyond the provisions of the *Ratio Studiorum*. The American spirit of freedom and its multiculturalism served as fertile ground for the unity of opposites within the Society itself. Ultramontanes and Republicans, conservatives and progressives, even different nationalities, some of which were already mentioned in the Formula of the Institute, let their respective particularisms dissolve to collaborate in the common mission.

The multicultural Americanism was able to combine with a certain French progressivism in the early 1930s. With *La Nouvelle Théologie*, Teilhard de Chardin, Gaston Fessard, and Henri de Lubac, alongside initiatives of an Augustin Béa, the Jesuits helped chart a new course for the church in the twentieth century. It was this movement that, during the Second Vatican Council, led to the election of Pedro Arrupe. He became the first of a series of missionary Superiors General of the order. Above all, he was the great promoter of the theology of inculturation so dear to African churches in the aftermath of the council, and the best articulator of the balance between faith and justice.

In these times of social and religious revolutions in the West, Arrupe maintained the optimism of the mystic that he was. The Society, under his leadership, adopted options toward the underprivileged that soon put the order at odds with the powerful and the conservative wing of the church and the Society. His interpretation of the council's spirit of *aggiornamento* proved a little too bold for the pontificates of Paul VI and John Paul II. Yesterday's friends turned their backs on the Jesuits. Their loyalty to the pope and the institutional church was questioned. And some Jesuits, amid this turmoil, thought of a reformed Jesuit order parallel to the one headed by Arrupe.

Arrupe received blows from all sides. He tried in vain to resign, until a cerebral thrombosis finally immobilized him in 1981, putting an end to the Society's most consequential Generalate of the twentieth century. In the meantime, Arrupe had touched many hearts among the Jesuits. With his same spirit, some of them were ready to succeed him and continue his work. It was he who named Jorge Bergoglio Provincial of Argentina in 1973. And when, in 1983, the General Congregation convened to elect his successor, Kolvenbach, the delegate from Venezuela was a young Arturo Sosa. Without a doubt, and each in his own way, all three claimed to be heirs of Pedro Arrupe. With them, Roman Catholicism and global Jesuitism witnessed the irruption at their center of the South and a practical implementation of liberation theology.

That an African grandmother could recognize a certain African quality in the election of Pope Francis, the first Jesuit in history, testifies that the spirit that animated the last Jesuit Superiors General and the directives of the General Congregations of the Jesuits had become ripe to produce a pope who was both deeply spiritual and resolutely social. Francis, like Arrupe or Sosa, belongs to an era in which the Society of Jesus worldwide opted for the preferential option for the poor. In this pontificate, and in continuation of the spirit of the 31st, 32nd, and 33rd General Congregations that has shaped Jesuit ethos since Vatican II, a turning point in history was also manifested that was long overdue. The history of the Society is above all that of an institution that is spiritual before it is social. This is its ethos; this is also the key to interpreting its history.

NOTES

INTRODUCTION

1. Joseph de Guibert, *The Jesuits: Their Spiritual Doctrine and Practice*, ed. George E. Ganss, trans. William J. Young (Saint Louis, MO: The Institute of Jesuit Sources, 1986), vii.

2. De Guibert, *The Jesuits*, 595.

3. Pedro Arrupe and Ruth Bradley, *One Jesuit's Spiritual Journey: Autobiographical Conversations with Jean-Claude Dietsch* (Saint Louis, MO: The Institute of Jesuit Sources, 1986), 63.

4. Claude Pavur, trans., *The Ratio Studiorum: The Official Plan for Jesuit Education* (Saint Louis, MO: The Institute of Jesuit Sources, 2005), vii.

5. Pavur, trans., *The Ratio Studiorum*, vii.

6. Claude Pavur, *In the School of Ignatius: Studious Zeal and Devoted Learning* (Boston, MA: Institute of Jesuit Sources, 2019), 11.

7. John W. O'Malley, Gauvin A. Bailey, and Steven J. Harris, *The Jesuits II: Cultures, Sciences, and the Arts, 1540–1773* (Toronto: University of Toronto Press, 2006), 452.

8. John W. O'Malley, "How the First Jesuits Became Involved in Education," in *The Jesuit Ratio Studiorum. 400th Anniversary Perspectives* (New York: Fordham University Press, 2000), 56–74.

9. Maria Clara Lucchetti Bingemer, "The Jesuits and Social Justice in Latin America," in *The Jesuits and Globalization: Historical Legacies and Contemporary Challenges* (Washington, DC: Georgetown University Press, 2016), 188–205.

10. Thomas P. Gaunt, "Jesuit Shift from Developed to Developing World," *CARA* 16, no. 4 (Spring 2011); Dana L. Robert, "Shifting Southward: Global Christianity Since 1945," *International Bulletin of Missionary Research* 24, no. 2 (April 2000): 50–58.

11. Laurenti Magesa, *What Is Not Sacred? African Spirituality* (Maryknoll, NY: Orbis Books, 2013).

12. John W. O'Malley, *The First Jesuits* (Cambridge: Harvard University Press, 1993).

13. Robert A. Maryks, ed., "The Quest for the Historical Ignatius," in *A Companion to Ignatius of Loyola. Life, Writing, Spirituality, Influence*, Brill's Companions to the Christian Tradition 52 (Boston, MA: Brill, 2014), 1–6.

14. William David Myers, "Ignatius and Luther: The History and Basis of a Comparison," in *A Companion to Ignatius of Loyola*, ed. Robert A. Maryks, Brill's Companions to the Christian Tradition 52 (Boston, MA: Brill, 2014), 141–58.

15. Myers, "Ignatius and Luther," 144.

16. John W. O'Malley, "The Many Lives of Ignatius of Loyola: Future Saint," in John W. O'Malley, ed., *Saints or Devils Incarnate? Studies in Jesuit History,* Jesuit Studies 1 (Boston, MA: Brill eBooks, 2013), 261.

17. O'Malley, "The Many Lives of Ignatius of Loyola," 264–65.

18. Ann Cole, *Becoming All Things to All Men: The Role of Jesuit Missions in Early Modern Globalization*, PhD diss., University of Arkansas, 2014.

19. David E. Mungello, *Curious Land: Jesuit Accommodation and the Origins of Sinology* (Honolulu: University of Hawaii Press, 1989); Stephen Schloesser, "Accommodation as a Rhetorical Principle. Twenty Years after John O'Malley's *The First Jesuits* (1993)," *Journal of Jesuit Studies* 1 (2014): 347–72.

20. Andrés I. Prieto, "The Perils of Accommodation: Jesuit Missionary Strategies in the Early Modern World," *Journal of Jesuit Studies* 4 (2017): 395–414.

21. *The Jesuits and Globalization. Historical Legacies and Contemporary Challenges* (Washington, DC: Georgetown University Press, 2016); Thomas Banchoff and José Casanova, "Introduction: The Jesuits and Globalization," in *The Jesuits and Globalization. Historical Legacies and Contemporary Challenges* (Washington, DC: Georgetown University Press, 2016), 1–26.

Notes

22. Luke Clossey, *Salvation and Globalization in the Early Jesuit Missions* (Cambridge, UK: Cambridge University Press, 2008), 1–40.

23. John T. McGreevy, "Restored Jesuits: Notes toward a Global History," in *The Jesuits and Globalization. Historical Legacies and Contemporary Challenges* (Washington, DC: Georgetown University Press, 2016), 131–46; John T. McGreevy, *American Jesuits and the World: How an Embattled Religious Order Made Modern Catholicism Global* (Princeton, NJ: Princeton University Press, 2016).

24. Sabina Pavone, "The History of Anti-Jesuitism: National and Global Dimensions," in *The Jesuits and Globalization. Historical Legacies and Contemporary Challenges* (Washington, DC: Georgetown University Press, 2016), 111–30.

25. Melinda McGarrah Sharp, "Globalization, Colonialism, and Postcolonialism," in *The Wiley-Blackwell Companion to Practical Theology*, ed. Bonnie J. Miller-McLemore (Malden, MA: Blackwell Publishers, 2012), 423.

26. Catherine M. Mooney, "Ignatian Spirituality, A Spirituality for Mission," *Mission Studies* 26 (2009): 192–213.

27. Daniel Franklin and E. Pilario, eds., *Globalization and the Church of the Poor* (London: SCM Press, 2015).

28. Pierre Antoine Fabre, "The First Fathers of the Society of Jesus," in *The Oxford Handbook of the Jesuits*, ed. Ines G. Zupanov (Oxford: Oxford University Press, 2018), 104.

29. Jonathan Kringelbach and Hélène Neveu Skinner, eds., *Dancing Cultures: Globalization, Tourism and Identity in the Anthropology of Dance*, Dance and Performance Studies 4 (New York: Berghahn Books, 2012).

30. Peter N. Stearns, ed., *Encyclopedia of Social History* (New York/London: Garland Publishing, 1994), 686.

31. Stearns, *Encyclopedia of Social History*, vi–vii.

32. Jean Luc Enyegue, "New Wine into Old Wineskins? African Reactions to Arrupe's Governing Vision (1965–1978)," *Archivum Historicum Societatis Iesu* 88, fasc. 176 (2019-II): 385–420.

33. E. Wesley Ely, "On Being a Catholic Physician. Embracing the Spiritual History," *The Linacre Quarterly* 82, no. 2 (2015): 114.

34. Mark S. Ferrara, *Sacred Bliss: A Spiritual History of Cannabis* (Lanham, MD: Rowman & Littlefield, 2016), 4.

35. Walter J. Ciszek with Daniel Flaherty, *He Leadeth Me* (San Francisco, CA: Ignatius Press, 1973), 199.

36. Ciszek and Flaherty, *He Leadeth Me*, 199.

37. Francesco Marchisano, "The Archival Patrimony of Religious Families as a Key to the Church's Pastoral Mission of Inculturation into the New Millennium," in *"Criptis Tradere et Fideliter Conservare": Archives as "Places of Memory" within the Society of Jesus*, ed. Thomas M. McCoog (Rome: Jesuit General Curia, 2003), 5.

38. Piret Paal et al., "Expert Discussion on Taking a Spiritual History," *Journal of Palliative Care* 32, no. 1 (2017): 19.

39. Paal et al., "Expert Discussion," 23.

40. Larissa Brewer-García, "Hierarchy and Holiness in the Earliest Colonial Black Hagiographies: Alonso de Sandoval and His Sources," *The William and Mary Quarterly* 76, no. 3 (2019): 486.

41. Assan Sarr, "Gender, Spirituality, and Economic Change in Rural Gambia: Agricultural Production in the Lower Gambia Region, c. 1830s–1940s," *African Economic History* 45, no. 2 (2017): 1–26.

42. Simon Skinner, "History *versus* Hagiography: The Reception of Turner's *Newman*," *Journal of Ecclesiastical History* 61, no. 4 (2010): 772.

43. Jean Luc Enyegue, "Writing African History in a Global World: The Intercultural Paradigm," *Equinox* 5, nos. 1/2 (2021): 33–54.

44. Fernand Braudel, "Les responsabilités de l'histoire," *Cahiers Internationaux de Sociologie* 10 (1951): 3.

45. Braudel, "Les responsabilités de l'histoire," 3.

46. Barbara A. Holmes, *Joy Unspeakable: Contemplative Practices of the Black Church* (Minneapolis, MN: Fortress Press, 2017), xxiii.

47. Jean Luc Enyegue, "Engelbert Mveng, Nouvelles pistes pour une épistémologie de l'histoire," in *Engelbert Mveng: Chantre de la libération du muntu*, ed. François-Xavier Akono (Cameroon: Press de l'UCAC, 2014), 193–209.

48. Birago Diop, "Souffles," *Présence Africaine* 12 (1951): 187–89.

CHAPTER 1

1. Miguel Angel Ladero Quesada, "La 'Reconquête,' clef de voûte du moyen âge espagnol," in *L'expansion occidentale (XIe–XVe*

siècle). Formes et conséquences (Paris: Editions de la Sorbonne, 2003), 26–30.

2. James Brodrick, *Saint Ignatius Loyola: The Pilgrim Years* (London: Burns & Oates, 1956), 23.

3. Brodrick, *Saint Ignatius Loyola*, 34–35.

4. John W. O'Malley, "Fulfillment of the Christian Golden Age under Pope Julius II: Text of a Discourse of Giles of Viterbo, 1507," *Traditio* 25 (1969): 265–338.

5. Elizabeth Rhodes, "Join the Jesuits, See the World: Early Modern Women in Spain and the Society of Jesus," in *The Jesuits II. Cultures, Sciences, and the Arts 1540–1773*, ed. John W. O'Malley et al. (Toronto: University of Toronto Press, 2006), 33–49.

6. Gilles Havard and Cécile Vidal, *Histoire de l'Amérique Française* (Paris: Flammarion, 2019), 39.

7. Brodrick, *Saint Ignatius Loyola*, 29.

8. Brodrick, *Saint Ignatius Loyola*, 29–31.

9. Adrian Hastings, *The Church in Africa, 1450–1950* (Oxford: Oxford University Press, 1994), 81.

10. Hastings, *The Church in Africa*, 83.

11. Hastings, *The Church in Africa*, 83.

12. J. B. Coulbeaux, *Histoire politique et religieuse de l'Abyssinie depuis les temps les plus recules jusqu'a l'avenement de Menelik II*, vol. 2 (Paris: Geuthner, 1929), 106.

13. Coulbeaux, *Histoire politique et religieuse*, 127–130.

14. Coulbeaux, *Histoire politique et religieuse*, 133.

15. C. F. Beckingham, "European Sources of Ethiopian History before 1634," *Paideuma* 33 (1987): 170–71.

16. Hastings, *The Church in Africa*, 83.

17. Theresa M. Earenfight, "Raising Infanta Catalina de Aragón to Be Catherine, Queen of England," *Anuario de Estudios medievales* 46, no. 1 (2016): 417–19.

18. Félix Labrador Arroyo, "La organización de la casa de Catalina de Austria, reina de Portugal (1523–1526)," *Cuadernos de historia moderna* 39 (2014): 16.

19. Jean Lacouture, *Jésuites: Les conquérants*, vol. 1 (Paris: Seuil, 1991), 117.

20. Lacouture, *Jésuites*, 179.

21. Sabina Pavone, "A Saint under Trial. Ignatius of Loyola between Alcalá and Rome," in *A Companion to Ignatius of Loyola: Life, Writings, Influence*, ed. Robert A. Maryks (Boston, MA: Brill, 2014), 48.

22. Alain Woodrow, *Les Jésuites: Histoire de pouvoirs* (Paris: Lattès, 1990), 30.

23. Charles André Bernard, "L'illumination de l'intelligence: Un trait de l'expérience mystique Ignatienne," *Gregorianum* 72, no. 2 (1991): 223–46.

24. *Rowing into the Deep. 36th General Congregation. Documents* (Rome: S.I. Curia, 2017), 97.

25. Stefania Pastore, "Unwise Paths: Ignatius Loyola and the Years of Alcalá de Henares," in *A Companion to Ignatius of Loyola. Life, Writings, Influence*, ed. Robert A. Maryks (Boston, MA: Brill, 2014), 35.

26. Pastore, "Unwise Paths," 25.

27. Pastore, "Unwise Paths," 40–41.

28. Pastore, "Unwise Paths," 31.

29. Pastore, "Unwise Paths," 35.

30. Pastore, "Unwise Paths," 38.

31. Pavone, "A Saint under Trial," 49.

32. Pastore, "Unwise Paths," 34.

33. José García de Castro Valdés, "Ignatius of Loyola and His First Companions," in *A Companion to Ignatius of Loyola: Life, Writings, Influence*, ed. Robert A. Maryks (Boston, MA: Brill, 2014), 67.

34. Linda Lanza and Marco Toste, "The Influence of Salamanca in the Iberian Peninsula: The Case of the Faculties of Theology of Coimbra and Évora," in *The School of Salamanca: A Case of Global Knowledge Production*, ed. Thomas Duve et al. (Leiden: Brill, 2021), 120.

35. Linda Lanza and Marco Toste, "The Influence of Salamanca in the Iberian Peninsula," 122.

36. Katherine Elliot van Liere, "Humanism and Scholasticism in Sixteenth-Century Academe: Five Student Orations from the University of Salamanca," *Renaissance Quarterly* 53, no. 1 (Spring 2000): 64.

37. Alfred Dufour, "Droit international et Chrétienté: Des origines espagnoles aux origins polonaises du droit international. autour du sermon 'De bellis justis' du canoniste polonais Stanislas de Skarbimierz, 1360–1431," in *Roots of International Law* (Leiden: Brill, 2014), 96–97.

Notes

38. William J. Courtenay, "Inquiry and Inquisition: Academic Freedom in Medieval Universities," *Church History* 58, no. 2 (1989): 173.

39. F. Desjardin, *Les Jésuites et l'université devant le parlement de Paris au XVIe siècle. Discours prononcé à l'ouverture de la conférence des avocats le 25 novembre 1876* (Paris: Librairie G. Baillière et Cie, 1877), 5.

40. Serge Lusignan, "Les pauvres étudiants à l'université de Paris," in *Le petit peuple dans l'occident médiéval. Terminologies, perceptions, réalités*, ed. Pierre Boglioni, Robert Delort, and Claude Gauvard (Paris: Editions de la Sorbonne, 2019), 340.

41. Lusignan, "Les pauvres étudiants à l'université de Paris," 343.

42. Sharon Farmer, "Young, Male and Disabled," in *Les petits peuple dans l'occident médiéval. terminologies, perceptions, réalités*, ed. Pierre Boglioni, Robert Delort, and Claude Gauvard (Paris: Editions de la Sorbonne, 2002), 442ff.

43. Sharon Farmer, "The Beggar's Body: Intersections of Gender and Social Status in High Medieval Paris," in *Monks and Nuns, Saints and Outcasts. Religion in Medieval Society*, ed. Sharon Farmer and Barbara H. Rosenwein (New York: Cornell University Press, 2000), 160.

44. Juan de Polanco, "De la vida de Iñigo antes que Dios le tocase," in *Mon. Ign. Fontes Narrativi*, I, 182–83.

45. Polanco, "De la vida de Iñigo antes que Dios le tocase," 199–201.

46. Jean-Pierre Molénat, "Communautés musulmanes de Castille et du Portugal. Les cas de Tolède et de Lisbonne," in *L'expansion occidentale (XIe–XVe siècle). Formers et conséquences* (Paris: Editions de la Sorbonne, 2003), 215ff.

47. Antonio Mestre Sanchis, "Reacciones en Espana ante la expulsion de los Jesuitas de Francia," *Revista de Historia Moderna, Los Jesuitas en la Espana del Siglo XVIII* 15 (1996): 112.

48. Amy G. Remensnyder, "Christian Captives, Muslim Maidens, and Mary," *Speculum* 82 (2007): 645.

49. Amy G. Remensnyder, "The Colonization of Sacred Architecture: The Virgin Mary, Mosques, and Temples in Medieval Spain and Early Sixteenth-Century Mexico," in *Monks and Nuns, Saints and Outcasts. Religion in Medieval Society*, ed. Sharon Farmer and Barbara H. Rosenwein (New York: Cornell University Press, 2000), 195, 197.

50. Paula Clarke, "The Mentality of a Used-Clothes Dealer of the XVth Century," in *Le petit peuple dans l'occident médiéval*, ed. Pierre Boglioni, Robert Delort, and Claude Gauvard (Paris: Editions de la Sorbonne, 2002), 499–507.

51. Lacouture, *Jésuites: Les conquérants*, 1:125.

52. Lacouture, *Jésuites*, 179–80.

53. Brodrick, *Saint Ignatius Loyola*, 26.

54. Paul F. Grendler, *Schooling in Renaissance Italy: Literacy and Learning, 1300–1600* (Baltimore, MD: Johns Hopkins University Press, 1989), 74ff.

55. Translation from the Latin: "*qui ex medio honorum cursu et a saeculari et terrena militia admirabili quadam ratione vocatus, ita se divino imperio regendum et formandum tradidit...*"

56. Antoine Foucher, "Nature et formes de l'"histoire tragique' a Rome," *Latomus* 59, fasc. 4 (December 2000): 774.

57. Kouky Fianu, "Alphabétisation et Définition Du Petit Peuple à La Fin Du Moyen Âge. Le Cas de Libraires Parisiens," in *Le petit peuple dans l'occident médiéval*, ed. Pierre Boglioni, Robert Delort, and Claude Gauvard (Paris: Editions de la Sorbonne, 2002), 647.

58. Jenni Kuuliala, *Saints, Infirmity, and Community in the Late Middle Ages* (Amsterdam: Amsterdam University Press, 2020), 190–91.

59. Farmer, "Young, Male and Disabled," 442.

60. Irina Metzler, "Disability in the Middle Ages: Impairment at the Intersection of Historical Inquiry and Disability Studies," *History Compass* 9, no. 1 (2011): 47.

61. Pat Thane, "Social Histories of Old Age and Aging," *Journal of Social History* 37, no. 1 (Autumn 2003): 95.

62. Farmer, "Young, Male and Disabled," 442.

63. Pavone, "A Saint under Trial," 50.

64. John Bossy and Peter Hebblethwaite, *Christianity in the West, 1400–1700* (Oxford/New York: Oxford University Press, 1985), 143.

65. Bossy and Hebblethwaite, *Christianity in the West*, 145.

66. Brodrick, *Saint Ignatius Loyola*, 22.

67. Pastore, "Unwise Paths," 38.

68. Santiago Arzubialde, *Ejercicios Espirituales de San Ignacio: Historia y análisis* (Bilbao: Mensajero, 2009), 167.

69. To obtain satisfaction, the confession had to be sincere (hence contrition, sorrow, and confession for one's sins), complete,

and the penance proportional to the sin committed, before receiving absolution. Cf. *Breve directorium ad confessarii ac confitentis munus rite obeundum concinnatum per M. Joannem Polancum Theologum Societatis Iesu*, Roma 1554 [MHSI 7, Ch P.IV, 13; MHSI 33, EpIgn. VI, 166–67; and 164, 176, 206]. See also Thomas N. Tentler, *Sin and Confession on the Eve of the Reformation* (Princeton, NJ: Princeton University Press, 1977).

70. Arzubialde, *Ejercicios espirituales de San Ignacio: Historia y análisis*, 168.

CHAPTER 2

1. Juan de Polanco, "Fundación y Confirmación de la Compañía de Jesús," in *Summ. Hisp. Polanci*, 209.

2. "Pedro de Ribadeneira," in Alain Guillermou, *The Life of Saint Ignace de Loyola* (Paris: Le Seuil, 1956), 209.

3. Guillermou, *Saint Ignace de Loyola*, 210.

4. Francis Xavier, "Letter to His Companions Residing in Rome. From Cochin, January 20, 1548," in Francis Xavier, *The Letters and Instructions of Francis Xavier*, trans. M. Joseph Costelloe, SJ, Series I–Jesuit Primary Sources, in English Translations; No. 10 (St. Louis, MO: Institute of Jesuit Sources, 1992), 169–80.

5. Engelbert Mveng, *Histoire du Cameroun* (Yaoundé: CEPER, 1984), 46.

6. Pacheco Pereira, *Esmeraldo de situ orbis: côte occidentale d'Afrique, du sud-marocain au Gabon*, ed. and trans. R. Mauny (Bissau: Portuguese Guinean Studies Center, 1956), 149–51.

7. Mveng, *Histoire du Cameroun*, 103–4.

8. Mveng, *Histoire du Cameroun*, 56.

9. Francis Xavier, *The Letters and Instructions of Francis Xavier*, 169–80.

10. Xavier, *The Letters*, 169–80.

11. Xavier, *The Letters*, 169–80.

12. Xavier, *The Letters*, 218.

13. Paul Dudon, *Saint Ignace de Loyola* (Paris: Beauchesne, 1934), 450.

14. Guillermou, *Saint Ignace de Loyola*, 214.

15. John O'Malley, *The First Jesuits* (Cambridge: Harvard University Press, 1993), 204.

16. Ignatius of Loyola, "Letter to the Senate of Messina, Rome, January 14, 1548," in Ignatius of Loyola, *Ignatius of Loyola: Letters and Instructions* (Saint Louis, MO: The Institute of Jesuit Sources, 2006), 233.

17. John Patrick Donnelly, ed., *Year by Year with the Early Jesuits. Selections from the "Chronicon" of Juan de Polanco* (St. Louis, MO: The Institute of Jesuit Sources, 2004), 71–89.

18. Claude Pavur, *In the School of Ignatius. Studious Zeal and Devoted Learning* (Boston, MA: Institute of Jesuit Sources, 2019), 5 and 18.

19. Ignatius, *Ignatius of Loyola: Letters and Instructions*, 238.

20. Dudon, *Saint Ignace de Loyola*, 450.

21. Dudon, *Saint Ignace de Loyola*, 453.

22. Dudon, *Saint Ignace de Loyola*, 461.

23. Dudon, *Saint Ignace de Loyola*, 475.

24. Ignatius of Loyola (by commission), "Letter to Antonio Araoz, Rome, September 4, 1548," in *Letters and Instructions*, 252.

25. Dudon, *Saint Ignace de Loyola*, 491–93.

26. Dudon, *Saint Ignace de Loyola*, 449.

27. Marc Bloch, *The Historian's Craft*, 1st American ed. (New York: Knopf, 1953), 29.

28. Bloch, *The Historian's Craft*, 41.

29. Bloch, *The Historian's Craft*, 75–76.

30. Dominique Bertrand, *Un corps pour l'esprit. Essai sur l'expérience communautaire selon les Constitutions de La Compagnie de Jésus* (Paris: Desclée De Brouwer, 1974), 14.

31. André de Jaer, *Faire corps pour la mission. lire Les Constitutions de La Compagnie de Jésus* (Brussels: Éditions Lessius, 1998), 10.

32. Ignatius of Loyola, *A Pilgrim Journey: The Autobiography of Ignatius of Loyola*, trans. Joseph N. Tylenda (San Francisco: Ignatius Press, 2001), nn. 99–100 and 186–87.

33. Ignace de Loyola, *Écrits*, ed. Maurice Giuliani (Paris: Christus/DDB, 1991), 318.

34. Hannes Siegrist, "Comparative History of Cultures and Societies: From Cross-Societal Analysis to the Study of Intercultural Interdependencies," *Comparative Education* 42, no. 3 (2006): 397.

35. Bloch, *The Historian's Craft*, 10.

36. Lynn Hunt, *Writing History in the Global Era*, 1st ed. (New York: W.W. Norton & Company, 2014), 55.

37. Hunt, *Writing History in the Global Era*, 59.

38. Ignace de Loyola, *Écrits*, 277.

39. Ignace de Loyola, *Écrits*, 270.

40. Doris Kearns Goodwin, *Team of Rivals: The Political Genius of Abraham Lincoln* (London: Penguin, 2009).

41. O'Malley, *The First Jesuits*, 30.

42. Norton Downs, *Basic Documents in Medieval History* (Princeton, NJ: Van Nostrand Co., 1959), 134–35.

43. Ignace de Loyola, *Écrits*, 277.

44. Ignace de Loyola, *Écrits*, 278.

45. See the accounts of Jerónimo Nadal, "On the Genuine Spirit of Our Society," in *Epistolae* (Madrid, 1898–1905), 2:45. See also O'Malley, *The First Jesuits* (Cambridge, MA: Harvard University Press, 1995).

46. Francisco de Borgia, "On Means of Preserving the Spirit of the Society and of Our Vocation," April 1569, https://jesuitportal .bc.edu/research/documents/1569_borgiapreservingthespirit/, accessed June 14, 2022.

47. Ignace de Loyola, *Écrits*, 292.

48. Cf. Dominique Bouhours, *The Life of Saint Francis Xavier of the Society of Jesus, Apostle of the Indies and of Japan*, trans. John Dryden (Dublin: printed for Ignatius Kelly, at the Stationers-Arms, in Mary's-Lane, Bookseller, 1743), preface by John Dryden.

49. Pedro de Ribadeneira, *The Life of Ignatius of Loyola*, trans. Claude Pavur (Saint Louis, MO: Institute of Jesuit Sources, 2014), 243.

50. Mary Woodstock, "A Letter of Very Reverend Father Mutius Vitelleschi on the Centenary of the Society," in *Select Letters of Our Very Reverend Fathers General to the Fathers and Brothers of the Society of Jesus* (Woodstock, MD: Woodstock College, 1900), 85–119, accessed June 14, 2022, https://jesuitportal.bc.edu/research/documents/1639 _vitelleschicentenary/.

51. Woodstock, "A Letter of Very Reverend Father Mutius Vitelleschi on the Centenary of the Society."

52. John W. Padberg, Martin D. O'Keefe, and John L. McCarthy, *For Matters of Greater Moment: The First Thirty Jesuit General Congregations* (Saint Louis, MO: The Institute of Jesuit Sources, 1994), 187.

53. Padberg, O'Keefe, and McCarthy, *For Matters of Greater Moment*, 172.

54. Padberg, O'Keefe, and McCarthy, *For Matters of Greater Moment*, 174.

55. Padberg, O'Keefe, and McCarthy, *For Matters of Greater Moment*, 201.

56. Padberg, O'Keefe, and McCarthy, *For Matters of Greater Moment*, 201.

57. Padberg, O'Keefe, and McCarthy, *For Matters of Greater Moment*, 204.

58. Padberg, O'Keefe, and McCarthy, *For Matters of Greater Moment*, 205–6.

59. "The Jesuit of Lyon," the author wrote at the time, "can be a calm Savoyard or a Comtois who is not always very convenient, a rough Auvergnat or a more mystical Ardéchois, a Lyonnais concerned with consideration, or a Provençal with a heart full of fantasy, camouflaging under his insouciance the art of living and the wisdom of the old civilized peoples" (cf. Anon, "Portrait of the Jesuit of Lyon," *Jésuites* [1953], 11).

60. Anon, "Portrait du Jésuite Lyonnais," *Jésuites* (1953), 13.

61. Robert A. Maryks, *The Jesuit Order as a Synagogue of Jews: Jesuits of Jewish Ancestry and Purity-of-Blood Laws in the Early Society of Jesus* (Leiden: Brill, 2010).

62. James Brodrick, *The Progress of the Jesuits (1556–79)* (New York: Longmans, Green, and Co., 1947), 5–6.

63. Brodrick, *The Progress of the Jesuits*, 67.

64. Brodrick, *The Progress of the Jesuits*, 78.

65. Downs, *Basic Documents in Medieval History*, 135.

66. Downs, *Basic Documents in Medieval History*, 135.

67. C. J. Ligthart and André Naze, *Le retour des Jésuites au XIXe siècle: La vie du P. Général J. Ph. Roothaan* (Namur: Culture et vérité, 1991), 94.

68. Ligthart and Naze, *Le retour des Jésuites au XIXe siècle*, 98.

69. Ligthart and Naze, *Le retour des Jésuites au XIXe siècle*, 131.

70. Ligthart and Naze, *Le retour des Jésuites au XIXe siècle*, 99.

71. Luis Maria Ortiz, "El clero en las eleccciones públicas," *Razón y Fe* 9 (1905): 214–28.

72. Venancio Minteguiaga, "Algo sobre las elecciones municipales," *Razón y Fe* 13 (1905): 141–56.

73. José Ramón Eguillor, Manuel Revuelta González, and Rafael M. Sanz de Diego, *Memorias del P. Luis Martín: General de la Compañía de Jesús (1846–1906)*, vol. 1 (Rome: Institutum Historicum S.I., 1988), 661–62.

74. Michel-Rolph Trouillot, *Silencing the Past: Power and the Production of History* (Boston, MA: Beacon Press, 1995), 110.

75. Trouillot, *Silencing the Past*, 113.

76. Peter Burke, *The French Historical Revolution: The Annales School, 1929–89*, Key Contemporary Thinkers (Stanford, CA: Stanford University Press, 1990), 61.

77. In the French introduction to the letter of Saint Ignatius to Nunez Barreto, the Ethiopian mission is referred to as *"reconquête spirituelle,"* that is, "spiritual reconquest." Cf. Saint Ignace de Loyola, *Lettres*, trans. Gervais Dumeige (Paris: DDB, 1956), 366.

78. John P. Donnelly, *Jesuit Writings of the Early Modern Period 1540–1640* (Indianapolis, IN: Hackett Publishing, 2006), n. 2, 132. The translation of the two letters is taken from this same book, and the page number in which the letter is found in the book will be put into brackets. The original date is August 13, not 17th as in Donnelly's translation. Cf. Ignacio de Loyola, "Al P. Pedro Canisio," in *Obras completas de Ignacio de Loyola* (Madrid: BAC, 1982), 923–31.

79. Saint Ignace de Loyola, *Lettres*, 133.

80. Saint Ignace de Loyola, *Lettres*, 134.

81. Saint Ignace de Loyola, *Lettres*, 135.

82. Saint Ignace de Loyola, *Lettres*, 136.

83. A series of three letters Ignatius wrote in 1555 to the emperor of Ethiopia and the patriarch of the new mission. The most important of these letters is: Ignacio de Loyola, "Recuerdos que podrán ayudar para la reducción de los reinos del Preste Juan a la unión de la Iglesia y religión católica, enviados al P. Juan Nunes," in *Obras completas de Ignacio de Loyola* (Madrid: BAC, 1982), 957–64. Also translated by Donnelly. The other letters are: Ignacio de Loyola, "Al P. Nunes Barreto, Roma, 24 Febrero 1555," in *Obras completas de Ignacio de Loyola* (Madrid: BAC, 1982), 965–66; Ignacio de Loyola, "Al Negus de Etiopia, Roma, 23 Febrero 1555," in *Obras completas de Ignacio de Loyola* (Madrid: BAC, 1982), 950–56.

84. Donnelly, *Jesuit Writings of the Early Modern Period*, 23.

85. Donnelly, *Jesuit Writings of the Early Modern Period*, 23.

86. *"Así el patriarca que esta en Alejandría o en el Cairo, siendo cismático y diviso desta santa Sede Apostólica, y del Sumo Pontífice, que es cabeza de todo el cuerpo de la Iglesia, el no rescibe para si vida de gracia ni autoridad, ni el puede dar a otro algún patriarca legítimamente"* (Ignacio de Loyola, "Al Negus de Etiopia, Roma, 23 Febrero 1555," 952–53.).

87. Donnelly, *Jesuit Writings of the Early Modern Period*, 25.

88. Donnelly, *Jesuit Writings of the Early Modern Period*, 24.

89. Donnelly, *Jesuit Writings of the Early Modern Period*, 24.

90. Donnelly, *Jesuit Writings of the Early Modern Period*, 25.

91. Donnelly, *Jesuit Writings of the Early Modern Period*, 26–27.

92. Donnelly, *Jesuit Writings of the Early Modern Period*, 29.

93. Donnelly, *Jesuit Writings of the Early Modern Period*, 31.

94. Prior to that official mission to Ethiopia, Saint Francis Xavier was the first Jesuit to reach the Estado da India—"the empire the Portuguese created from Mozambique to Macau administered from the great Indian metropolis of Goa" (Glenn J. Ames, "Serving God, Mammon, or Both?: Religious 'vis-à-vis' Economic Priorities in the Portuguese 'Estado Da India,' c. 1600–1700," *The Catholic Historical Review* 86, no. 2 (April 2000): 194–95.). Francis Xavier en route to Goa spent two months in Mozambique and Malindi from September 1541. See Festo Mkenda, *Mission for Everyone: A Story of the Jesuits in Eastern Africa, 1555–2012* (Nairobi: Saint Paul, 2013), 39.

95. Philip Caraman, *The Lost Empire: The Story of the Jesuits in Ethiopia* (Notre Dame, IN: University of Notre Dame Press, 1985), 10.

96. Donnelly, *Jesuit Writings of the Early Modern Period*, 31.

97. Herve Pennec, *Des Jesuites au royaume du Pretre Jean (Ethiopie)* (Paris: C. C. Calouste Gulbenkian, 2003), 129.

98. Pennec, *Des Jesuites*, 136. Also: Caraman, *The Lost Empire: The Story of the Jesuits in Ethiopia*, 1.

99. Note that Philip Caraman argues that in 1583 only Francisco Lopez still survived in the first mission, although Pennec believes that Antonio Fernandez, who sent a letter to Father Francisco Borgia, General of the Society in 1591, was still in Ethiopia. See Herve Pennec, "La mission jesuite en Ethiopie au temps de Pedro Paez (1583–1622) et ses rapports avec le pouvoir ethiopien," *Ressegna di studi etiopici* 36 (1992): 84.

100. Pennec, "La mission jésuite en Ethiopie," 85.

101. Pennec, *Des Jesuites*, 150.

102. Pennec, "La mission jésuite en Ethiopie," 91.

103. Pennec, "La mission jésuite en Ethiopie," 83.

104. Cf. Philip Caraman, "Pedro Paez," in *Diccionario histórico de la Compañía de Jesús* (Madrid: Universidad Pontificia Comillas, 2001).

105. Pennec, *Des Jesuites*, 134.

106. Herve Pennec, "La mission jesuite en Ethiopie au temps de Pedro Paez (1583–1622) et ses rapports avec le pouvoir ethiopien (Deuxieme partie: Le temps de la seduction, 1603–1612)," *Ressegna di studi etiopici* 37 (1993): 146.

107. Pennec, *Des Jesuites*, 199.

108. Claire Bosc-Tiesse, "A Century of Research on Ethiopian Church Painting: A Brief Overview," *Journal of Ethiopian Studies* 42, nos. 1/2 (2009): 1–23.

109. Wendy Laura Belcher, "Sisters Debating the Jesuits: The Role of African Women in Defeating Portuguese Proto-Colonialism in Seventeenth-Century Abyssinia," *Northeast African Studies* 13, no. 1 (2013): 121–66. This article shows how women in the court opposed both the emperor and the Jesuits and became key players in the uprising against the emperor that led to the expulsion of the Jesuits in 1632.

110. Pennec, "La mission jésuite en Ethiopie au temps de Pedro Páez (1583–1622) et ses rapports avec le pouvoir ethiopien (Deuxième partie: Le temps de la séduction, 1603–1612)," 163.

111. "Ja hoie, padre amantíssimo a jurisdição eclesiástica toda esta na mão da Companhia que ella acertou em nome das anta Igreja" (see Pennec, *Des Jesuites au royaume du Pretre Jean [Ethiopie]*, 156, 229). My translation: "And today, Dear Father, I have the joy to announce you that the entire ecclesiastical jurisdiction is in the hands of the Society, and that was made on behalf of the Holy Church."

112. Pennec, "La mission jesuite en Ethiopie au temps de Pedro Paez (1583–1622) et ses rapports avec le pouvoir ethiopien," 81.

113. Pennec, *Des Jesuites*, 35, 148.

114. Dale H. Moore, "Christianity in Ethiopia," *Church History* 5, no. 3 (September 1936): 280–81.

115. On Mendez, see Mkenda, *Mission for Everyone*, 96–118.

116. C. F. Beckingham, "The Itinerario of Jeronimo Lobo," *Ressegna di studi etiopici* 21 (1965): 167.

117. Caraman, *The Lost Empire: The Story of the Jesuits in Ethiopia*, 142.

118. Fikru Negash Gebrekidan, "Ethiopia and Congo: A Tale of Two Medieval Kingdoms," *Callaloo* 33, no. 1 (2010): 230.

119. In Goa, that battle focused on religious symbols, and the resistance was as ferocious as in Ethiopia. See Paul Axelrod and Michelle A. Fuerch, "Flight of the Deities: Hindu Resistance in Portuguese Goa," *Modern Asian Studies* 30, no. 2 (1996): 387–421.

120. We cannot apply "Counter-Reformation" in this case even if the content of the reforms looks similar, simply because Ethiopia was not a Reformed country.

121. Ines G. Zupanov, "Prosélytisme et pluralisme religieux: Deux expériences missionnaires en Inde aux XVIᵉ et XVIIᵉ siècles," *Archives de sciences sociales des religions* 39, no. 87 (1994): 36.

122. Theodore Natsoulas, "A Failure of Early French Expansionism in Africa: The French-Jesuit Effort in Ethiopia at the Turn of the 18th Century," *Journal of Ethiopian Studies* 36, no. 1 (2003): 5.

123. pennec, "la mission jesuite en Ethiopie (Deuxieme partie)," 151.

124. pennec, "la mission jesuite en Ethiopie (Deuxieme partie)," 152–53.

125. pennec, "la mission jesuite en Ethiopie (Deuxieme partie)," 152–53.

126. pennec, "la mission jesuite en Ethiopie (Deuxieme partie)," 167.

CHAPTER 3

1. Harvey Cox, *Fire from Heaven. The Rise of Pentecostal Spirituality and the Reshaping of Religion in the Twentieth-First Century* (Cambridge, MA: Da Capo Press, 2001), 244.

2. J. Kwabena Asamoah-Gyadu, *Contemporary Pentecostal Christianity: Interpretation from an African Context* (Eugene, OR: Wipf and Stock Publishers, 2013), 147–52.

3. Ludovic Lado, *Catholic Pentecostalism and the Paradoxes of Africanization* (Leiden: Brill, 2009).

4. R. Andrew Chesnut, Steven Engler, and Bettina E. Schmidt, "The Spirit of Brazil: Charismatic Christianity among the World's

Largest Catholic and Pentecostal Populations," in *Handbook of Contemporary Religions in Brazil* 13 (Leiden: Brill, 2017), 81–82.

5. Todd Hartch, *The Rebirth of Latin American Christianity* (Oxford/New York: Oxford University Press, 2014), 117.

6. Hartch, *The Rebirth of Latin American Christianity*, 118.

7. Edward L. Cleary and Timothy Steigenga, *The Catholic Charismatic Renewal: Revitalization Movements and Conversion* (New Brunswick, NJ: Rutgers University Press, 2019), 153.

8. Cleary and Steigenga, *The Catholic Charismatic Renewal*, 153.

9. M. Antoni J Üçerler, "The Jesuits in East Asia in the Early Modern Age: A New 'Areopagus' and the 'Re-Invention' of Christianity," in *The Jesuits and Globalization*, ed. Thomas Banchoff and José Casanova (Washington, DC: Georgetown University Press, 2016), 36–37.

10. Francis X. Clooney, *Western Jesuit Scholars in India: Tracing Their Paths, Reassessing Their Goals* (Leiden: Brill, 2020), 6–7.

11. Roberto De Nobili, *Preaching Wisdom to the Wise*, trans. Anand Amaladass and Francis X. Clooney (St. Louis, MO: The Institute of Jesuit Sources, 2000), 27.

12. Andrew C. Ross, *A Vision Betrayed: The Jesuits in Japan and China, 1542–1742* (Maryknoll, NY: Orbis Books, 1994), 42–43.

13. Ross, *A Vision Betrayed*, 74.

14. Joan-Pau Rubiés, "The Concept of Cultural Dialogue and the Jesuit Method of Accommodation: Between Idolatry and Civilization," *AHSI* 74, fasc. 147 (2005): 239.

15. Jacques Gernet, *China and the Christian Impact: A Conflict of Cultures* (Cambridge, UK: Cambridge University Press, 1985).

16. Rubiés, "The Concept of Cultural Dialogue," 243.

17. De Nobili, *Preaching Wisdom to the Wise*, 37.

18. Rubiés, "The Concept of Cultural Dialogue," 276.

19. Leonardo Sacco, "Matteo Ricci and the Metaphor of the Bridge between Civilizations. Some Critical Remarks," *Storia, antropologia e scienze del linguaggio* 34, fasc. 1 (2019): 41–116.

20. Joan-Pau Rubiés, "The Jesuits and the Enlightenment," in *The Oxford Handbook of the Jesuits*, ed. Ines G. Zupanov (Oxford: Oxford University Press, 2018), 2.

21. Max Weber, *The Protestant Ethic and the Spirit of Capitalism*, trans. Stephen Kalberg (New York: Oxford University Press, 2011).

22. Michael Novak, *The Catholic Ethic and the Spirit of Capitalism* (New York: The Free Press, 1993).

23. Ross, *A Vision Betrayed*, 43.

24. Ross, *A Vision Betrayed*, 42.

25. Eugenio Menegon, *Ancestors, Virgins, & Friars: Christianity as a Local Religion in the Late Imperial China* (Cambridge, MA: Harvard University Asia C.H.Y.I., 2009), 2.

26. Menegon, *Ancestors, Virgins, & Friars*, 5.

27. Menegon, *Ancestors, Virgins, & Friars*, 7.

28. Ambrose Mong, "Catholic Missions in China: Failure to Form Native Clergy," *International Journal for the Study of the Christian Church* 19, no. 1 (2019): 36.

29. Mong, "Catholic Missions in China," 36.

30. Mong, "Catholic Missions in China," 36.

31. Albert Monshan Wu, *From Christ to Confucius: German Missionaries, Chinese Christians, and the Globalization of Christianity, 1860–1950* (New Haven, CT: Yale University Press, 2016), 4.

32. Monshan Wu, *From Christ to Confucius*, 4.

33. Bárbara Reyes, *Private Women, Public Lives: Gender and the Missions of the Californias*, 1st ed. (Austin: University of Texas Press, 2009).

34. Wendy Laura Belcher, "Sisters Debating the Jesuits: The Role of African Women in Defeating Portuguese Proto-Colonialism in Seventeenth-Century Abyssinia," *Northeast African Studies* 13, no. 1 (2013): 121–66.

35. Jean Luc Enyegue, "The Adulteresses Were Reformers: The Perception and Position of Women in the Religious Fight of Fernando Poo, 1843–1900," *Journal of Jesuit Studies* 4 (2018): 215–32.

36. Víctor M. Fernández et al., *The Archeology of the Jesuit Missions in Ethiopia, 1557–1632* (Leiden: Brill, 2017), 451–53.

37. Tracy Neal Leavelle and Project Muse, *The Catholic Calumet: Colonial Conversions in French and Indian North America*, 1st ed. (Philadelphia: University of Pennsylvania Press, 2012), 8.

38. Adina Ruiu, "Conflicting Visions of the Jesuit Missions to the Ottoman Empire, 1609–1628," *Journal of Jesuit Studies* 1 (2014): 261.

39. Ruiu, "Conflicting Visions of the Jesuit Missions," 261.

40. Ines G. Zupanov, *Disputed Missions: Jesuit Experiments and Brahmanical Knowledge in Seventeenth-Century India* (New Delhi: Oxford University Press, 1999), 115.

41. Elisa Frei, "Signed in Blood: Negotiating with the Superiors General about the Overseas Missions," *Studies in the Spirituality of Jesuits* 51, no. 4 (Winter 2019): 1–54.

42. Catherine M. Mooney, "Ignatian Spirituality, A Spirituality for Mission," *Mission Studies* 26 (2009): 192–213.

43. Ines G. Zupanov, "'I Am a Great Sinner': Jesuit Missionary Dialogues in Southern India (Sixteenth Century)," *Journal of the Economic and Social History of the Orient* 55 (2012): 419.

44. Tobias Winnerling, "The Spiritual Empire of the Society of Jesus," *Itinerario* 40, no. 2 (2016): 215–37.

45. Ulrike Strasser, "Copies with Souls: The Late Seventeenth-Century Marianas Martyrs, Francis Xavier, and the Question of Clerical Reproduction," *Journal of Jesuit Studies* 2 (2015): 562.

46. Franco Mormando and Jill G. Thomas, *Francis Xavier and the Jesuit Missions in the Far East* (Chestnut Hill, MA: Boston College Burns Library, 2006), 9.

47. Mormando and Thomas, *Francis Xavier and the Jesuit Missions in the Far East*, 11.

48. Pedro de Ribadeneira, *Vida del P. Ignacio de Loyola, fundador de la religión de La Compañía de Jesús* (Madrid: Alonso Gómez, 1583).

49. Mormando and Thomas, *Francis Xavier and the Jesuit Missions in the Far East*, 13–14.

50. Pedro de Ribadeneira, *Tratado en el qual se da razón del Instituto de la Religión de la Compañía de Jesús* (Madrid: Colegio de la Compañía de Jesús, 1605).

51. David G. Schultenover, "Luis Martín García, the Jesuit General of the Modernist Crisis (1892–1906): On Historical Criticism," *The Catholic Historical Review* 89, no. 3 (2003): 439–40.

52. Gilbert J. Garraghan, "The Jesuit Quadricentennial, 1940," *The Catholic Historical Review* 26 (April 1940): 340.

53. Garraghan, "The Jesuit Quadricentennial, 1940," 340.

54. Thierry Meynard, *The Jesuit Reading of Confucius: The First Complete Translation of the Lunyu (1687) Published in the West* (Leiden: Brill, 2015), 7.

55. Mungello, *Curious Land*, 249.

56. Meynard, *The Jesuit Reading of Confucius*, 71.

57. Strasser, "Copies with Souls," 566.

58. Strasser, "Copies with Souls," 569.

59. T. Frank Kennedy, "Jesuits and Music: The European Tradition, 1547–1622" (PhD diss., Santa Clara, CA, University of California Santa Clara, 1982), 193–96.

60. Kennedy, "Jesuits and Music," 200.

61. Mormando and Thomas, *Francis Xavier and the Jesuit Missions in the Far East*, 13.

62. Mormando and Thomas, *Francis Xavier and the Jesuit Missions in the Far East*, 9–10.

63. Mormando and Thomas, *Francis Xavier and the Jesuit Missions in the Far East*, 10–11.

64. Giovanni Girolamo Soprani, *La vie, les miracles, et la canonization de S. Ignace de Loyola. Tirée des informations authentiques du procez de sa canonization fait à La Rote et à la Congregation Des Rites* (Rouen: Richard L'Allemant, 1629), 188.

65. Girolamo Soprani, *La vie, les miracles*, 194.

66. Juan Eusebio Nieremberg, "P. Luis Gonzalez de Cámara," in *Varones ilustres de la Compañía de Jesús*, vol. 6, 9 vols. (Bilbao: Administración del Mensajero del Corazón de Jesús, 1887), 491–541.

67. Ignatius of Loyola, *A Pilgrim Journey.*

68. Juan Eusebio Nieremberg, "Juan Nuñes Barreto," in *Varones ilustres de la Compañía de Jesús*, vol. 2 (Bilbao: Administració de "El Mensajero del Corazón de Jesús," 1889), 376–77.

69. Nieremberg, "Juan Nuñes Barreto," 383.

70. Ralph A. Austen, "The Metamorphoses of Middlemen: The Duala, Europeans, and the Cameroon Hinterland, ca. 1800–ca. 1960," *The International Journal of African Studies* 16, no. 1 (1983): 1–24.

71. James William Brodman, *Ransoming Captives in Crusader Spain: The Order of Merced on the Christian-Islamic Frontier* (Philadelphia: University of Pennsylvania Press, 1986), ix.

72. Nieremberg, "Juan Nuñes Barreto," 385.

73. Nieremberg, "Juan Nuñes Barreto," 387.

74. Nieremberg, "Juan Nuñes Barreto," 387.

75. Nieremberg, "Juan Nuñes Barreto," 388.

76. Les références bibliques insérées par moi.

77. Nieremberg, "Juan Nuñes Barreto," 389.

78. Nieremberg, "Juan Nuñes Barreto," 392.

79. Nieremberg, "Juan Nuñes Barreto," 392.

80. Nieremberg, "Juan Nuñes Barreto," 404.

81. Nieremberg, "Juan Nuñes Barreto," 406.

82. Pennec, "La mission jesuite en Ethiopie," 91.

83. Pennec, "La mission jesuite en Ethiopie," 83.

84. A. H. M. (Arnold Hugh Martin) Jones and Elizabeth Monroe, *A History of Abyssinia* (Oxford: Clarendon Press, 1935), 89.

85. *Varones ilustres* 2:441.

86. *Varones ilustre* 2:441.

87. Jim E. Banta et al., "The Global Influence of the Seventh-Day Adventist Church on Diet," *Religions* 9, no. 251 (n.d.): 1–25.

88. *Varones ilustres* 2:442.

89. *Varones ilustres* 2:443.

90. *Varones ilustres* 2:454.

91. *Varones ilustres* 2:459.

92. *Varones ilustres* 2:445–46.

93. *Varones ilustres* 2:447–449.

94. *Varones ilustres* 2:455.

95. David Mathew, *Ethiopia, the Study of a Polity, 1540–1935* (London: Eyre & Spottiswoode, 1947), 40.

96. Pennec, "La mission jesuite en Ethiopie," 146.

97. Mathew, *Ethiopia, the Study of a Polity, 1540–1935*, 42–43.

98. Pennec, "La mission jesuite en Ethiopie," 79.

99. Pennec, "La mission jesuite en Ethiopie," 81.

100. Mathew, *Ethiopia, the Study of a Polity*, 52

101. Mathew, *Ethiopia, the Study of a Polity*, 52–53.

102. Mathew, *Ethiopia, the Study of a Polity*, 55.

103. C. R. Markham, "The Portuguese Expeditions to Abyssinia in the Fifteenth, Sixteenth, and Seventeenth Centuries," *The Journal of the Royal Geographical Society of London* 38 (1868): 10.

104. Markham, "The Portuguese Expeditions to Abyssinia," 11.

105. C. F. Beckingham, "European Sources of Ethiopian History before 1634," *Paideuma* 33 (1987): 170–71.

106. Alex Garganigo, "William without Mary: Mourning Sensibly in the Public Sphere," *The Seventeenth Century* 23, no. 1 (2008): 105.

107. Garganigo, "William without Mary," 107.

108. Bouhours, *The Life of Saint Francis Xavier of the Society of Jesus*, Dedication.

109. Louis G. Kelly, "The Other Dryden," *Livius* 8 (1996): 87.

110. Kelly, "The Other Dryden," 88.

111. John Spurr, "The Piety of John Dryden," in *The Cambridge Companion to John Dryden*, ed. Steven N. Zwicker (Cambridge, UK: Cambridge University Press, 2004), 242.

112. Bouhours, *The Life of Saint Francis Xavier of the Society of Jesus*, Dedication.

113. Kelly, "The Other Dryden," 88.

114. Kelly, "The Other Dryden," 88.

115. Bouhours, *The Life of Saint Francis Xavier of the Society of Jesus*, 233.

116. Bouhours, *The Life of Saint Francis Xavier of the Society of Jesus*, 305.

117. Larissa Juliet Taylor, "God of Judgment, God of Love: Catholic Preaching in France, 1460–1560," *Historical Reflections* 26, no. 2 (Summer 2000), 264.

118. E. Davister, "Le Nègre est-il capable d'affection?," *Missions belges* (1912), 100.

119. Davister, "Le Nègre est-il capable d'affection?," 100.

120. Davister, "Le Nègre est-il capable d'affection?," 105.

121. Mgr. Van Hée, "Le Séminaire de Lemfu," *Revue missionnaire des Jésuites belges* 8 (July 1932): 350.

122. A. Brielman, "Une des oeuvres principales du missionnaire: L'école," *Missions belges* 9 (1907): 100.

123. Alexandre Brou, *Cent ans de missions, 1815–1934. Les Jésuites missionnaires au 19e et au 20e siècle* (Paris: Editions Spes, 1935), 85.

124. "Vicariat apostolique du Kwango: Statistiques, 1937–1938," *Revue missionnaire des Jésuites belges* 18 (January 1939): 26.

125. Brou, *Cent ans de missions, 1815–1934*, 72.

126. Brou, *Cent ans de missions, 1815–1934*, 73.

127. A. Scott Moreau, *Contextualization in World Mission: Mapping and Assessing Evangelical Models* (Grand Rapids, MI: Kregel Publications, 2012), 19.

128. Mark A. Noll, *The Rise of Evangelicalism. The Age of Edwards, Whitefield and Wesleys* (Downers Grove, IL: InterVarsity Press, 2003), 18–19.

129. Thomas Haweis, *Evangelical Principles and Practice* (London: Oliver, 1962), v.

Notes

130. Mark Hutchinson and John Wolffe, *A Short History of Global Evangelicalism* (Cambridge, UK: Cambridge University Press, 2012), 26.

131. Hutchinson and Wolffe, *A Short History of Global Evangelicalism*, 29.

132. Hutchinson and Wolffe, *A Short History of Global Evangelicalism*, 30.

133. Juan Eusebio Nieremberg, "P. Marcial de Lorenzana, SJ," in *Varones ilustres SI*, vol. 4 (Bilbao: Administració de "El Mensajero del Corazón de Jesús," 1889), 379.

134. Nieremberg, "P. Marcial de Lorenzana, SJ," in *Varones ilustres SI* 4:375–376.

135. Nieremberg, "P. Marcial de Lorenzana, SJ," in *Varones ilustres SI* 4:377.

136. Nieremberg, "P. Marcial de Lorenzana, SJ," in *Varones ilustres SI* 4:377.

137. T. Frank Kennedy, "Music and the Jesuit Mission in the New World," *Studies in the Spirituality of Jesuits* 39, no. 3 (Fall 2007): 8.

138. Kennedy, "Music and the Jesuit Mission in the New World," 15–16.

139. John K. Thornton, "Conquest and Theology. The Jesuits in Angola, 1548–1650," *Journal of Jesuit Studies* 1, no. 2 (2014): 259.

140. Linda M. Heywood, "The Angolan-Afro-Brazilian Cultural Connections, Slavery and Abolition," *A Journal of Slave and Post-Slave Studies* 20, no. 1 (1999): 16.

141. Heywood, "The Angolan-Afro-Brazilian Cultural Connections, Slavery and Abolition," 16.

142. Heywood, "The Angolan-Afro-Brazilian Cultural Connections, Slavery and Abolition," 19.

143. Heywood, "The Angolan-Afro-Brazilian Cultural Connections, Slavery and Abolition," 14–15.

144. Heywood, "The Angolan-Afro-Brazilian Cultural Connections, Slavery and Abolition," 15–16

145. Mattheus Cardoso, *Le catéchisme kikongo de 1624*, trans. Francois Bontick (Brussels: Académie royale des sciences d'Outre-Mer, 1978); Antonio Do Coucto, *Gentilis angollae in fidei mysteriis eruditus: Opusculum Reginae Fidelissimae Mariae i jussu denuo excussum* (Lisbon: Olisipone, 1784).

CHAPTER 4

1. Robert Molyneux, "A Funeral Sermon," *Woodstock Letters* 13, no. 3 (1884): 297–302.

2. Molyneux, "A Funeral Sermon," 296.

3. Molyneux, "A Funeral Sermon," 298.

4. Molyneux, "A Funeral Sermon," n. 1, 297.

5. Molyneux, "A Funeral Sermon," 299.

6. Joseph M. Finotti 1817–1879, *Peter Claver: A Sketch of His Life and Labors on Behalf of the African Slave* (Boston, MA: Lee and Shepard, 1868).

7. Molyneux, "A Funeral Sermon," 299.

8. Molyneux, "A Funeral Sermon," 300.

9. Molyneux, "A Funeral Sermon," 302.

10. Urbano Valero Agundez, *El proyecto de renovacion de La Compania de Jesus (1965–2007)* (Bilbao: Mensajero-Sal Terrae, 2011), n. 27.

11. Alexandra Merle, "El *De rege* de Juan de Mariana (1599) y la cuestión del tiranicidio: ¿un discurso de ruptura?," *Criticon* Online (2014): 89–102.

12. Philippe Lécrivain, *les premiers siècles jésuites: Jalons pour une histoire, 1540–1814* (Paris: Lessius, 2016), 249.

13. Lécrivain, *Les premiers siècles jésuites*, 250.

14. Lécrivain, *Les premiers siècles jésuites*, 251.

15. Lécrivain, *Les premiers siècles jésuites*, 251.

16. "Des persécutions excitées contre nous," *Jesuit Missionaries in New France* (MNF) IV, 173, II, Ch. 2, nos. 1–14, pp. 656–65, at p. 658–59.

17. "Des persécutions que nous avons souffert en 1637," MNF IV, 52, II, Ch. 1, nos. 9–13, pp. 134–241, at p. 136.

18. "Assemblée générale de tout le païs où on délibère de notre mort," MNF IV, 52, II, Ch. 2, nos. 1–5, at pp. 142–47.

19. "Des persécutions que nous avons souffert en 1637," MNF IV, 52, II, Ch. 1, nos. 9–13, pp. 134–241, at p. 175.

20. "Des persécutions que nous avons souffert en 1637," 142.

21. See Jose del Rey Fajardo, *Expulsión, extinción y restauración de los Jesuitas en el nuevo reino de Granada, 1767–1815* (Bogota: Editorial Pontificia Universidad Javeriana, 2014), 256–61.

Notes

22. Isaac Disraeli, *Despotism: Or, the Fall of the Jesuits; A Political Romance* (London: John Murray, 1811), vii.

23. Xavier Walter, *La troisième mort des missions de Chine* (Paris: François-Xavier de Guibert, 2008), 29–39.

24. L.-J. Rogier, G. de Bertier de Sauvigny, and Joseph Hajjar, *Nouvelle histoire de l'eglise. siècle des lumières, révolutions, restaurations (1715–1800)*, vol. 4 (Paris: Seuil, 1966), 91.

25. Rogier, de Bertier de Sauvigny, and Hajjar, *Nouvelle histoire de l'eglise* 4:93.

26. Lécrivain, *Les premiers siècles jésuites*, 529.

27. Jean Lacouture, *Jésuites: Les conquérants*, vol. 1 (Paris: Seuil, 1991), 415.

28. M. Batllori, "Entre la supresión y la restauración de la Compañía de Jesús," *Archivum historicum Societatis Iesu* 43 (January 1974): 368.

29. Kendall Brown, "Jesuit Wealth and Economic Activity within the Peruvian Economy: The Case of Colonial Southern Peru," *The Americas* 44, no. 1 (1987): 41–42.

30. Jonathan Wright, "From Immolation to Restoration: The Jesuits, 1773–1814," *Theological Studies* 75, no. 4 (2014): 731–33.

31. Maurice Whitehead, "The Lavalette Affair and the Flight from St. Omers, 1762," in *English Jesuit Education: Expulsion, Suppression, Survival, Restoration, 1762–1803* (Burlington, VT: Ashgate, 2013), 44.

32. Whitehead, "The Lavalette Affair and the Flight from St. Omers, 1762," 44.

33. Wright, "From Immolation to Restoration: The Jesuits, 1773–1814."

34. Antonio Zarandona, *Historia de la extincion y restablecimiento de la Compania de Jesus*, ed. Ricardo Cappa, vol. 3, 3 vols. (Madrid: Luis Aguado, 1890).

35. Jean-Marc Rohrbasser, "Le tremblement de terre de Lisbonne: Un mal pour un bien?," *Annales de démographie historique* 2, no. 120 (2010): 199ff.

36. Zarandona, *Historia de la extincion y restablecimiento de la Compania de Jesus* 3:8.

37. Zarandona, *Historia de la extincion y restablecimiento de la Compania de Jesus* 3:8.

38. Rocío Peñalta Catalán, "Voltaire: Una reflexión filosófico-literaria sobre el terromoto de Lisboa de 1755," *Revista de filología románica* 26 (2009): 194.

39. Peñalta Catalán, "Voltaire: Una reflexión filosófico-literaria sobre el terromoto de Lisboa de 1755," 194.

40. Lécrivain, *Les premiers siècles jésuites*, 552.

41. Maurice Whitehead, "Jesuit Secondary Education Revolutionized: The Académie Anglaise, Liège, 1773–1794," *Paedagogica Historica* 40, nos. 1/2 (April 2004): 34.

42. Wright, "From Immolation to Restoration: The Jesuits, 1773–1814," 736.

43. Whitehead, "Jesuit Secondary Education Revolutionized," 33.

44. Whitehead, "Jesuit Secondary Education Revolutionized," 39.

45. Del Rey Fajardo, *Expulsión, extinción y restauración de los Jesuitas en el nuevo reino de Granada, 1767–1815*, 511–17.

46. Del Rey Fajardo, *Expulsión, extinción y restauración*, 511–17.

47. John W. O'Malley, *Los Jesuitas y los Papas: Cinco siglos de historia* (Bilbao: Mensajero, 2017), 135–36.

48. Jan Roothaan, "Al P. Antonio Morey: Filipinas y misiones ultramares, 29 April 1852," in Archivum romanum Societatis Iesu (ARSI), "Missiones litterae, 1832–62."

49. Roothaan, "Al P. Antonio Morey."

50. Marc Lindeijer, "Aptus ad gobernandum. The Formation of Fr. Jan Roothaan in the Principles and Practices of Good Governance of the Restored Society of Jesus, 1823–1829," in *The Survival of the Jesuits in the Low Countries, 1773–1850* (Leuven: Leuven University Press, 2019), 233–53.

51. ARSI, *Fondo "P. Jan Philip Roothan SJ," Amsterdam, 23 Novembre 1785—Roma, 8 Maggio 1853*, vol. 7 (Roma: ARSI, 2014), accessed, April 16, 2022, http://www.sjweb.info/arsi/documents/Inventario_Roothaan_Vol2.pdf.

52. Peter Beckx, "Anthony Anderledy," *Letters and Notice* 13, no. 2 (July 1884).

53. Beckx, "Anthony Anderledy."

54. Anonymous, "The V.R. Peter Beckx, Twenty-Third General of the Society of Jesus, 1795–1887," *Letters and Notices* 16, no. 2 (1887).

55. Anonymous, "The V.R. Peter Beckx, Twenty-Third General of the Society of Jesus."

56. Anonymous, "The V.R. Peter Beckx, Twenty–Third General of the Society of Jesus."

57. Manuel Revuelta, "América hispánica," in *DHCJ* 1:147.

58. Anonymous, "The V.R. Peter Beckx, Twenty–third General of the Society of Jesus."

59. Anonymous, "The V.R. Peter Beckx, Twenty–third General of the Society of Jesus."

60. Anonymous, "Varia: A Useful Book," *Woodstock Letters* 15, no. 2 (1886).

61. James H. Hutson, *The Founders on Religion: A Book of Quotations* (Princeton, NJ: Princeton University Press, 2005), 45.

62. Hutson, *The Founders on Religion*, 44.

63. Hutson, *The Founders on Religion*, 45.

64. Hutson, *The Founders on Religion*, 45.

65. Daniel L. Schlafy, "The 'Russian' Society and the American Jesuits: Giovanni Grassi's Crucial Role," in *Jesuit Survival and Restoration*, ed. Robert Maryks (Boston, MA: Brill, 2015), 358.

66. Catherine O'Donnell, "John Carroll, the Catholic Church, and the Society of Jesus in Early Republican America," in *Jesuit Survival and Restoration*, ed. Robert Maryks (Boston, MA: Brill, 2015), 371.

67. Schlafy, "The 'Russian' Society and the American Jesuits: Giovanni Grassi's Crucial Role," 361–62.

68. Schlafy, "The 'Russian' Society and the American Jesuits: Giovanni Grassi's Crucial Role," 360.

69. Schlafy, "The 'Russian' Society and the American Jesuits: Giovanni Grassi's Crucial Role," 363.

70. Daniel Rops, *L'Eglise des révolutions*, vol. 6 (Paris: Fayard, 1960), 715.

71. Rops, *L'Eglise des révolutions*, 719.

72. Mary Elizabeth Brown, "The Making of Italian–American Catholics: Jesuits Work on the Lower East Side, New York, 1890's–1950's," *The Catholic Historical Review* 73, no. 2 (1987): 195–210.

73. Robert Bruce Mullin, "North America," in *A World History of Christianity*, ed. Adrian Hastings (Grand Rapids, MI: Eerdmans, 1999), 434.

74. Rops, *L'Eglise des révolutions*, 6:720.

75. Mullin, "North America," 434.

76. Rops, *L'Eglise des révolutions*, 6:727.

77. Rops, *L'Eglise des révolutions*, 6:729.

78. Gilbert J. Garraghan, *The Jesuits of the Middle United States*, vol. 1 (New York: America Press, 1938), 47–49.

79. "Les controverses américanistes finirent par diviser la hiérarchie américaine. Les questions relatives à l'éducation catholique américaine séparèrent les libéraux, menés par l'archevêque John Ireland et l'évêque John Kean et leurs partisans, des conservateurs menés par l'archevêque Michael Corrigan." "The Americanist controversies ended up dividing the American hierarchy. Questions of American Catholic education separated the liberals, led by Archbishop John Ireland and Bishop John Kean and their supporters, from the conservatives led by Archbishop Michael Corrigan." Cf. Paul Kahan, "The 'Latin Question' as Microcosm: The Americanist Controversies Writ Small," *American Catholic Studies* 118, no. 1 (Spring 2007): 49.

80. Gilbert J. Garraghan, *The Jesuits of the Middle United States*, vol. 3 (New York: America Press, 1938), 434.

81. Garraghan, *The Jesuits of the Middle United States* 3:429.

82. Kahan, "The 'Latin Question' as Microcosm: The Americanist Controversies Writ Small," 48.

83. Gilbert J. Garraghan, *The Jesuits of the Middle United States*, vol. 2 (New York: America Press, 1938), 535–36.

84. Garraghan, *The Jesuits of the Middle United States* 3:423–34.

85. Gerald McKevitt and Thomas Worcester, "Jesuit Schools in the USA, 1814–c. 1970," in *The Cambridge Companion to the Jesuits, Cambridge Companions to Religion* (Oxford: Oxford University Press, 2008), 278.

86. McKevitt and Worcester, "Jesuit Schools in the USA," 282.

87. McKevitt and Worcester, "Jesuit Schools in the USA," 283.

88. McKevitt and Worcester, "Jesuit Schools in the USA," 286.

89. John T. McGreevy, *American Jesuits and the World: How an Embattled Religious Order Made Modern Catholicism Global* (Princeton, NJ: Princeton University Press, 2016), 2.

90. McGreevy, *American Jesuits and the World*, 4.

91. Peter McDonough and Eugene C. Bianchi, *Passionate Uncertainty. Inside the American Jesuits* (Berkeley, CA: University of California Press, 2002), 1.

92. McDonough and Bianchi, *Passionate Uncertainty*, 3.

93. McDonough and Bianchi, *Passionate Uncertainty*, 2.

94. Peter McDonough, *Men Astutely Trained. A History of the Jesuits in the American Century* (New York: The Free Press, 1992), xvi.

95. All quoted by Raymond A. Schroth, *The American Jesuits: A History* (New York: New York University, 2007), 49–50.

96. Schroth, *The American Jesuits*, 49–50.

97. McKevitt and Worcester, "Jesuit Schools in the USA," 278.

98. Jean-Baptiste Amadieu and Simon Icard, eds., *Du jansénisme au modernisme: La bulle Auctorem Fidei, 1794, Pivot du magistère romain* (Paris: Beauchesne, 2020).

CHAPTER 5

1. Arturo Sosa, SJ, *Walking with Ignatius: In Conversation with Darío Menor* (Chicago, IL: Loyola Press, 2021), 115.

2. Urbano Valero, *Pablo VI y los Jesuitas: Una relación intensa y complicada, 1963–1978* (Bilbao: Mensajero, 2019), 69.

3. Valero, *Pablo VI y los Jesuitas*, 94–95.

4. Valero, *Pablo VI y los Jesuitas*, 97.

5. Valero, *Pablo VI y los Jesuitas*, 101.

6. Valero, *Pablo VI y los Jesuitas*, 101.

7. Valero, *Pablo VI y los Jesuitas*, 101.

8. Valero, *Pablo VI y los Jesuitas*, 166.

9. Valero, *Pablo VI y los Jesuitas*, 178.

10. Gianni La Bella, *Los Jesuitas: Del Vaticano II al Papa Francisco* (Bilbao: Mensajero, 2019), 191.

11. Gianni La Bella, *Pedro Arrupe, Supérieur Général des Jésuites, 1965–1983: Le gouvernement d'un prophète, Suivi d'un témoignage d'Adolfo Nicolás, "Huit rencontres avec P. Pedro Arrupe"* (Brussels: Editions Française, 2009), 194–95.

12. La Bella, *Los Jesuitas: Del Vaticano II al Papa Francisco*, 230–36.

13. Peter Hans Kolvenbach, *The Road from La Storta: Peter-Hans Kolvenbach, on Ignatian Spirituality* (St. Louis, MO: Institute of Jesuit Sources, 2000).

14. Peter Hans Kolvenbach, *Fous pour le Christ* (1998), Jesuit Historical Institute in Africa (JHIA) Collection, *General Stacks* (SB 4700. L7 1998).

15. Peter Hans Kolvenbach, *Men of God: Men for Others* (New York: Alba House, 1990).

16. Peter Hans Kolvenbach, *La formacion del Jesuita* (Rome: Curia General de la Compañia de Jesus, 2003).

17. Peter Hans Kolvenbach, *The Characteristics of Jesuit Education* (Bombay: Anand-Gujarat, 1987); Peter Hans Kolvenbach, *Discursos Universitarios* (2008), JHIA Collection, *General Stacks* (BX 4705. K65 2008).

18. Peter Hans Kolvenbach, *A nos collaborateurs et collaboratrice. Un merci tres cordial!* (1992), *General Stacks* (SB 433. K65 1992).

19. Peter Hans Kolvenbach and Joseph Pittau, *Understanding and Discussion: Approaches to Muslim-Christian Dialogue* (Rome: Centre "Cultures & Religions," Pontifical Gregorian University, 1998).

20. Adolfo Nicolás, "Homélie de la Messe de Remerciements," *AR* 24, Fasc. I, no. 2, no. Documenta Congregationis Generalis (2008): 629.

21. Nicolás, "Homélie de la Messe de Remerciements," 630.

22. Nicolás, "Homélie de la Messe de Remerciements," 631.

23. Festo Mkenda and Michael Amaladoss, *The Way, the Truth and the Life: A Confluence of Asia, Europe and Africa in Jesus of Nazareth; A Souvenir Publication in Honour of Fr Adolfo Nicolás SJ* (Nairobi: Jesuit Historical Institute in Africa, 2017), 10–11.

24. General Curia, SJ, "General Congregation 35. Historical Introduction," *AR* 24, Fasc. I, no. 2, no. Documenta Congregationis Generalis (2008): 163.

25. Mkenda and Amaladoss, *The Way, the Truth and the Life*, 10–11.

26. See Mkenda and Amaladoss, *The Way, the Truth and the Life*, 8.

27. See Ogbu Kalu, Sheridan Gilley, and Brian Stanley, "Ethiopianism and the Roots of Modern African Christianity," in *The Cambridge History of Christianity*, vol. 8 (Cambridge: Cambridge University Press, 2001), 588.

28. Pope Benedict XVI, "Africae Munus," November 19, 2011, no. 13, accessed January 5, 2022, https://www.vatican.va.

29. Joseph Opdebeek, SJ, and Cyrille Van den Driessche, "Notes et informations sur l'influenza," *Missions belges de la Compagnie de Jésus* 17 (1919): 22.

30. Opdebeek and Van den Driessche, "Notes et informations sur l'influenza," 22.

31. J. M. Katzenellenbogen, "The 1918 Influenza Epidemic in Mamre," *SAMT* 74, no. 1 (1988): 362.

32. I. De Pierpont, "Comment les missionnaires font des routes au Congo," *Mission belges* (1910), 181–85.

33. Editors, "Fondation de cinq nouveaux villages chrétiens au Kwango," *Missions belges* (1901): 148–49.

34. Msgr. Van Hée, "Le séminaire de Lemfu," *Revue missionnaire des Jésuites belges* 8 (July 1932): 350–54.

35. A. Renard, "Mission du Kwango: Au service des malades," in *Missions belges de la Compagnie de Jésus: Congo, Bengale, Ceylan* (Brussels: Charles Bulens, 1908), 24.

36. Renard, "Mission du Kwango," 24.

37. E. Davister, "Le Nègre est-il capable d'affection?," *Missions belges* (1912): 100–105.

38. J. van Wing, "Mission du Kwango: Vingt-cinquième anniversaire de la mission," *Missions belges de la Compagnie de Jésus* 17 (1919): 44.

39. Elizabeth Outka, *Viral Modernism: The Influenza Pandemic and Interwar Literature* (New York: Columbia University Press, 2019), 200.

40. Outka, *Viral Modernism*, 200.

41. Karl Rahner, *Foundations of Christian Faith: An Introduction to the Idea of Christianity* (New York: Crossroad, 1978), 431.

42. Rahner, *Foundations of Christian Faith*, 440–41.

43. Outka, *Viral Modernism*, 201.

44. Outka, *Viral Modernism*, 201.

45. Outka, *Viral Modernism*, 216.

46. Ignatius of Loyola, *The Spiritual Exercises of St Ignatius of Loyola* (New York: Vintage, 2000), no. 329.

47. Ignatius of Loyola, *The Spiritual Exercises*, no. 332.

48. Maurice Giuliani, *La experiencia de los ejercicios espirituales en la vida* (Bilbao: Mensajero-Sal Terrae, 1992), 47.

49. Giuliani, *La experiencia de los ejercicios espirituales en la vida*, 50–51.

50. Ignatius of Loyola, *Saint Ignatius of Loyola: Personal Writings*, trans. Joseph A. Munitiz and Philip Endean (London: Penguin Books, 1996), 123.

51. Ignatius of Loyola, *Ignatius of Loyola: Letters and Instructions* (St. Louis, MO: The Institute of Jesuit Sources, 2006), 18–19.

52. Ignatius of Loyola, *Ignatius of Loyola: Letters and Instructions*, 21.

53. Rahner, *Foundations of Christian Faith*, 456.

54. "In Memoriam. A Short Account of Fr. Vito Carrozzini, SJ," *Woodstock Letters* 6 (May 1, 1877): 127–28.

55. "In Memoriam," 127.

56. Michael Barkun, "Religion and Conflict from Independence to the Civil War," in *The Cambridge History of Religions in America*, ed. Stephen J. Stein (Cambridge, UK: Cambridge University Press, 2012), 165–66.

57. Chester Gillis, "American Catholics, 1800–1950," in *The Cambridge History of Religions in America*, ed. Stephen J. Stein (Cambridge, UK: Cambridge University Press, 2012), 254.

58. Randall M. Miller and Stephen J. Stein, "Religion and the Civil War," in *The Cambridge History of Religions in America* (Cambridge, UK: Cambridge University Press, 2012), 204.

59. Joseph M. Finotti (1817–1879), *Peter Claver: A Sketch of His Life and Labors in Behalf of the African Slave* (Boston, MA: Lee and Shepard, 1868).

60. John R. Slattery (1851–1929) and Bertrand Gabriel Fleuriau (1693–1773), *The Life of St. Peter Claver, SJ: The Apostle of the Negroes* (Philadelphia: H. L. Kilner, 1893).

61. "Our Indians and Negroes," *Jesuit Missions* 11, no. 4 (April 1937): 87.

62. "Our Indians and Negroes," 87.

63. Thomas Richard Murphy, "'Negroes of Ours': Jesuit Slaveholding in Maryland, 1717–1838" (PhD diss., University of Connecticut, 1998), https://opencommons.uconn.edu/dissertations/AAI9831883/.

64. John F. Quinn, "'Three Cheers for the Abolitionist Pope!' American Reaction to Gregory XVI's Condemnation of the Slave Trade, 1840–1860," *The Catholic Historical Review* 90, no.1 (2004): 67–93.

65. "In Memoriam," 126.

Notes

66. "The Influenza Pandemic at Camp Meade," *Woodstock Letters* 48, no. 1 (1918): 9.

67. "The Influenza Pandemic at Camp Meade," 9.

68. Engelbert Mveng, *Si quelqu'un...* (Tours: Mame, 1962).

69. Engelbert Mveng, *Histoire du Cameroun*, 1st ed. (Paris: Presence Africaine, 1963), 487.

70. John K. Thornton, *Africa and Africans in the Making of the Atlantic World, 1400–1680* (New York: Cambridge University Press, 1992).

71. Stephen D. Behrendt, A. J. H. Latham, and David Northrup, *The Diary of Antera Duke: An Eighteenth-Century African Slave Trader* (New York: Oxford University Press, 2010).

72. Ralph A. Austen and Jonathan Derrick, *Middlemen of the Cameroons Rivers: The Duala and Their Hinterland, c. 1600–c. 1960* (New York: Cambridge University Press, 1999).

73. Diana Wylie, *Starving on Full Stomach: Hunger and the Triumph of Cultural Racism in Modern South Africa* (New Brunswick, NJ: Rutgers University Press, 2001).

74. David Northrup, *Africa's Discovery of Europe, 1450–1850*, 2nd ed. (New York: Oxford University Press, 2009).

75. Gregory Mann, "Immigrants and Arguments in France and West Africa," *Comparative Studies in Society and History* 45, no. 2 (2003): 362–85.

76. Arturo Sosa, A., "Homily of Feast of Saint Peter Faber, in Memory of Father Pedro Arrupe with the Jesuits, Religious Sisters, and Retreatants" (Chapel of the Nagatsuka Residence and Spirituality Center of Saint John of Gotō in Hiroshima, August 2, 2019). Cf. "Collection Arturo Sosa," JHIA, Nairobi. Not classified.

77. Arturo Sosa, A., "Cinquante ans du Secrétariat pour la justice sociale et l'écologie intégrale," November 4, 2019. Cf. "Collection Arturo Sosa," JHIA, Nairobi, non classé.

78. Sosa, "Cinquante ans du Secrétariat pour la justice sociale et l'écologie intégrale."

79. Arturo Sosa, A., "23 de Enero: 20 años de revolución burgesa," *SIC* (1978): 15–17.

80. Sosa, "23 de Enero," 17.

81. Arturo Sosa, A., "Por qué coinciden Venezuela y Estados Unidos. Un problema de seguridad nacional (Americana)," *SIC* 41, no. 401 (1983): 4.

82. Sosa, "Por qué coinciden Venezuela y Estados Unidos," 4.

83. Sosa, "Por qué coinciden Venezuela y Estados Unidos," 5.

84. Luis Ugalde, "El alarmante déficit exterior," *SIC* 42, no. 412 (1979): 69.

85. La Redacción, "El escándalo del cemento," *SIC* 42, no. 412 (1979): 70.

86. Juan Carlos Navarro, "Gasto público, ingreso petrolero y distribución del ingreso," *SIC* 42, no. 412 (1979): 62–64.

87. Grupos Cristianos de Base, "Las informaciones de puebla," *SIC* 42, no. 412 (1979): 95–96.

88. Jean Pierre Wyssenbach, "Los barrios cuentan su historia," *SIC* 42, no. 412 (1979): 74–76.

89. Angelina Pollak-Eltz, "Movimientos religiosos en el mundo de hoy," *SIC* 42, no. 412 (1979): 81–82.

90. Arturo Sosa, A., "El 23 de Enero de 1983," *SIC* 46, no. 452 (1983): 74–75.

91. Arturo Sosa, A., "Avatares de la política nacional," *SIC* 47, no. 466 (1984): 262.

92. Arturo Sosa A., "Democracia Amenazada," *SIC* 48, no. 476 (1985): 266–73.

93. Arturo Sosa A., "Democratizar a Venezuela," *SIC* 48, no. 475 (1985): 206–7.

94. Sosa, "Democratizar a Venezuela," 206–7.

95. Arturo Sosa A., "Estado y democratización en Venezuela," *SIC* 51, no. 506 (1988): 253.

96. Arturo Sosa A., "La muerte del presidente," *SIC* 55, no. 542 (1992): 60.

97. Sosa, "La muerte del presidente," 60.

98. Arturo Sosa A., "Los escenarios electorales: La enfermedad del presidente, el militarismo, la oposición y otros elementos," *SIC* 739 (2011): 394.

99. Arturo Sosa A., "Iglesia y profundización de la democracia," *SIC* 55, no. 546 (1992): 252.

100. Sosa, "Iglesia y profundización de la democracia," 254.

101. Arturo Sosa A., "Los Jesuitas en el momento actual," *SIC* 46, no. 460 (1983): 436.

102. Sosa, "Los Jesuitas en el momento actual," 436.

103. Sosa, "Los Jesuitas en el momento actual," 438.

104. Arturo Sosa A., "Los Jesuitas: Dispersos y diversos," *SIC* 575 (June 1995): 196.

105. Sosa, "Los Jesuitas: Dispersos y diversos," 198.

106. Sosa, "Los Jesuitas: Dispersos y diversos," 198.

CONCLUSION

1. Loïc de Cannière, "We Will Be a More Ignatian Society," *CIS* 11, no. 2 (1980): 24.

2. Gerardo Bustillos H., "Bolivia Will Be Sending Out Missionaries," *CIS* 11, no. 2 (1980): 91.

3. David Martin, *Tongues of Fire: The Explosion of Protestantism in Latin America* (Oxford: Blackwell, 1993).

4. Karl Rahner, "A Letter to a Young Jesuit in the Charismatic Renewal," in *Jesuits and the Charismatic Renewal* (Rome: Centrum Ignatianum Spiritualitatis, 1984), 131–34.

5. Rahner, "A Letter to a Young Jesuit in the Charismatic Renewal," 131–34.

6. Rahner, "A Letter to a Young Jesuit in the Charismatic Renewal," 131–34.

7. Ignacio Iglesias, "Service at the Frontiers in Ignatian Sources," *CIS* 81 (1996): 7–19, here 7 and 10.

8. Iglesias, "Service at the Frontiers in Ignatian Sources," 7, 10.

9. John W. O'Malley, "The Ministries of the Early Jesuits: Social Disciplining or Discerning Accommodation?," *CIS* 81 (1996): 29.

10. O'Malley, "The Ministries of the Early Jesuits," 33.

INDEX

Index

Ottomans, 65
Outka, Elizabeth, 160, 161–62
Oviedo, André de, 88–89

Paal, Piret, xix
Páez, Pedro, 61, 62, 91–92
Palmeiro, Andrés, 83
Pamplona, 1–3, 34, 184
Pandemic (Spanish flu), 159–63
Papacy and Jesuits, 109,
    110, 115
Paradoxes, 183–84
Paraguay, 103, 118, 121–22
Paris, 21–22, 42, 53
Pastore, Stefania, 18
Paul III, Pope, 41–43, 110
Paul IV, Pope, 111
Paul V, Pope, 66
Paul VI, Pope, 99, 149–52, 153
Pavur, Claude, xiv
Peak experience, xviii–xix
Penitence, 17, 32–33
Pérez, Carlos Andrés, 172,
    173, 174
Pérez, Juan, 7
Persecution, 31, 163–66
Philip II, 89
Philip IV, 64
Pietism, 101
Pius VI, Pope, 124, 128, 145
Pius VII, Pope, 128–29
Pius XI, Pope, 149
Pius XII, Pope, 149
Polanco, Juan de, xvi, 80, 111
Politics, 52, 55–56, 112–13, 170
Porto, 120–21
Portugal, 39–40, 120–22
Poverty, 23, 42, 89, 156, 178
Presbyterianism, 100

Prestor John, 58–59, 65
Propaganda, 124–26
Protestantism, 14, 57, 66, 135,
    137, 143, 164
Puebla Conference, 172
Puritanism, 100

Rahn, Harold, 71
Rahner, Karl, 161, 163, 181–82
Ratio Studiorum, xiv, 41, 66,
    126–27, 132
Reason/rationalism, 72–75, 143,
    144, 182
Reconquista, 5–6, 15, 20, 56–57
Recruitment, 41–42
Rejadell, Teresa, 162
Religious Freedom Act, 178
Religious freedom/liberty, 134,
    135, 138, 185
Renovation Reading, 134
Republicanism, 134–35
Restoration, Jesuit, 109–10,
    130–34, 144
Reyes, Bárbara O., 77
Rezzi, Luigi, 129
Ribadeneyra, Pedro de, xv, 38,
    50, 112
Ricci, Lorenzo, 122, 124
Ricci, Mateo, 73
Rite of profession, 37
Rodrigues, Simon, 22
Roothaan, Jerome, 55, 130–32,
    134
Ross, Andrew, 73
Roupnel, Gaston, xx
Rubiés, Joan-Pau, 73, 74
Rugieri, 81
Ruiu, Adina, 78
Russia, 127–29